What
Citizens
Need to Know
About
Economics

SRS

U.S.NEWS
& WORLD REPORT

What Citizens Need to Know About Economics

Editors

Eleanor Goldstein, Editor, Social Issues Resources Series, Inc.
Joseph Newman, Editor, U.S. News & World Report Books

Writer

Richard Van Scotter, Ph.D.

Staff Editors

Elaine Weingarten
Seth Cagin
Ann Gazourian

Revised Edition 1983
Copyright © 1978 by U.S. News & World Report, Inc.
2300 N Street N.W., Washington, D.C. 20037

ISBN 0-89193-303-4 *(What Citizens Need to Know About Economics)*

Library of Congress Catalogue Card No. 78-13877
Printed in the United States of America

Orders and inquiries:
Social Issues Resources Series, Inc. (SIRS)
P.O. BOX 2507
Boca Raton, Florida 33427
Telephone: (305) 994-0079
Toll Free: 1-800-327-0513 (except AK, FL & HI)

What Citizens Need to Know About Economics

Contents

Introduction

Not a day passes without reference in the news to economic principles.

Is the FED raising or lowering the "discount rate?" Has the CPI advanced or declined? Is GNP growing or shrinking? What is the dollar exchange rate? Answers to questions such as these and others are important if we want to buy a house, look for a job, invest in the stock market, put money in the bank, buy a new car, start a business or take a trip to a foreign country. The "economic indicators" provide information for Americans in the worlds of work and commerce.

Every economic principle described in this book is relevant and commonplace. Obscure economic terms are not included. Those principles described provide a structure for a continuing understanding of how our economic system works.

For an economist, a "picture is worth a thousand words." Graphs, models and statistics are an economist's tools. However, because of the dynamic nature of economics, any data is out-dated by the time it is published. Statistics can describe where the economy "has been" at any given time, they can tell where "it is," but they can't always project accurately where it "will be" in the future.

Many graphics are included in this book—most show long-term trends, some short-term. In looking at the statistics, always be aware that they are representational. For current statistics, it's necessary to obtain data from other sources.

Economics is about some of the most important aspects of our lives. It describes what a society will produce and who will get what of the scarce resources. This book has been written with the hope that it will provide a foundation for an ongoing interest and involvement in this vital subject.

Chapter 1

Economics

> - *Economics is the study of the allocation of scarce resources.*
>
> - *Almost everything a human being needs to stay alive has become scarce.*

One of the miracles of contemporary American life is the quantity of stores to be found throughout the country, most of them bulging with an astounding variety and number of goods. It is difficult to imagine something that can't be bought somewhere. Many of us hardly notice the phenomenon because we have become so accustomed to it. But it's one of the first things that amazes the foreign visitor when he or she visits a modern shopping center.

Every day millions of consumers purchase billions of products manufactured by millions of producers. It's an amazing activity. Economics describes how it all happens. It is concerned with analyzing the production, distribution, and consumption of goods and services.

Though goods flow in and out of our stores in a greater volume than anywhere else in the world, there is not enough of everything to satisfy everyone. As we acquire more and more things, we want more, so there never is enough, and we discover an extraordinary phenomenon: *scarcity amid plenty*. Desires are always greater than the economy's capacity to fulfill them.

A common dream that many share is to be turned loose in a sumptuous department store, free to choose anything the heart may desire. In reality, when most of us go to a department store, or a supermarket, discount house, or drugstore, we are restricted in what we can buy. We must choose a limited number of items from the multitude on the shelves. We have a fixed amount of money and must decide between different options— —a pair of shoes *or* a new shirt, a record *or* a

book, a television *or* a refrigerator.

Since there cannot be enough of everything to satisfy everyone, what should be produced? How much of each item should be produced? And who is to get what is produced?

These are some of the basic questions with which economics is concerned. Since everyone is affected by the answers to these questions, an understanding of economic concepts is very helpful to every citizen, as an individual and as a member of society.

Goods and services

Two basic components of an economic system are *business enterprises* and *households*. Businesses produce *goods* and *services;* households consume them. Clothes, food, cars, stereos, books, and other material items are *economic goods*. They cost money—or have economic value. It takes skill and effort to create goods. People want them, and a limited number are available. Therefore, goods are *scarce* and have a price.

People who clean clothes, sell the food, service the cars, and repair stereos provide *economic services*. They do something to or for items or people, but do not produce material objects.

Goods and services that are not scarce do not have economic value. A person does not have to give up anything to acquire *free goods*. The air one breathes is valuable, but also abundant and, therefore, is free. However, if a person uses air conditioning, the resulting cool air becomes an economic good. Air conditioning costs money.

For city dwellers, water is an economic good. To a hiker, high in the mountain, who only has to dip a canteen into a flowing stream, water is a free good. Abundance creates cheaper goods; scarcity makes a good more expensive.

Models and tools

In analyzing the relations between producers and consumers, economists use various tools. These include statistics, tables, graphs, and models. A model is a representation of reality. It may be a picture or a diagram, a blueprint, or a dress pattern. The economist makes and uses models to better understand the economy. The closer the economist's model is to reality, the more useful it is.

Economics is a relatively new science. It is by no means an exact science, nor nearly as predictable as mathematics and physics. The reason is that economics, unlike other sciences, is determined by the behavior of humans—as consumers, workers, business managers, and public officials. It is often difficult to predict how people will react in different situations. This unpredictability of human behavior makes it difficult for economists to construct accurate models.

Nonetheless, economists analyze, measure, develop theories, and predict consequences of what may or may not happen. They use models to understand how prices are established, to determine how much is being produced, and to measure

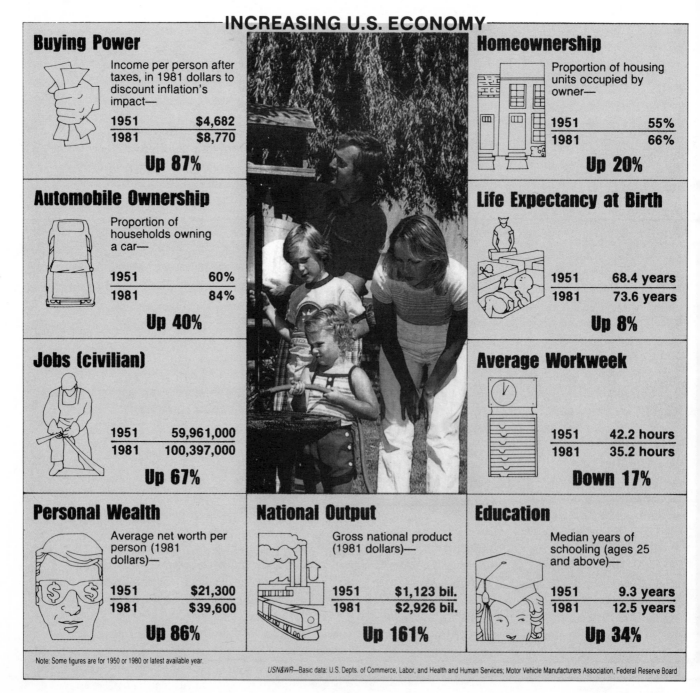

INCREASING U.S. ECONOMY

Buying Power
Income per person after taxes, in 1981 dollars to discount inflation's impact—

1951	$4,682
1981	$8,770

Up 87%

Automobile Ownership
Proportion of households owning a car—

1951	60%
1981	84%

Up 40%

Jobs (civilian)

1951	59,961,000
1981	100,397,000

Up 67%

Personal Wealth
Average net worth per person (1981 dollars)—

1951	$21,300
1981	$39,600

Up 86%

National Output
Gross national product (1981 dollars)—

1951	$1,123 bil.
1981	$2,926 bil.

Up 161%

Homeownership
Proportion of housing units occupied by owner—

1951	55%
1981	66%

Up 20%

Life Expectancy at Birth

1951	68.4 years
1981	73.6 years

Up 8%

Average Workweek

1951	42.2 hours
1981	35.2 hours

Down 17%

Education
Median years of schooling (ages 25 and above)—

1951	9.3 years
1981	12.5 years

Up 34%

Note: Some figures are for 1950 or 1980 or latest available year.

USN&WR—Basic data: U.S. Depts. of Commerce, Labor, and Health and Human Services; Motor Vehicle Manufacturers Association, Federal Reserve Board

inflation or unemployment and other important aspects of the economy.

The economist also uses charts and graphs to show what is happening in the economy, and what changes have taken place in prices, total production, wages, unemployment, interest rates, profits and many other measures. For the economist, "A picture is worth a thousand words."

Measurements

Keeping track of the economy is a task that occupies thousands of specialists. By keeping an eye on a few key figures, known as *economic indicators,* a person can get a good idea as to where the economy is going. This is important for the investor, the businessman, or the consumer facing major decisions about changing jobs or making a big purchase. Charts, graphs, and tables are used to show this information and data.

Microeconomics and macroeconomics

There are two basic ways in which economists view activity: they study the parts or look at the whole. *Microeconomics* involves analyzing the parts or elements that go into the economy. It deals with the behavior of a consumer, the activities of a business firm or an industry, and the output of a worker.

Macroeconomics looks at the whole picture. It groups together all households and industries, and deals with such things as total national income, total level of employment, general price levels and total expenditures. It also includes the study of national economic growth and development.

Public sector and private sector

In a *free enterprise system,* the goal is for individual businesses and firms to operate as freely as possible, with as few restraints from government as possible. This private sector of the economy produces goods and services for profit. There may be activities that the private sector cannot or will not undertake because these activities are unprofitable or require too much capital: building roads, building and maintaining armies, or running a postal service. In such cases the public sector performs these tasks using tax revenues. It is a continuing debate as to which activities the private sector should handle and which ones the public sector should handle. Should the health care of individuals be in the private sector or the public sector? Should parks be run for profit in the private sector or for the public good in the public sector? As society becomes increasingly complex, these questions become harder to answer.

A microeconomic view of a part of the economy	A macroeconomic view of the economy

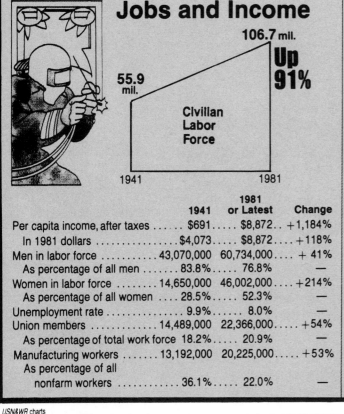

Jobs and Income

55.9 mil. — 106.7 mil.
Up 91%
Civilian Labor Force
1941 — 1981

	1941	1981 or Latest	Change
Per capita income, after taxes	$691	$8,872	+1,184%
In 1981 dollars	$4,073	$8,872	+118%
Men in labor force	43,070,000	60,734,000	+41%
As percentage of all men	83.8%	76.8%	—
Women in labor force	14,650,000	46,002,000	+214%
As percentage of all women	28.5%	52.3%	—
Unemployment rate	9.9%	8.0%	—
Union members	14,489,000	22,366,000	+54%
As percentage of total work force	18.2%	20.9%	—
Manufacturing workers	13,192,000	20,225,000	+53%
As percentage of all nonfarm workers	36.1%	22.0%	—

Economy

$125 bil. — $2,957 bil.
Up 2,266%
Total Output of Goods and Services (GNP)
1941 — 1981

	1941	1981 or Latest	Change
Total output in 1981 dollars	$782 bil.	$2,957 bil.	+278%
Government spending	$29 bil.	$990 bil.	+3,314%
As percentage of GNP	23.0%	33.5%	—
Housing starts (units)	706,000	1,100,000†	+56%
Auto production	3,780,000	6,400,000†	+69%
U.S. direct investment abroad	$7.3 bil.*	$213.5 bil.	+2,825%
Foreign direct investment in U.S.	$2.9 bil.*	$65.4 bil.	+2,155%
Exports of goods and services	$6.1 bil.	$364.1 bil.	+5,869%
As percentage of total output	4.9%	12.3%	—

USN&WR charts

Economic Indicators: Tracking The U.S. Economy

Keeping track of the economy is a task that occupies thousands of specialists.

Economists use a few key figures—indicators, indexes and statistics—that can be useful to the investor, business manager and general public. They contain important information for the worker facing a major decision about changing jobs or for the consumer considering a big purchase.

Here are the reports to watch.

Gross national product—This is the broadest measure of the economy's performance. Issued every three months by the Commerce Department, it is the best estimate of the total dollar value of the nation's output of goods and services. Movements in many areas of

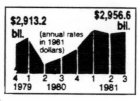

$2,913.2 bil. — $2,956.6 bil. (annual rates in 1981 dollars) 4 1 2 3 4 1 2 3 / 1979 1980 1981

the economy are closely related to changes in GNP, making it a good analytic tool. In particular, watch the annual rate of growth or decline in "real" or "constant" dollars. This eliminates the effects of inflation, so that the actual volume of production is measured. Remember, though, that frequent revisions of GNP figures sometimes change the picture of the economy.

Industrial production—Issued monthly by the Federal Reserve Board, this index shows changes in the physical output of America's factories, mines and electric and gas utilities. The index tends to move in the same direction as the economy, making it a good guide

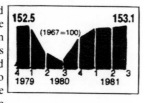

152.5 — 153.1 (1967=100) 4 1 2 3 4 1 2 3 / 1979 1980 1981

to business conditions between reports on GNP. Detailed breakdowns of the index give a reading on how individual industries are faring.

Leading indicators—This boils down to one number the movement of a dozen statistics that tend to predict—or "lead"—changes in the GNP. The monthly index issued by the Commerce Department includes such things as layoffs of workers, new orders placed by manu-

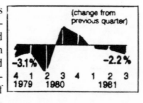

(change from previous quarter) -3.1% — -2.2% 4 1 2 3 4 1 2 3 / 1979 1980 1981

facturers, changes in the money supply and the prices of raw materials. If the index moves in the same direction for several months, it's a fair sign that total output will move the same way in the near future.

Personal income—A monthly report from the Commerce Department, this shows the before-tax income received by people in the form of wages and salaries, interest and dividends, rents and other payments such as Social Security, unemployment and pensions. As a measure

(annual rates in 1981 dollars) $2,441.8 bil. $2,365.7 bil. 4 1 2 3 4 1 2 3 / 1979 1980 1981

of individuals' spending power, the report helps explain trends in consumer buying habits, a major part of total GNP. When personal income rises, it often means that people will increase their buying. But note a big loophole: Excluded are the billions of dollars that change hands in the so-called underground economy—cash transactions that are never reported to tax or other officials.

Retail sales—The Commerce Department's monthly estimate of total sales at the retail level includes everything from cars to a bag of groceries. Based on a sample of retail establishments, the figure gives a rough clue to consumer attitudes. It can also indicate future con-

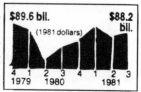

$89.6 bil. — $88.2 bil. (1981 dollars) 4 1 2 3 4 1 2 3 / 1979 1980 1981

ditions: A long slowdown in sales can lead to cuts in production.

Consumer prices—Issued monthly by the Labor Department, this index shows changes in prices for a fixed market basket of about 360 goods and services. The most widely publicized figure is for all urban consumers. A second, used in labor contracts and some govern-

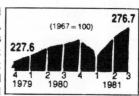

(1967=100) 276.7 227.6 4 1 2 3 4 1 2 3 / 1979 1980 1981

ment programs, covers urban wage earners and clerical workers. Both are watched as a measure of inflation, but many economists believe that flaws cause them to be wide of the mark.

Producer prices—This is a monthly indicator from the Labor Department showing price changes of goods at various stages of production, from crude materials such as raw cotton, to finished goods like clothing and furniture. An up-

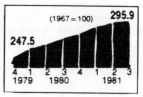

(1967=100) 295.9 247.5 4 1 2 3 4 1 2 3 / 1979 1980 1981

ward surge may mean higher consumer prices later. The index, however, can miss discounts and may exaggerate rising price trends. Watch particularly changes in the prices of finished goods. These do not fluctuate as widely as crude materials and thus are a better measure of inflationary pressures.

Employment—The percentage of the work force that is involuntarily out of work is a broad indicator of economic health. But another monthly figure issued by the Labor Department—the number of payroll jobs—may be better for spotting

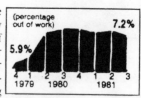

(percentage out of work) 7.2% 5.9% 4 1 2 3 4 1 2 3 / 1979 1980 1981

changes in business. A decreasing number of jobs is a sign that firms are cutting production.

Housing starts—A pickup in the pace of housing starts usually follows an easing of credit conditions—the availability and cost of money—and is an indicator of improvement in economic health. This monthly report from the Commerce Department also includes the number of

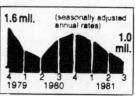

1.6 mil. (seasonally adjusted annual rates) 1.0 mil. 4 1 2 3 4 1 2 3 / 1979 1980 1981

new building permits issued across the country, an even earlier indicator of the pace of future construction.

Chapter 2

Basic Questions

- *People's "wants," or desires, far exceed their "needs," or basic requirements.*

- *Each society decides "who" will get "what."*

Just to stay alive requires a certain amount of food and shelter from harsh weather. For millions of years, people had little more than that. In most of the world today, people still have little more than the essentials with which to stay alive. They live at a bare *subsistence* level. How different life is for many in the United States, where automobiles, televisions, stereos, telephones and refrigerators are commonplace. Most of these marvels have been invented and produced in the last hundred years.

In order to stay alive every person has *needs*. Most people have *wants* which far exceed their needs. The society in which a person lives affects a person's needs. Americans "need" clothes, shoes, a place to live, an education, pencils, pens, books, and many other items in order to survive in their society. Most would feel deprived without a telephone, a car, a television or refrigerator, although they don't need these items for survival.

Economists talk about needs and wants when they describe *scarcity*. Wants far exceed needs for almost everyone. Major economic questions are how to satisfy needs, and how to decide which wants should be satisfied. The consumer, by deciding what to buy; the producer, by deciding what to manufacture; and the government, by deciding how to regulate, all enter into the picture.

There just aren't enough resources to go around for everyone to have everything. Some basic decisions have to be made as to how to distribute the scarce resources. Each society has to decide that question. In American society, many of the decisions are made by people who buy things *(consumers)* and people who make them *(producers).*In economic terms, these also are called *households* and *businesses*. People decide what they want from a wide assortment of choices and, when they make purchases, they are letting businesses know what to produce. Government often intervenes to regulate—perhaps to see that businesses are fair to consumers. Government itself uses many scarce resources for what is considered the good of society—a new missile, a highway system, or the development of a national park.

The challenge of an economic system is to assure enough *production* of goods and services to provide for its people, and to arrange for the *distribution* of this production.

Economic questions

An economic system faces basic questions in solving these problems:

1) **What** to produce?

2) **Who** will produce?

3) **How much** to produce?

4) **To whom** to distribute?

The first question confronting an economic system is **what to produce.** Should the society

5

produce ships and missiles or hospitals and homes; small cars or large cars, or fewer cars and more trains; gas energy, oil energy or solar energy? A society's goal might be the production of goods and services that people want and will use. On the other hand, producing too many cars, even though the people may want them, could lead to harmful, even disastrous, consequences—crowded highways, congested downtowns, traffic deaths and air pollution. Often there are competing goals: Most people want cars but they also want clean air. Can society provide a car for everyone and clean air at the same time?

Who will produce is another question that must be answered by economic systems. A basic problem of production is to mobilize human energy. Without enough production, many people will not be part of the productive process. Jobs must fit the skills of the work force, and they must be located where the workers are. When these conditions are not met, the result is *unemployment*—a chronic problem of many economic systems. Individual firms cannot concern themselves with total employment for the nation. Only government is in a position to assess the whole picture and develop policies that will aid in overall employment.

This leads to a third basic economic question: **How much to produce.** We want to produce enough goods and services of the proper kind to insure employment for all who can work. But we also want to direct production so that the supply of a good or service matches the demand for it. When this match does not occur, either prices will be driven up (demand is greater than supply) or inventories on producers' shelves will pile up and workers will be laid off (supply is greater than demand). Only on rare occasions in our economy has total supply equaled total demand. When supply and demand are not equal, the results may be recession or inflation.

Another goal, related to how much to produce, is economic growth. A constant increase in the size of national production, both to accommodate a growing population and to increase the material standard of the population, has been achieved in the past. Many people question whether growth can continue at such a pace.

Finally, an economic system must decide **to whom to distribute the output.** Should the output be distributed more to some people than to others? What distribution is proper and fair? Should the economic pie of a society be divided evenly? The distribution of output is a very controversial issue.

The goals of any society are determined by the people as they speak through their public officials. If the goals are not met, there is often unrest, sometimes leading to revolution. In a democratic country where citizens can vote for change, eco-

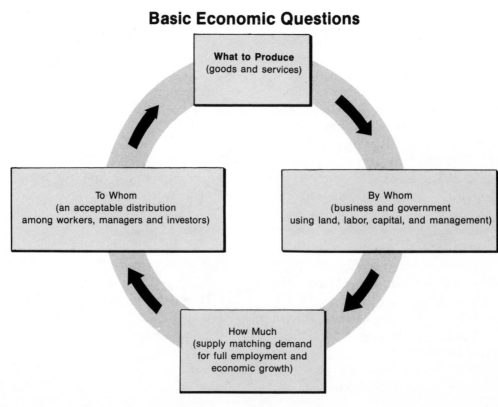

Basic Economic Questions

What to Produce
(goods and services)

To Whom
(an acceptable distribution
among workers, managers and investors)

By Whom
(business and government
using land, labor, capital, and management)

How Much
(supply matching demand
for full employment and
economic growth)

nomic issues are resolved at the polls. In a totalitarian country the issues are settled by the leaders without consulting the public.

People can go hungry in the midst of fertile land. They can be cold even though there is coal underground. They can be without a house in the middle of a forest. Natural resources on the surface and under the surface of the earth have to be put to use to feed, heat, and shelter people. Unrecognized, and left in their natural states, resources do little to satisfy the needs and wants of people.

Factors of production

A nation's production depends on the resources it has and how it uses them. Business enterprises decide what types of resources to use; they also combine resources. Their goal is to obtain the best mix, or most efficient use of resources for maximum production. These resources are called *factors of production.* They can be grouped into four categories: *land, labor, capital,* and *management.*

Land refers to natural resources, including all the earth's soil and water, as well as everything found on, above, and below them. Land also provides the space we need to live and to carry out our activities. Air is a land resource, as is soil and mineral deposits, such as oil and iron ore.

Labor consists of the human services which are used in production. It includes all of the people in the labor force: the factory worker, the farmer, the doctor, writer, clerk, waitress, actor, plumber, beautician, and everyone else who has a job.

Capital is goods produced by people to be used in the further production of other goods. All of the machines and equipment in the society are capital. The barber's scissors and chair, the writer's pencil and typewriter, and the huge equipment of a steel mill are all considered capital.

The **manager,** or entrepreneur, is the person who organizes and directs the other three factors and assumes risk in the production process.

Like the economic resources of the consumer or household, these factors of production tend to be scarce. Capital tends to be the most scarce of all the factors, because it takes the other three factors to create it. You have to have natural resources, workers, and someone who knows how to put them together, the entrepeneur or manager, in order to create capital.

Economics involves money. For the use of any factor of production, there is a payment. From one point of view, these payments are the *costs of production.* From another point of view, payments are *incomes earned.* These incomes have names that coincide with the factors: to land goes a payment called *rent;* labor earns *wages;* the payment that accrues to capital is *interest;* and the monetary return to entrepreneurs is *profit.*

Factors of Production

Each of the factors of production receives payments known as *incomes earned.*

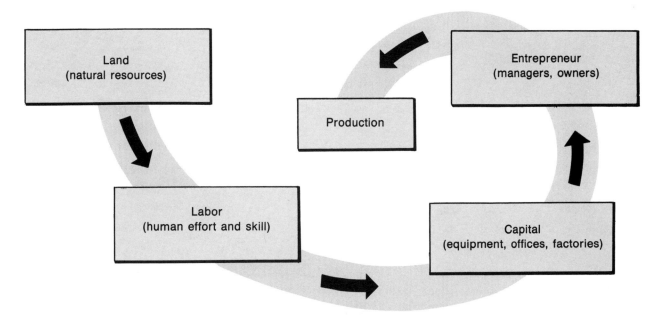

7

Events That Shaped The U.S. Economy

1849
Gold Rush to California.

1861
Civil War begins, followed by the abolition of slavery in 1865.

1862
Passage of the Homestead Act, giving public land to pioneers at a nominal fee.

CLAIM

1869
Accelerating the movement west, cross-country rail link completed at Promontory Point, Utah.

1890
Sherman Antitrust Act is passed to slow the growth of business monopolies.

MONOPOLY

1893
Sharp recession leads to railroad failures and sets the stage for adoption of a gold standard in 1900.

1901
U.S. Steel, formed from assets of $1.4 billion, becomes the largest U.S. company. At same time, major expansions in autos, electrical appliances, textiles—all fed by a wave of immigrant workers.

1913
Federal income tax enacted. Rates range from 1 to 7 percent. Withholding doesn't begin until 1943. Federal Reserve System created to shore up the national banking system and aid financially strapped banks.

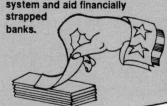

1941
U.S. entry into World War II adds steam to what would become the second-longest business boom on record. Women enter the work force in great numbers.

1944
Bretton Woods agreement creates International Monetary Fund, the framework of the international financial system.

1947
Taft-Hartley Act curtails labor movement's power by allowing the government to regulate unions.

1964
President Lyndon Johnson launches Great Society programs that greatly increase government spending on health, food and antipoverty programs. At the same time, Vietnam War expands, planting the seeds for double-digit inflation.

1789

Congress establishes U.S. Treasury—first step in government regulation of the economy.

1792

New York Stock Exchange begins and starts largest capital market in the world.

1803

Size of U.S. doubles by the Louisiana Purchase from France, encouraging westward expansion and development of canals, railroads.

1837

Depression brought on by reckless speculation and failure of the state banking system.

1873

Beginning of a six-year depression, brought on by overexpansion of railroads and other businesses. Leads to major banking reforms.

1882

John D. Rockefeller organizes the Standard Oil Trust, which controlled about 90 percent of refined oil and symbolized new era of big business.

1886

American Federation of Labor is founded—the real birth of the U.S. labor movement.

1887

Interstate Commerce Act sets up the first federal regulatory body, which initially concentrated on the railroads.

1929

Stock-market crash followed by Great Depression, whose after shocks lasted until World War II.

1933

Franklin Roosevelt takes office. His New Deal programs, particularly public works and new financial agencies, vastly expand government role in the economy.

1935

Social Security Act passes. Today 36 million persons receive more than 155 billion dollars in annual benefits.

1935

National Labor Relations Act protects the right of labor to organize and engage in collective bargaining. Three years later, first minimum wage enacted.

1970

Creation of the Environmental Protection Agency. Begins era of wider government regulation of the workplace and consumer products.

1971

U.S. no longer will surrender gold for dollars in foreign exchange. Value of the dollar begins to float against other currencies.

1973

Yom Kippur War between Israel and Egypt leads to oil embargo imposed by Arab oil-exporting nations. World energy prices soar, adding to the sharp inflation of the 1970s.

1981

U.S. public debt reaches $1 trillion, symbolic of the growth in government spending that has spurred a new drive to restrain the government's role in the economy.

9

Chapter 3
Basic answers

- *Societies solve basic economic questions of who will get what by either competing for scarce resources or cooperating and sharing scarce resources.*

- *Capitalism is based on competition; socialism is based on cooperation.*

The workings of our modern society are intricate. Thousands of tasks must be performed by millions of people every day or life would become chaotic. If garbage collectors, or coal miners, or bus drivers, or letter carriers, or telephone repairers, or grocers do not do their jobs, we're all in trouble. On any day, the community could break down if something serious goes wrong.

People began to depend on one another for survival in primitive times, and they have had to do so ever since. There are three ways for societies to accomplish the work that needs to be done: They can organize by doing things according to *tradition;* they can have *authoritarian rule;* they can let each individual look after his or her own *self-interest*.

Who will do the work?

Tradition, or *custom,* and authoritarian rule, also known as *command,* were the most common ways to get work done throughout most of history. Gradually, over hundreds of years, a new system of doing the work of society developed. This was a system in which each person looked after his or her own self-interest. Each person would do as he or she wanted, whether it was baking bread, producing weapons, farming the land, and then sell his or her products for *profit,* or *gain*. This is known as the *market system*. This system is not as simple as custom or command. It staggers the mind to wonder how all the work in society can get done if people look after their own interests without regard to the well-being of others. Who

will do the hard, tedious jobs and the dangerous work if no one is there to command others to do it, or if custom does not keep them in line?

An "invisible hand"

The market system developed and spread from nation to nation, yet few people understood what was happening. A teacher of philosophy, Adam Smith, was intrigued by the way in which the market system worked. In 1776, he published a book entitled, *Inquiry Into the Nature and Causes of the Wealth of Nations.*

The market system, Smith reasoned, was guided by an "invisible hand." He described how "the private interests and passions of men" could lead in the direction "which is most agreeable to the interest of the whole society."

Adam Smith's book was the first complete treatment of *capitalism*. Later, other writers of economics described various aspects of the system. But it was Smith who demonstrated how a system in which people looked after their own individual interests could solve the problems of producing and distributing goods and services for a whole society.

A blueprint for socialism

In 1851, another monumental book, that took eighteen years to write, was published. It was called *Das Kapital* (Capital). The authors were Karl Marx and Friedrich Engels, and their subject also was the capitalist economic system. Unlike Adam Smith, Marx and Engels did not admire

Adam Smith

Karl Marx

capitalism. They saw it as a system that creates misery, oppression, slavery, degradation, and exploitation because it depends on one person using the labor of another for profit. Marx, the more significant of the two writers, envisioned a classless society, not divided on the basis of property. He believed that society as a whole, meaning the people, should own all the means of production. Marx's society was called *socialism* (or *communism*). In this economic system, all people were to work according to their ability, and to receive according to their needs. In the beginning, this system would require central planning to ensure the welfare of all the people; eventually, the people could guide the system cooperatively, and the centralized control would "wither away."

Adam Smith analyzed and described capitalism. Karl Marx analyzed capitalism and designed a blueprint for socialism. Today these are the basic economic systems in the world. Most societies have some aspects of both capitalism and socialism.

The overriding characteristic of capitalism is that *capital,* or the means of production, is owned privately—by private businesses or individuals. Capitalism also is called the "private enterprise" or "free enterprise" system.

In socialist economies the means of production are owned socially—by the people through their government—or, to the extent that there is private industry, the government is responsive to social needs. Socialist nations provide many services for their citizens: medical care, education, welfare and retirement benefits.

Capitalism

Capitalists believe that individuals will make the most productive contribution to society if they are free to choose their own economic activity. Capitalism is based on *competition* among producers as well as workers.

Adam Smith, in **The Wealth of Nations,** wrote that each producer and worker, eager to improve his economic status, would strive to provide a better good or service than his competitor; provide the good or service at the lowest possible cost or price; and try to improve the product or work. In this manner, *competition* in the economy would determine what was produced, ensure product quality, establish just prices and wages, and stimulate invention and ingenuity. This, Smith believed, was the *"invisible hand"* of the market operating for the social good.

The government's role was minimal, so the system was called laissez-fairism, or *laissez-faire capitalism*—a French expression meaning "to let do" or to let people do as they choose. The system Smith

11

Adam Smith's "Invisible Hand" Disappears

What kind of economy does the U.S. have? It's a unique blend, the experts point out, that differs from that of all other nations.

In 1776, Adam Smith proclaimed the classical law of political economics.

Every person in pursuing his self-interest, the Scottish economist-philosopher wrote in *The Wealth of Nations,* is guided, as if by an "invisible hand," to serve the common good. Thus, Smith declared, any interference by government with free competition is almost certain to be harmful.

Now, after two centuries, that hands-off—or laissez-faire—doctrine has given way to the hand of government in managing economies nearly everywhere.

The U.S. operates a mixed economy: Free-enterprise capitalism combined with government regulation of industry and government-provided social benefits.

Compared with other economies, says Paul Samuelson, the Massachusetts Institute of Technology author of popular textbooks on economics, the U.S. has the least government ownership, the least direct control of industry and ranks "a little below the middle" in terms of welfare-state benefits.

Japan, Australia, Spain and Greece are among countries that provide lesser benefits than does the United States. Britain, Canada and Scandinavian countries provide more, mainly because of national health plans.

The Communist world operates the most controlled economies, relying heavily on government ownership of production and centralized planning. In the Soviet Union, the typical factory is state owned, private enterprise is negligible, and production is directed toward benefiting the state rather than the private individual.

Both Russia and China have run their economies via five-year plans designed to give central direction to agriculture and industry through government-imposed production quotas. In recent years, however, the two Communist giants have flirted with Western-style profit incentives to boost their poor economic performances.

Elsewhere, state ownership exists in varying degrees throughout much of Europe, where governments own air-lines, railroads, utilities and significant shares of industry.

In Britain, for example, where Prime Minister Thatcher is trying to change direction, the government owns the steel, transportation, shipbuilding and aerospace industries and substantial portions of the oil and auto industries.

In France, the Socialist Mitterrand government plans to expand nationalization from 11 percent of industrial production to 18 percent, or about the level in Britain. An initial Mitterrand target: The French banking system.

The U.S., on the other hand, engages in little direct ownership of production, except for some regional power systems such as the Tennessee Valley Authority and some transportation systems such as Amtrak.

Because it avoids nationalization, the U.S. regulates business more tightly than do most other industrialized nations. "In terms of antitrust, the environment, employment of minorities and other respects," says Robert Higgs of the University of Washington, "we regulate more than the Europeans do."

A government's influence over its economy is reflected by its share of the gross national product. In the U.S., government spending at all levels accounts for about one third of total national output. This compares with about 50 percent in the nations of the European Economic Community.

The U.S. bears a heavier defense burden. But a key difference between the size of government in the U.S. and Europe is the cost of social welfare. It accounts for about 12 percent of the U.S. national product, compared with an average of 20 percent in Europe.

Subsidized income. David Wyss of the London office of Data Resources, Inc., an American economics firm, estimates that about twice as much personal income comes from the state in Europe as in the United States. Here, for example, unemployment compensation is limited to 39 weeks. In Britain, the unemployed are paid for a year and then qualify for other benefits.

To pay for this generosity, European governments collect a much higher percentage of taxes from their citizens than Americans are used to paying. Though taxes on income, particularly investment income, in countries such as Britain and Sweden are quite high, a key difference between Europe and the United States is the extent of indirect taxation.

In Britain, for example, the value-added, or sales, tax is 15 percent, compared with the average of less than 4 percent that Americans pay in state and local sales taxes.

Higgs notes that both Japan and West Germany "do less to distort investment incentives than the U.S. does" through its tax system.

Japan, the major industrial power in Asia, is unique. Government plays a significant, though indirect, role. It chooses industries to be developed, sees that they are assisted by the private financial system and insures that companies provide extensive benefits to their workers.

In effect, the Japanese government and industry work together to achieve progress, in contrast to the adversarial relationship between the government and business in the United States.

So, the economy's "invisible hand," described by Adam Smith in 1776 as the personal pursuit of self-interest, has increasingly become, in the U.S. as well as in all other industrialized nations, the hand of government. □

Three Forms of Pollitical Economies

How they work today—

CAPITALISM

Production: Private individuals own land and businesses, operating them for profit. The market, mainly, determines what goods are sold at what prices.

Pay: Wages are set between employes and management at individual firms, with workers often represented by unions.

Government: It regulates business largely by telling firms what not to do. It stimulates output through incentives and usually provides tax-supported social benefits.

COMMUNISM

Production: The state owns the sources of production, managed by bureaucrats. Central planners set production quotas.

Pay: Government sets wages. Free trade unions are taboo.

Government: Establishes production plans and objectives by central committees.

SOCIALISM

Production: Elected government gradually takes control of key industries. Authorities often plan output for use rather than profit.

Pay: Strong trade unions bargain with management, often serve as the fountainheads of socialism.

Government: It allocates resources, uses taxing power to redistribute wealth.

described has produced enormous wealth over the past 200 years. The motivation to produce, work, and invent resulted in steady economic development. But uncontrolled economic activity led to serious problems that Smith did not foresee—inherent flaws in the capitalist blueprint. Where unrestrained self-interest and competition have prevailed, the larger needs of society have often gone unmet.

As some businesses became more successful and powerful, they drove competitors out. This led to *monopolies* (where one business dominates) in many industries. Competition, the driving force underlying the economic system, was lost. With a plentiful labor market, powerful business owners kept wages low and working conditions poor. In addition, capitalism proved to be vulnerable to recession and inflation. Periodically, production declined, unemployment increased, consumption decreased, and profits dried up—in a downward cycle. When recessionary conditions deepened, depression would set in. Eventually, downward cycles were offset by upward trends bringing prosperity. But often this new cycle brought new problems—rising prices and inflation.

To remedy these problems, governments intervened and laissez-fairism underwent modification. "Trust-busting" curtailed monopolistic practices to encourage competition; labor unions grew to provide power for the workers; eventually, government financial policies were developed to counteract economic slumps and inflation.

Marxist socialism or communism

Karl Marx was the major architect of the economic systems developed in the Soviet Union, Eastern Europe, China, and Cuba. A central idea of Marxist thought is that workers should control the *means of production*. Marx argued that if the factories and farms were under control of private owners, the workers would be exploited. This exploitation, Marx wrote, would lead from discontent to revolution, and inevitably to the collapse of capitalism.

With workers controlling the means of production, Marxists theorized that they would form a "dictatorship of the Proletariat" which would carry out the ideals of socialism. When this was achieved, the government would "wither away," and the true state of communism would come into being. However, in reality, officials of the communist party, not the workers, control the means of production. And no communist government has yet "withered away."

A second major idea of Marxism is a *commitment to equality*. The wealth of a nation should be shared evenly among workers, and no working family or individual should go without the basic necessities of life. The principle: "from each according to his ability, to each according to his needs" is a Marxist ideal. In practice, however, citizens are assured a basic living, but workers in communist countries are generally paid according to what they produce.

To some extent, all modern socialist nations derive their goals from Marxist economic theory. They advocate central planning and controls to achieve "socially useful" production. In a capitalist country, a good or service will be produced if it can bring a profit, even though it may be trivial.

Under a communist government, the officials set forth basic economic objectives, and a central planning board implements these policies. The farms, factories, mines, railroads, construction firms, and retail stores are owned and operated by the state. A central planning board draws up production plans and sets goals or objectives. The controlled economic system in the Soviet Union and other communist countries has succeeded in achieving rapid industrial growth during the past several decades.

Democratic socialism

Great Britain, the Scandinavian countries, and much of Western Europe have socialist governments. However, nationalization of industries is far less than 100 percent. Sweden, Denmark, and Norway have nationalized only the industries considered crucial to the economy, or those that private companies couldn't handle. Great Britain has nationalized major industries like coal mining, electric power, gas, railways, highway freight transportation, inland canal transportation, and the Bank of England, in order, 1) to reorganize many small, inefficient units of production, 2) to rejuvenate stagnant industries with state investment, and 3) to control basic industries for rational economic planning goals. They have also socialized the health programs in the nation.

In other socialist nations, private industry is regulated to serve the public interest. The government exercises control over prices, wages, interest rates, capital development, and even production and employment.

The major aim of *democratic socialists* is to provide social services. This is achieved through taxation. Taxes on personal incomes are as high as 90 percent in some nations. Business earnings, too, are highly taxed. The vigor with which industry and taxation is controlled often depends on the political climate in these nations. Generally, when the mood of the citizens is toward social reform, labor party or social democratic representatives are voted into office. When taxation, business control, and too many regulations overwhelm the public, conservatives are elected.

For tax dollars, the people receive extensive social services. This is the most distinctive feature of modern democratic socialism. These economic systems provide many benefits: annual child allowances, tuition-free education through college, free hospital care, sick pay, unemployment insurance, and retirement benefits. Other services may include free family planning, treatment for alcohol and drug addiction, and maternity allowances.

Third World socialism

Most Third World nations (countries which prefer not to align themselves with either of the two major blocs led by the United States and the Soviet Union) are socialist or lean toward socialism. In many less-developed countries, the government is in the best position to mobilize capital for economic growth. Capital, or wealth, is difficult to accumulate, and is usually under the control of a few families. Most people have no opportunity to accumulate wealth to start up a business or farm. Only the government is in the position to create or borrow funds for large-scale development in these countries.

A mixed economy

Capitalism has evolved well past the pure model outlined by Adam Smith, just as today's socialism is very different from the Marxist model. Most modern capitalist nations are best described as mixed economies. Capitalists have adopted various socialistic practices, including national health insurance, work disability coverage, social security, unemployment insurance, subsidies to specific industries, and regulations of industrial practices and products.

American capitalism has been an inspiration to many nations of the world. Its greatest achievement has been its steady and extraordinarily high level of economic growth. Most Americans are paid well enough to have ample purchasing power. We are a wealthy society.

Marx wrote that capitalism has within it the "seeds of its own destruction." American capitalism has overcome many shortcomings and survived many crises largely through government intervention in the nation's economy. The government over the years has regulated the money supply by pumping money into the economy during economic slumps, employing or giving financial assistance to the unemployed, and coming to the aid of hard pressed industries, such as automobile manufacturing.

Chapter 4

Consumers

- *Consumers vote with their dollars on what should be produced in the marketplace.*

- *Since the consumer does not have the ability to determine product safety, he or she needs advice and protection.*

In a market system, the consumer is the real boss. The dollar is the vote. If a person is willing to spend money for something, he or she is saying, in effect, "I like it. I'm glad you produced that." Consumers voice approval, or disapproval when they buy or don't buy, just as voters do when they cast ballots at the polls. Consumers have *wants*. When these wants are backed by a willingness and ability to pay, it constitutes *demand*. Consumer demands are satisfied by goods and services produced by others, who receive something in exchange (usually money).

People's decisions about where to live and work, what to buy or pass over, and how much to save, are at the heart of the "free" market system. Business and government take their cues from consumers, adjusting plans to meet their wants and needs. The study of consumers, business firms, and government, particularly as they affect prices in the market, is the subject of *microeconomics*. Microeconomics is concerned with the parts of the economy.

The power of the consumer has been impeded in our modern economic society. Given the large number of choices that must be made and the amount of information that must be understood, the consumer can be overwhelmed, confused, and persuaded. The pattern of influence from consumer to producer can become reversed. The intelligent consumer today must be educated, analytical and shrewd. In recent years, consumers have banded together to obtain fair treatment in the market place.

Consumers make choices

Every day, the nation's millions of consumers spend more than $5 billion. This amounts to about $25 for each man, woman and child. Their purchases account for almost two-thirds of all the money spent each year, with government and business accountable for the rest.

The real cost of an economic product can be measured in terms of what a person must give up to obtain it. Ultimately, we give up leisure time to work and earn money, which we exchange for goods or services. We balance the relative costs and values of goods and services. The satisfied consumer is the one who has done a competent job in calculating. Sometimes, the consumer's calculating is methodical; other times, it is intuitive. The time a consumer spends in making choices (looking for sales, scanning ads, and clipping coupons) is also an economic good whose value should be considered.

About 70 percent of the average household's spending goes for necessities: housing, food, clothes and health care. To be able to afford these items and still have money left for nonessentials, such as travel and entertainment, most families watch their budgets. The money that a household has to spend after necessities have been taken care of is known as *discretionary income*. The same problem of matching limited resources with seemingly endless demands confronts businesses and public agencies.

No one is born knowing how to make economic choices. It's a trial and error process that dates back to the candy counter, when a child learns

Demands Lead to Production

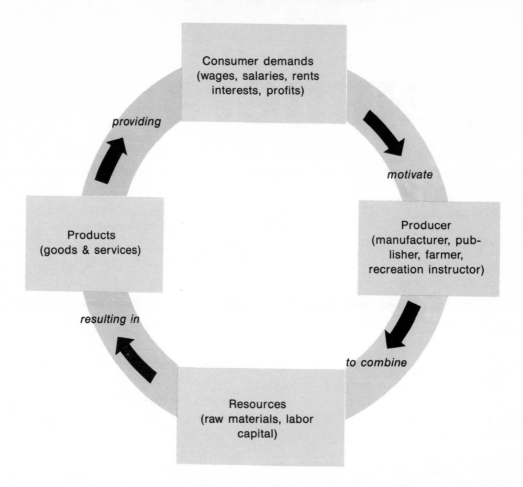

there isn't enough money to buy all that he wants, and that some things don't taste as good as others. The next time, he is wiser and more selective. Later, dissatisfied with a limited allowance, he might take a job to earn money to buy more. He then becomes a producer as well as a consumer, and makes a decision about how to use one of the most valuable resources—time.

Law of diminishing utility

Shoes are a need for most people in our society. The first pair has a very high value, or utility. It might even be important to have several pairs, maybe tennis shoes, a pair of hiking boots and a pair for parties. After the needs for different shoes have been satisfied, additional pairs become less necessary. At some point, the value of another pair of shoes would be a disadvantage. Two hundred pairs of shoes would be a real nuisance. It would be hard to find space to store them all, and it would be a problem to decide which ones to wear each day. What is true for shoes is true for everything else a person might buy. This principle is the *law of diminishing utility*.

The amount of satisfaction a person gets from a good or service is called *utility*. Generally, the more of a particular thing a person has, the less utility he or she receives from additional items. That is, the first item has the most value, while succeeding items have less and less value. With enough money, a consumer will continue to purchase a good or service until its utility matches its price tag. When its utility is less than its cost, the consumer will stop buying.

The revised sequence

It is said that the consumer is the real boss because what he or she decides to buy determines what will be produced. In our modern economy, this is not always true; while consumers are the ones who make decisions about what to buy, businesses do not sit idly by while the consumer makes up his or her mind. The economist John Kenneth Galbraith remarked that in our conventional thinking, the direction of power in the market is from the consumer to the producer. However, with the growth of large businesses, sophisticated technology, scientific management,

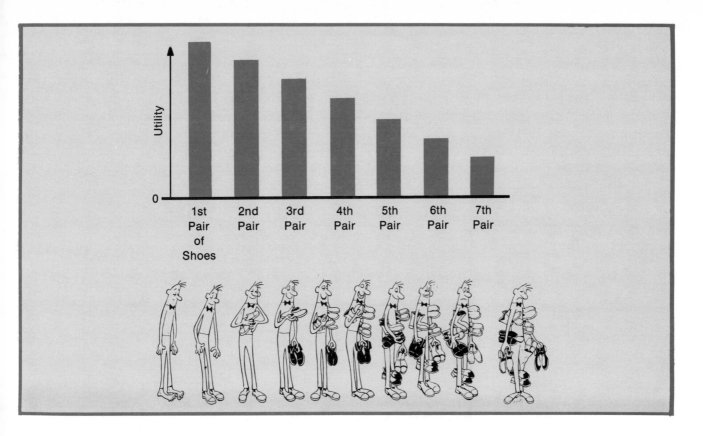

advertising, and market planning, the consumer is less than king. To some extent the direction of power in the marketplace has been reversed. Galbraith called this the *revised sequence.* When businesses spend many years and millions of dollars designing a model change for a new automobile, they want some assurance that the car will be appealing to the consumer. They, therefore, survey the market for consumer preferences, and they also influence the market. The major source of this influence is advertising. The revised sequence prevails among many industries today. From automobiles to washing machines to motion pictures, advertising influences people to buy items that they don't even know they need or want.

Consumers battle back

A major economic question is what role the government should play in protecting the consumer. The concept of "caveat emptor," meaning "let the buyer beware," dates back to early capitalism. However, in our complex society the buyer cannot do the necessary research and investigation to determine if a product is safe or reliable. Therefore, the government has a role to play in testing and evaluating products offered in the marketplace. The desirable degree of testing and regulation is a persistent political debate. Some people want to allow business to have a free hand to produce and sell what they choose. Others believe that the consumer must be protected by laws from unsafe products and inadequate services. The federal government now receives an estimated 10-million consumer complaints a year.

In a trillion-dollar economy, even this volume of complaints is a drop in the bucket. Still, it is significant. The rising number of complaints in recent years reflect several developments:
● In an age of mass production and rising costs, craftsmanship and good service is on the wane.
● With high prices cutting deeper into many family budgets, buyers want to make every penny count.
● Consumers have come to believe they have a right to expect high quality work when they pay for it.
● Finally, there has been striking growth in the network of consumer protection agencies at the local and state level. There are more than six hundred agencies now in operation.

The great bulk of complaints flooding Washington wind up in four agencies:

Consumer Product Safey Commission. An independent regulatory agency created in 1972, it has set safety standards for thousands of consumer products. The commission can take an offender to court and impose fines up to $500,000 for violations of its standards.

Office of Consumer Affairs. Established by Executive Order in 1971 as an arm of the White House, it is now part of the Department of Health and Human Services. Through pamphlets and a biweekly newsletter, the office warns consumers against fraudulent business practices and shoddy merchandise.

Food and Drug Administration. The FDA is a division of the Department of Health and Human Services, and since 1931 has been charged with protecting the health of Americans against impure and unsafe foods, drugs and cosmetics.

The FDA is empowered to recall an unsafe or ineffective product.

Federal Trade Commission. In operation since 1915, the FTC is an independent agency that handles complaints about false or deceptive advertising, fake warranties and guarantees, and mislabled manufactured goods. It has the power to investigate complaints and take a manufacturer to court to end improper practices.

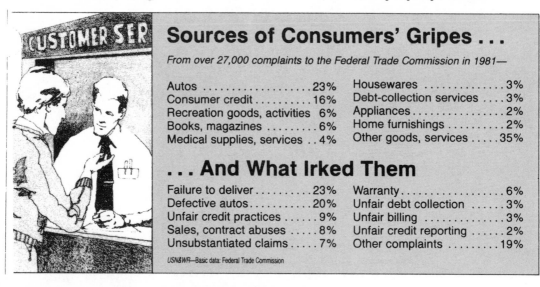

Sources of Consumers' Gripes . . .

From over 27,000 complaints to the Federal Trade Commission in 1981—

Autos 23%	Housewares 3%
Consumer credit 16%	Debt-collection services 3%
Recreation goods, activities 6%	Appliances 2%
Books, magazines 6%	Home furnishings 2%
Medical supplies, services . .4%	Other goods, services 35%

. . . And What Irked Them

Failure to deliver 23%	Warranty 6%
Defective autos 20%	Unfair debt collection 3%
Unfair credit practices 9%	Unfair billing 3%
Sales, contract abuses 8%	Unfair credit reporting 2%
Unsubstantiated claims 7%	Other complaints 19%

USN&WR—Basic data: Federal Trade Commission

Consumer spending

Of each $100 in outlays after taxes—

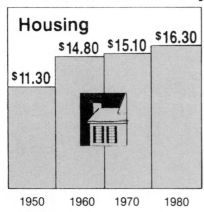

Housing

$11.30 — 1950
$14.80 — 1960
$15.10 — 1970
$16.30 — 1980

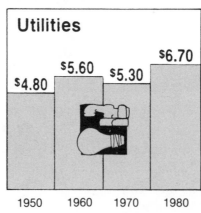

Utilities

$4.80 — 1950
$5.60 — 1960
$5.30 — 1970
$6.70 — 1980

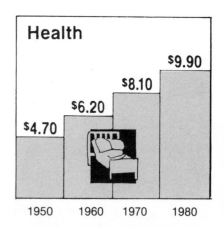

Health

$4.70 — 1950
$6.20 — 1960
$8.10 — 1970
$9.90 — 1980

Clothes

$12.40 — 1950
$9.90 — 1960
$8.90 — 1970
$7.40 — 1980

Food and Drink

$28.10 — 1950
$25.00 — 1960
$22.30 — 1970
$20.70 — 1980

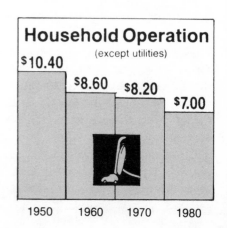

Household Operation
(except utilities)

$10.40 — 1950
$8.60 — 1960
$8.20 — 1970
$7.00 — 1980

Chapter 5
The cost of living

> - *The cost of living is influenced by many things, including the weather and foreign trade.*
>
> - *As the cost of living increases, the standard of living decreases.*

Americans traditionally focus on their earnings as an indicator of relative *standard of living*. We compare wages with others, and we measure our changing prospects by looking at raises in salary and comparing our earnings with what they were in years past. This emphasis on income may fail to indicate accurately how our economic life is progressing in terms of our true standard of living or quality of life. Some economists feel that the *cost of living* may be more important than income in determining economic status. One may receive a substantial raise in salary, but if the cost of living rises at a greater rate because of inflation, a person may actually be worse off economically than before. On the other hand, a modest rise in one's income may be more significant than it appears if, at the same time, the costs of the items we need or want do not rise, or if, as in rare cases, they decline.

It is often said that the value of the dollar has decreased, or that it is worth only 75 cents or 50 cents compared to a dollar of 10 or 20 years ago. This is another way to say that the dollar can only buy what 50 cents could buy at a previous time because the costs of what we buy have risen. For this reason, government officials and economists are keenly concerned with the cost of living. Not only time periods in our lives, but where we live, influence our cost of living. Because of geographic factors, such as climate, our costs of heat and air conditioning may differ from region to region in the United States, and the costs of products and food are influenced by local food and goods production. Consequently, moving to another city to

take a job paying more money may not be a wise economic move if the new location has a substantially higher cost of living that will cancel out the income gain.

The cost of living is influenced by factors as diverse as the weather and the price of oil. Good growing weather produces abundant crops, and food prices go down. Floods, droughts, or frosts cause crop shortages and food prices go up. If oil-producing nations raise their prices and gas prices at the pump go up, so does the cost of nylon stockings, plastics and all other petroleum-based products.

Since the cost of items purchased is a vital factor in determining the prosperity, decline, or general standard of the economy, government and business leaders need a system to measure the changing cost of living. Today, many labor wage contracts and pension benefits are tied to the cost of living to guarantee that one's income keeps pace with any increase in consumer costs.

Consumer Price Index

The *consumer price index,* or CPI, is calculated periodically by the Federal Bureau of Labor Statistics (BLS) to keep tabs on the changing cost of living. The products and services that consumers commonly buy are considered in determining the general cost of living. This total group of items is divided into categories: food, housing, apparel, transportation, medical care, entertainment, and other. In computing the overall index, each category is given a weight, depending on what percentage the items in that category represent in an average person's budget. The CPI is not only calculated for the total group of about 400 items, but is calculated for changes in each of the categories. Prices from various locations in the country are considered to determine a national average. Since food is such an important item in a family's cost of living, a CPI on a hypothetical *"market basket"* of typical food purchases is regularly announced. The "market basket" would include items such as milk, eggs, bread, steak, poultry and vegetables.

In computing the CPI, a base year is selected. The number 100 is assigned to the base year in order to make comparisons. If the CPI figure this year were 185, it would mean that prices in general were 85 percent higher than in the base year. In the adjacent graph, the base year is 1975. The overall consumer price index rose between 1975 and 1982 from 100 to 178.6, or a rise of about 78 percent. ***U.S. News & World Report*** calculated its own "market basket" index from food prices in eight cities around the U.S., using items used in the BLS's food category. As indicated, often the price changes in one category differ significantly from the overall CPI.

The base period is usually a year in which prices were neither especially high or low. The base period also should be one in the not-too-distant past. It is important, when comparing prices over a period of time, that similar products are used as a basis for computing the index. A tomato is a tomato, whether it was bought in 1960 or today, but a medium-sized automobile today is considerably different from what it was in 1960. The year 1975 is a good base year for comparing prices in the early 1980s.

The CPI and how it is calculated become involved in much political controversy. Political leaders in office do not like to see the CPI rise significantly during their terms because voters will blame them for inflation and vote them out of office. Businesses and governments must pay higher salaries and pensions when the CPI rises.

Most economists agree that the index exaggerates the cost of living. In recent years, they say, the overall increase in the CPI exceeded an average consumer's actual costs by as much as 2 percent. For example:

● Rising housing prices and mortage-interest rates were a chief source of the nation's inflation. Yet, the vast majority of Americans did not buy a new house. Most homeowners still are paying modest mortgages on homes that were purchased prior to the recent price surge.

● High gasoline prices caused nationwide transportation costs to climb 18.2 percent during 1979. As a result, many automobile drivers cut back on their consumption of gas. Automobile sales also declined. But the consumer price index was not altered to reflect the reduction in automobile travel caused by the gas crunch.

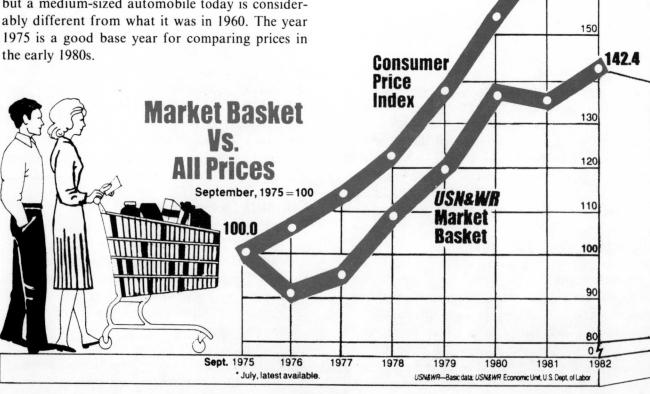

Market Basket Vs. All Prices

September, 1975 = 100

100.0

Consumer Price Index

178.6*

142.4

USN&WR **Market Basket**

170
160
150
130
120
110
100
90
80
0

Sept. 1975   1976   1977   1978   1979   1980   1981   1982

* July, latest available.

USN&WR—Basic data: USN&WR Economic Unit, U.S. Dept. of Labor

Inflation by Decade

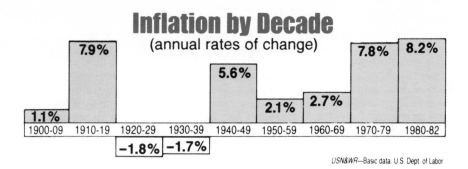

(annual rates of change)

1.1%	7.9%	−1.8%	−1.7%	5.6%	2.1%	2.7%	7.8%	8.2%
1900-09	1910-19	1920-29	1930-39	1940-49	1950-59	1960-69	1970-79	1980-82

USN&WR—Basic data: U.S. Dept. of Labor

● Food prices rose, led by big increases for beef and veal. Here again, the government's statistics failed to recognize that many shoppers simply stopped buying these products when the prices got too high. Instead, they bought less expensive foods.

● A number of municipalities cut taxes in response to citizen pressure. For these residents, the cost of home ownership declined. But their experience does not fit with government statistics showing that the cost of home ownership rose.

● Although the consumer price index shows that medical costs rose 9.3 per cent in 1979, many American workers enjoyed health-care benefits financed fully by their employers. Therefore, these workers did not feel the full brunt of rising medical costs.

● Since 1975, the consumer price index has been used to trigger automatic cost-of-living increases in Social Security benefits. Yet the index does not reflect the buying patterns of elderly Americans. Retired people seldom buy such expensive items as houses or cars.

Buying Power of 1900 Dollar

(as deflated by the consumer price index)

1900 $1 1930 50¢

1960 28¢ 1982 9¢

Living Standards— U.S. Still Ranks High

ZURICH

DESPITE RISING PRICES and persistent recession, American paychecks still go further than those in any other part of the world.

That's the conclusion of a new study by the Union Bank of Switzerland here. It surveyed prices and wages in business centers of the non-Communist world during the first half of 1982 and compared the purchasing power of typical paychecks. The result, said the bank, is that, on the whole, living standards in U.S. cities outstripped those in other lands.

In Los Angeles, for instance, an employe has to work only about half as long as a Londoner to pay for a basic package of goods, services and housing. The contrast is even greater with workers in such spots as Tokyo, Rio de Janeiro and Singapore.

Much of the American lead is the result of fatter paychecks. Even after deductions, hourly pay in New York in 12 occupations ranging from an unskilled factory worker to a departmental manager averaged $7.60. That compared with $6.70 in Tokyo and $5.70 in Düsseldorf, key cities whose goods compete vigorously with those made in the United States.

When it comes to the cost of daily living, U.S. city dwellers are more fortunate than many others. An assortment of basic goods and services priced at $945 in Los Angeles would come to $1,388 in Tokyo, the bank said. It explained that it tried to base its survey generally on what a European family of three would commonly buy.

Some of the greatest variations show up in housing costs. The bank found that rents for unfurnished three-room apartments covered in its survey ran from $2,160 a month to $170, or even lower where rates are subsidized.

The charts show how three U.S. cities compare with other major centers.

Hours of Work Needed to Bu

City	Hours
Los Angeles	195.5
Zurich	196.9
Toronto	207.5
Chicago	210.0
Johannesburg	217.9
Amsterdam	235.3
Düsseldorf	243.9
Sydney	246.0
Brussels	249.4
Stockholm	250.7
Vienna	266.3
New York	268.0
Paris	272.4
Madrid	302.9
Tel Aviv	320.7
London	381.1
Bahrain	394.1
Milan	397.6
Caracas	430.9
Tokyo	529.
Rio de Janeiro	
Hong Kong	
Panama City	
Manila	
Singapore	

Comparing Prices Shoppers Pay

City	Food (39 items)	Rent (3-room, unfurnished apartment per month)	Auto (medium priced, four door)	Gasoline (1 gallon, premium)	TV (22-in colo
Amsterdam	$187	$ 290	$ 7,433	$2.50	$ 6
Bahrain	$375	$1,030	$ 8,020	$ .74	$ 7
Brussels	$208	$ 440	$ 6,415	$2.21	$ 6
Caracas	$305	$ 830	$ 9,814	$ .33	$ 9
Chicago	$284	$ 720	$ 9,838	$1.36	$ 6
Düsseldorf	$228	$ 520	$ 7,391	$2.12	$ 7
Hong Kong	$257	$1,530	$ 9,219	$1.69	$ 5
Johannesburg	$192	$ 260	$ 7,863	$2.23	$ 8
London	$215	$ 720	$ 9,495	$2.19	$ 5
Los Angeles	$245	$ 560	$ 8,700	$1.49	$ 4
Madrid	$198	$ 400	$ 8,252	$2.54	$ 8
Manila	$187	$ 460	$ 8,539	$2.37	$ 9
Milan	$202	$ 300	$ 8,340	$2.75	$ 5
New York	$281	$ 980	$ 8,148	$1.48	$ 5
Panama City	$196	$ 980	$ 7,000	$2.25	$ 5
Paris	$225	$ 520	$ 8,073	$2.68	$ 8
Rio de Janeiro	$194	$ 610	$ 9,752	$2.70	$ 6
Singapore	$292	$1,360	$17,710	$1.83	$ 4
Stockholm	$280	$ 310	$ 9,301	$2.39	$ 9
Sydney	$230	$ 600	$ 7,978	$1.51	$ 7
Tel Aviv	$128	$ 170	$11,774	$2.10	$ 8
Tokyo	$554	$2,160	$ 5,440	$2.84	$ 5
Toronto	$250	$ 480	$ 5,645	$1.26	$ 8
Vienna	$210	$ 440	$ 7,574	$2.52	$ 8
Zurich	$306	$ 640	$ 7,561	$2.31	$1,0

ackage of Basic Goods, Services

656.7
712.1
720.0
1,237.8
1,455.0

Note: Package of basic goods includes food, clothing, housing, other needs. Pay based on average of 12 occupations after taxes.

ring, 1982)

...en's ...thes (...ieces)	Men's Clothes (6 pieces)	Bus (6 miles on local transport)	Telephone (monthly rate)	Cigarettes (20 Marlboros)	Whisky (0.7 liter)	Hotel (double room, breakfast)
...97	$317	$ .63	$ 8.82	$1.20	$ 7.46	$ 93
...96	$596	$ .13	$10.36	$ .78	$13.47	$159
...82	$385	$ .52	$ 6.85	$ .97	$ 8.65	$ 96
...28	$659	$ .29	$ 6.86	$1.14	$20.72	$104
...94	$490	$ .90	$ 3.30	$ .95	$ 9.14	$156
...82	$331	$ .91	$11.49	$1.31	$ 7.43	$100
...02	$330	$ .28	$ 5.99	$ .63	$ 7.32	$102
...07	$329	$ .46	$ 3.02	$ .78	$ 7.48	$ 89
...90	$387	$1.03	$ 8.67	$1.70	$10.98	$164
...79	$462	$ .85	$ 9.24	$ .85	$ 8.37	$122
...38	$336	$ .27	$ 3.98	$ .89	$ 9.14	$ 54
...64	$ 93	$ .15	$ 7.76	$ .41	$14.42	$ 98
...79	$290	$ .15	$ 4.63	$1.14	$ 5.30	$ 97
...34	$492	$ .75	$11.24	$ .88	$12.98	$152
...80	$575	$ .17	$10.51	$ .80	$12.02	$105
...57	$376	$ .53	$14.12	$1.14	$ 9.22	$150
...45	$236	$ .24	$ 2.58	$ .11	$53.21	$ 85
...82	$306	$ .30	$ 9.21	$ .92	$14.63	$122
...80	$442	$ .68	$ 5.65	$1.85	$19.25	$123
...48	$437	$ .67	$ 8.22	$1.15	$13.50	$110
...91	$295	$ .26	$ 3.81	$ .83	$10.32	$ 71
...32	$486	$ .50	$ 7.50	$1.21	$34.54	$133
...50	$346	$ .60	$ 8.71	$ .97	$ 9.76	$105
...76	$315	$ .91	$ 9.98	$1.75	$10.55	$ 95
...72	$365	$ .61	$10.18	$1.13	$18.56	$110

Note: Food prices are those in supermarkets; rents are for medium-priced apartments, including most utilities, women's clothing is for medium-priced summer dress, jacket, skirt, panty hose, day shoes, men's clothing is for medium-priced two-piece suit, blazer, shirt, socks, shoes, telephone is single-party service, hotel rates include service in first-class hotel. Prices are computed on the basis of exchange rates in the spring of 1982

USN&WR—Basic data: Union Bank of Switzerland

How Long It Takes to Make Ends Meet

What most would call necessities of life—a car, gasoline, electricity and shelter, to name a few—required far more working time to acquire in 1982 than they did 10 years earlier. The typical manufacturing worker, for instance, needed to work almost 13 hours a month just to pay ordinary electric and natural-gas bills, compared with about 7 hours in 1972.

Against these setbacks, most foods took slightly less working time to buy, as did a movie ticket and a six-pack of beer.

On the whole, however, the buying power of the average factory worker's paycheck has fallen every year since 1978. For a glimpse at what happened—

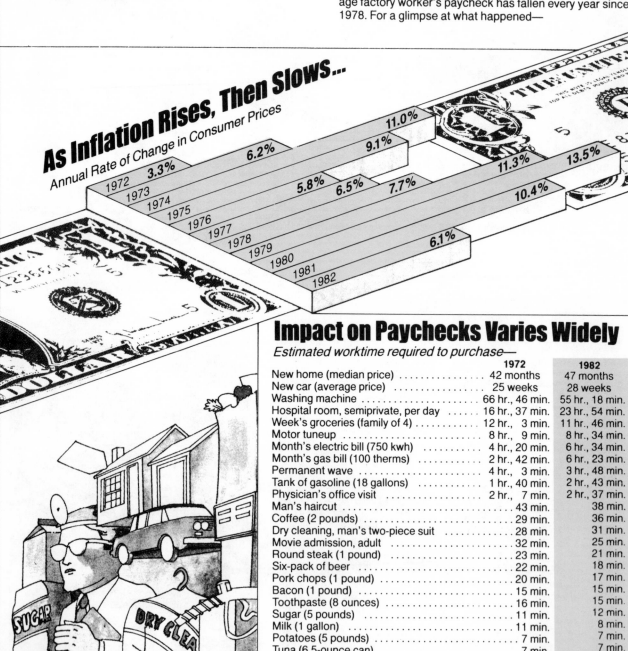

As Inflation Rises, Then Slows...
Annual Rate of Change in Consumer Prices

Year	Rate
1972	3.3%
1973	6.2%
1974	11.0%
1975	9.1%
1976	5.8%
1977	6.5%
1978	7.7%
1979	11.3%
1980	13.5%
1981	10.4%
1982	6.1%

Impact on Paychecks Varies Widely
Estimated worktime required to purchase—

	1972	1982
New home (median price)	42 months	47 months
New car (average price)	25 weeks	28 weeks
Washing machine	66 hr., 46 min.	55 hr., 18 min.
Hospital room, semiprivate, per day	16 hr., 37 min.	23 hr., 54 min.
Week's groceries (family of 4)	12 hr., 3 min.	11 hr., 46 min.
Motor tuneup	8 hr., 9 min.	8 hr., 34 min.
Month's electric bill (750 kwh)	4 hr., 20 min.	6 hr., 34 min.
Month's gas bill (100 therms)	2 hr., 42 min.	6 hr., 23 min.
Permanent wave	4 hr., 3 min.	3 hr., 48 min.
Tank of gasoline (18 gallons)	1 hr., 40 min.	2 hr., 43 min.
Physician's office visit	2 hr., 7 min.	2 hr., 37 min.
Man's haircut	43 min.	38 min.
Coffee (2 pounds)	29 min.	36 min.
Dry cleaning, man's two-piece suit	28 min.	31 min.
Movie admission, adult	32 min.	25 min.
Round steak (1 pound)	23 min.	21 min.
Six-pack of beer	22 min.	18 min.
Pork chops (1 pound)	20 min.	17 min.
Bacon (1 pound)	15 min.	15 min.
Toothpaste (8 ounces)	16 min.	15 min.
Sugar (5 pounds)	11 min.	12 min.
Milk (1 gallon)	11 min.	8 min.
Potatoes (5 pounds)	7 min.	7 min.
Tuna (6.5-ounce can)	7 min.	7 min.
Eggs, dozen	9 min.	6 min.
Cigarettes, pack	7 min.	6 min.
Chicken (1 pound)	6 min.	5 min
White bread (1 pound)	4 min.	4 min.

Note: Figures are based on average hourly wage in manufacturing—$3.82 in 1972 and $8.50 in 1982, and assume a 40-hour workweek.

USN&WR—Basic data: U.S. Depts. of Agriculture, Commerce and Labor and Federal Home Loan Bank Board

Chapter 6

Consumer credit

- *Credit has enabled a huge expansion of the economy.*

- *While credit can improve one's standard of living it must be used cautiously or disaster can occur.*

Dr. Morello, a physician in Mexico City, is building a house for his family. The foundation of the house was first laid four years ago. Dr. Morello goes to the local meeting place for workers and hires men to do concrete work for him, or lay brick, or lay tile, or put in plumbing. As each job is accomplished, he pays the workers in cash. Dr. Morello often waits several months after one task is completed before starting another. He has to wait to accrue more cash.

Ed Baker, a physician in Denver, Colorado, is also building a house for his family. The foundation of the house was laid four months ago. Dr. Baker went to a bank and borrowed money for a construction loan. Many tasks are accomplished simultaneously on his house. Stone-masons, carpenters, and plumbers might all be at work on the same day. Dr. Baker didn't have to worry about having the cash to pay the workers' salaries. The bank loan provided enough money for paying workers and buying materials. Dr. Baker's house is almost completed after four months. Dr. Morello's house still has a long way to go after four years.

The use of credit in the United States has enabled expansion of the economy, providing goods and services to Americans on a scale greater than any place else in the world at any time in history.

Years ago, most consumers were reluctant to go into debt; people used credit only in emergencies. The use of consumer credit has expanded rapidly in recent years, and today is used to buy homes, automobiles, furniture, appliances, gasoline, vaca-tions, hospital care, flowers—just about anything a person might want.

Consumers' debt in the past twenty years has increased nearly ten times. Altogether, American consumers owe more than $1.8 trillion, most of it for home mortgages.

Nearly every household owes some money or has some debts, usually in the form of car loans, house mortgages and charges on credit cards. On these loans, people pay *interest,* a percentage of the amount borrowed. Interest is the price paid for the use of money. The interest has to be high enough to make it worthwhile for lenders to give up funds that they might use for other purposes.

The wise use of credit

Debt can be a good thing, provided a family can meet the schedule of payments for loans or credit cards. Buying a home is one example of a wise debt. It would take years for the average family to save enough to buy a home with cash. Many would never make it, while a large share of their income would still go for housing in the form of rent. A mortgage loan from a bank or other lending institution lets them live in and enjoy their homes while they are paying off their debt. During periods of prosperity, when real estate prices are rising, the homeowner also benefits from ownership of increasingly valuable property.

Buying an automobile or household goods on credit permits the consumer to have the use of a product sooner and, in times of inflation, to purchase it at a lower cost than in the future. The use of credit cards has the advantage of consolidating many time-payments for a number of items, thereby reducing the time spent in paying bills and making it easier to account for how much is owed.

Still, buying on credit poses at least two major risks for the consumer: 1) borrowing costs money; high interest rates could make the item purchased a bad buy, and 2) it makes spending too easy for some people. Consumers have to be very careful not to borrow more money than they can afford to pay back.

When debt is too high

American consumers, influenced by easy access to credit, have built up a tremendous amount of debt. When the U.S. economy slumps, people's ability to pay their debts is impaired. The result can be a rash of *personal bankruptcies,* as there were during the recession of the early 1980s.

The excessive use of credit can be a factor in bringing about a recession. Although consumer spending generates sales dollars and stimulates retail business, too much spending can be unhealthy for the economy.

When consumers save, they make money available to businesses to build and modernize. This creates jobs and helps U.S. firms compete more effectively with foreign companies. Saving and investing money may help to increase productivity in a sluggish economy. A balance between spending and saving is necessary. Sometimes citizens are urged to buy, sometimes they are urged to save, depending upon the state of the economy.

Truth-in-Lending

In 1969, Congress passed a bill called the ***Truth-in-Lending Act,*** that required lenders to provide borrowers with certain basic information: the total amount of the loan, the number of payments, the amount of payments, the total amount paid over the period of the loan, and the annual rate of interest.

Interest on some debts is computed on the total amount: If the debt is $1200 at 10 percent interest and is paid off in a year, the payments are $112 per month for 12 months. Other debts are *amortized*—as each payment reduces the amount of the debt, interest is paid only on the declining balance. It is to the advantage of the borrower to have a debt which can be amortized.

It pays to shop around for a loan and find the best source. Interest rates will vary widely among different types of lending agencies and banks. On the average, credit unions are the cheapest source of borrowing, and small loan companies, the most expensive. If it were necessary to borrow $500 in order to purchase a refrigerator, the amount of interest to be paid on a one-year loan would vary considerably. Different credit institutions might charge the following interest:

Credit unions .... $45-$60
Banks......................... $50-$75
Small loan companies.......... $90-$120
Installment purchase credit...... $60-$80

The extension of credit has enabled people to

People in Trouble

Nonbusiness Bankruptcies: 304,248 / 211,348 / 182,249 (1971, 1976, 1982)

Mortgage Foreclosures: 16,060 / 9,029 (1st half/2nd half 1978, 1979, 1980, 1981)

Note: Years ended June 30 through 1979, March 31 thereafter. USN&WR—Basic data: Administrative Office of the U.S. Courts, Federal Home Loan Bank Board. Note: Figures are for mortgages by Insured savings associations.

buy far more products than their incomes might permit, and it has made possible the huge expansion in the economy. But, just as there are risks for the consumer who may abuse credit and buy more than he or she can afford, there are dangers for the whole economy if it expands too far. Too much spending may result in a too rapid increase in prices. Too little spending may result in a sluggish economy.

Who owes the national debt

The total national debt now exceeds $5 trillion dollars. Economists look at three major categories of borrowers—businesses, individuals and governments.

The fastest debt growth has been business borrowing.

Individuals owe more than 35 percent of all debt, a share that has remained steady over the years. Home mortgages account for nearly two-thirds of this debt.

Governments borrow large sums to finance their budgets when taxes do not provide sufficient revenue. Government debt is a cause for concern because government borrowing competes for money and may drive up interest rates for businesses and individuals.

Personal Bankruptcy

PORTER, Tex.

Michael and Paula Randall got drawn into the whirl of the credit carrousel until they fell off in a heap.

"It finally caught up with us," says Michael, a 25-year-old assistant maintenance supervisor for a Houston manufacturing plant. To avoid losing their home, he and his wife declared bankruptcy two years ago.

That wasn't the way it was supposed to end when the Randalls purchased their version of the American dream in 1979: A three-bedroom, two-bath brick house for $48,000. To celebrate, they bought and bought. "We weren't watching what we were doing," Michael admits.

The Randalls bought an expensive car and all sorts of home furnishings. Their utility bill was triple what they had been paying. An adoption attempt cost more than expected.

Then came the bill juggling. "We would pay one bill one month and another the next," Paula recalls. "I don't know how we managed to shuffle them for as long as we did."

One bill the couple couldn't continue to shuffle was the mortgage, which fell nearly $1,400 in arrears. When their lender threatened foreclosure, the Randalls filed for bankruptcy. In all, they owed $13,610.

Bankruptcy took "a load off my shoulders" by keeping creditors at bay, says Michael. The couple's debts are being paid off over 50 months. Debt and mortgage payments are deducted directly from Michael's paycheck. The Randalls now pay for most purchases with cash. Once they get out of hock, Paula vows, "we'll never be back in debt again."

NORTH RIDGEVILLE, Ohio

Terry Winchester's high hopes of becoming a successful entrepreneur were dashed in less than five years by the volatile economy.

"If interest rates hadn't gone sky-high, if residential construction hadn't dropped to next to nothing and if unemployment had stayed down," Winchester says now, "I'd have a very prosperous business today."

Instead, the 40-year-old operator of a now defunct home-insulation company in this Cleveland suburb is considering bankruptcy.

Home insulation seemed like "one of the better businesses to be in" back in 1977 when he started, Winchester recalls. "The economy was booming, people were employed, houses were selling, utility bills were rising and people were becoming more energy conscious," he says. "The future seemed pretty rosy."

So rosy, in fact, that Winchester invested $30,000 in machines that blow insulation into wall panels, and other equipment. He hired 10 people. The investment paid off handsomely, for a while. His sales volume leaped quickly to $300,000 a year, mostly in jobs for builders of new homes. But, in late 1979, the market soured while Winchester's costs began to soar, rising by nearly 40 percent over the next two years. He couldn't meet builder demands for price cuts.

Business plummeted. New-home contracts fell to fewer than 50 from 150. Jobs on existing homes dropped to 20 from 50. Debt payments were difficult to meet. By the winter of 1981, Winchester was down to two employes. He dismissed them in April, closed his business and, owing $70,000, moved in with his parents.

Now he has put his equipment up for sale and is talking with a lawyer about bankruptcy and other options. "I could never really catch up," Winchester reflects. "The jobs were getting scarcer, and the bills kept coming."

ATLANTA

Roger Louis Curry is a man of principle who now is on a toboggan slide toward bankruptcy.

"When you get something, you should pay for it," the 30-year-old chiropractor declares. "That's what my mother taught me, and I believe it."

But Curry didn't, or couldn't, follow his mother's wisdom. He now owes $30,000 that must be paid out of his $20,000-a-year salary.

Curry's 1975 car already has been repossessed. He has put himself in the hands of a credit-counseling service. He fears that his dream of opening his own office is in jeopardy.

Curry says the divorce three years ago was his undoing. "When we broke up, the income wasn't there," Curry recalls. Under the terms of the settlement, he says, his spouse got the children, "and I got all the bills"—$19,000 in debts that included student loans for himself and his ex-wife plus $10,000 owed the Internal Revenue Service in back taxes.

In retrospect, Curry concedes that he "did not have enough discipline" to resist easy credit. The couple bought appliances, clothes, gasoline and a Caribbean vacation, among other things, on credit.

Today, he has only $180 a month left for food and other expenses after paying his rent and consolidated debt.

Curry feels he's in a no-win game. Interest on the debt is high. The IRS and other creditors are demanding bigger payments. One way out would be to earn more by opening a private practice. But that requires money, which he doesn't have, or a good credit record, which he doesn't have either.

Who Owes The Nation's $5 Trillion Debt

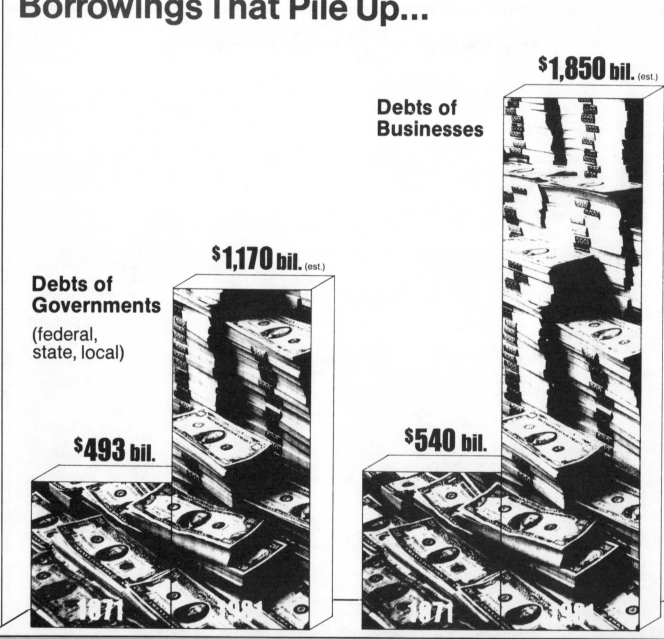

Borrowings That Pile Up...

Debts of Businesses — $1,850 bil. (est.)

Debts of Governments (federal, state, local) — $1,170 bil. (est.)

$493 bil. — $540 bil.

Up $677 billion, or 137%   Up $1,310 billion, or 243%

$1,930 bil. (est.)

$666 bil.

1971

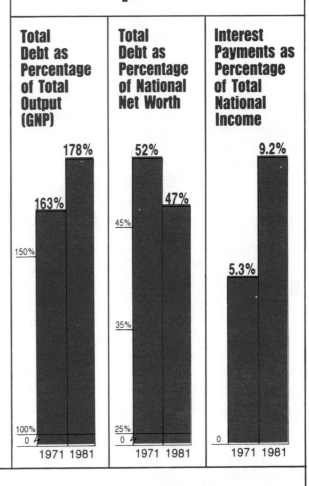

...And Their Impact

Total Debt as Percentage of Total Output (GNP)		Total Debt as Percentage of National Net Worth		Interest Payments as Percentage of Total National Income	
163%	178%	52%	47%	5.3%	9.2%
1971	1981	1971	1981	1971	1981

150%

100%
0

45%

35%

25%
0

All debt, apportioned to every adult American, now amounts to about $30,000 per person, compared with about $12,500 in 1971.

USN&WR charts—Basic data: Federal Reserve Board, 1981 estimates by *USN&WR* Economic Unit

Chapter 7

Business

- *The U.S. economy is characterized by millions of small businesses, but a few large corporations make the largest share of the profits.*

- *There is an optimum size for a company beyond which it become inefficient.*

A few generations ago, an American family could produce most of the food and clothing it needed to sustain itself. Those days are gone, replaced by an era in which almost everyone plays a specialized role in a complex network of producers and consumers. Today, business enterprises bring together workers, raw materials, machinery, and money to make a product or perform a service.

A business enterprise can be as simple as a single person producing one item or as complicated as a giant corporation with many subdivisions manufacturing hundreds of products. Businesses depend on consumers. To succeed, a business must offer goods and/or services that customers want, at prices they will pay. It must also operate efficiently enough to make a profit. Around 15 million U.S. firms of all sizes are producing goods ranging from autos to chewing gum, and providing services ranging from filling a tooth to serving thousands of meals at a convention. Eighty percent of all businesses employ fewer than twenty persons. At the opposite extreme, there are several thousand large firms which employ hundreds or thousands of workers each. More than 750,000 persons work for General Motors, and American Telephone & Telegraph employs almost as many. The annual sales of these two companies are greater than $20 billion each.

Large business firms account for most of the goods and services produced in our economy. When measured by sales value, a little more than one percent of all manufacturing firms produce almost two-thirds of the manufactured goods.

A business enterprise may begin with the *entrepreneur*—a person who sees a need, figures out how to meet it, and is willing to take risks. That person must put together the other factors of production: *land, labor* and *resources*.

Sometimes, starting a business is a matter of seeing new ways to combine existing products and methods. Henry Ford did not invent the automobile, but he initiated the assembly-line method of production to manufacture cars economically. Ray Kroc, founder of McDonald's, did not invent the hamburger or the drive-in restaurant, but he thought of a way to sell a product of standardized quality with quick service, at a low price.

Economist John Kenneth Galbraith has explained how the concept of entrepreneurship has been transformed with the growth of *large corporations*. In his book, **The New Industrial State**, he described how modern corporations are guided by management teams of engineers, scientists, or business specialists rather than by the adventurous, risk-taking individual who heads a company alone. The heads of such companies as IBM, General Motors, and U.S. Steel would not be described as daring entrepreneurs. Unlike the early days of American industry, few of these people's names are household words. High-level executives depend upon advice from research and planning teams to guide the operations of most big businesses today. Still, modern-day tycoons exist. The computer industry has many young entrepreneurs who have successfully started fast-growth companies. Steven Jobs, who founded Apple Computer Company when he was in his early twenties, is an example.

Sole proprietorship

The simplest form of business is the *sole proprietorship*, which is a business owned and operated by an individual. This is also the most popular type, accounting for nearly 80% of all U.S. businesses. Many TV technicians, plumbers, doctors, dentists and small shopkeepers operate sole proprietorships. Some are family businesses handed down through generations; others may have been purchased from previous owners. Thousands of new businesses are started each year in the United States. The rate of failure for a new business is very high, but some develop into successful enterprises.

The trend to big business

Large corporations account for more than 85 percent of all business sales receipts in this country, and their share has been rising. Why the trend toward big business? One reason is the public demand for products—cars, televisions, dishwashers and tape recorders—that cannot be manufactured efficiently by small businesses. These goods require large outlays of capital for research and development, automated equipment, highly skilled labor, and large sales forces—money only big business can raise.

Thus, the large corporation has come to dominate the business side of today's economy. The 500 largest companies in America account for more than 50 percent of all sales and earn more than three-fourths of all corporate profits. One example of a large company is General Motors, which has annual revenues exceeding the total production value (gross national product) of all but seventeen of the nations in the world.

The corporation is the preferred form of business venture for another reason. If a corporation is legally declared bankrupt, the owners (stockholders) may lose everything they have invested in it, but they usually cannot be required to pay the corporation's debts. The owner's risk, therefore, is limited.

In a corporation, ownership is divided into shares of *stock* that are offered and sold to investors. Investors purchase shares in the hope of receiving a portion of future profits through *dividends* (that share of a company's profits distributed to shareholders) and with the expectation that the value of the stock will increase as the company grows.

The stock market

Many people get their main impression of how business is faring from daily reports of the ups and downs of the stock market.

Stock prices, in some ways, are a gauge of the nation's economic health. The trading of stocks and bonds not only reflects the ebb and flow of

Ways of Organizing Production under Private Enterprise
Four Types of Businesses

Type of Organization	Formation	Ownership	Control and Management	Net Profits or Losses
Sole Proprietorship	Individual decision of person who starts business or buys from another	Individual	By owner or persons delegated by owner	Profits to owner; losses borne by owner
Partnership	By agreement between associates (Partners)	Jointly by two or more individuals	By partners or persons they delegate	Shared according to partnership agreement
Corporation	Organized by associates, or a person; legalized through state charter	Stockholders, according to number of shares	Board of directors elected by stockholders	Dividends to stockholders according to number of shares
Cooperative	By agreement among interested parties; usually incorporated under special laws for cooperatives	Member-patrons	Board of directors elected by the members	Profits distributed to members according to amount of purchases

When You Buy Stocks—

Here's what happens when you decide to buy shares listed on the New York Stock Exchange, a chain of events similar to that for transactions on other major securities markets:

1. Select a local broker, talk over investment plans and place an order.

2. You tell the broker to buy, say, 100 shares in XYZ Auto, at either a specific price or "at the market."

3. The broker phones or wires the order through his main office to the brokerage's member on the floor of the exchange.

4. The floor broker goes to the area where XYZ Auto is being traded, finds a broker offering to sell and makes a bid.

5. When price is agreed upon, the two floor brokers report the trade to their offices. Customers are notified.

6. The buyer has five business days to pay for the stock. The seller also has five days to deliver his shares to his broker. When he does, his certificate is canceled; a new one is mailed to the buyer.

jobs, goods, and services, but also influences them.

The stock market represents an enormous amount of wealth. Millions of people have investments in corporations; they own shares of the stock issued by a corporation—or hold *equity capital.* Institutions, such as pension funds, insurance companies, and bank trust departments are major stockholders that hold stock for the benefit of millions of individuals.

Initially, stock is sold by a corporation to raise money. Once all the shares are sold, further trading occurs between individuals. Most of the trade on the stock exchanges, such as the New York Stock Exchange, is between individuals.

The equity capital system has provided a great stimulus to American business: It raises money for growth while sharing the risk of losses with stockholders. In turn, stockholders, as legal owners, share in the decisions and profits of business.

There are two types of stock—*preferred* and *common.* Both types represent shares of ownership in a company, but preferred stock carries certain advantages. All of a company's stockholders have the right to share in its profits by receiving dividends, but preferred stockholders are first in line. If a company goes bankrupt and is forced to sell its assets, preferred stockholders are compensated for their shares as soon as the creditors have been paid. Common stockholders are repaid after

creditors and preferred stockholders, if any money remains.

Common stockholders do have the right to vote for company directors and, thus, have a hand in managing the company. Preferred stockholders do not have this power. In good years, it's possible that the dividends received by common stockholders may be larger than those paid to preferred owners because preferred stock carries a fixed dividend rate, while the common stockholders' dividend can vary.

Even people who do not own stocks feel more confident, more inclined to spend, if stocks climb. A long sinking spell on Wall Street is likely to make the public cautious. The stock market's influence goes beyond its immediate impact. If a company's stock is rising, it is more likely to issue new shares to raise money to expand and modernize its plants, thus generating both business and jobs.

While the efficiency of U.S. stock exchanges is the envy of most of the world, equity capital has its drawbacks for the economy. Corporate management knows it has a responsibility to stockholders to keep dividend rates up and protect the value of their shares of stock. It feels the pressure to maximize profits in the short run, and may not spend on equipment and plant changes which might lead to increased production in the future.

The typical buyer of stocks looks for two returns

on his money: 1) regular dividends that increase and 2) a rise in the price of the stock so it can be sold for more than he paid. Those prospects are constantly studied by shareholders, other investors who think they might buy the stock, and analysts in big investment houses. A stock's price in the short run is a a composite of all these appraisals.

Any unexpected event that challenges this assessment shows up quickly in a price change. If earnings per share go down when they were expected to go up, or if a new product turns out to be a failure, or if a company's markets are taken over by competitors with cheaper or better wares, a stock's price is sure to fall. An unforeseen increase in profits or the announcement of a major invention could send a stock soaring.

Through all of this, the Securities and Exchange Commission (SEC) keeps an eye on things. Its job is to prevent the investor from being fleeced through dishonest touting of securities, misleading reports on a company's fortunes or unfair trading practices.

But even the best-informed investor has no guarantee against losses. It's not just events in the affairs of individual companies that affect stock prices. Broad economic tides raise or lower the earnings of business as a whole, and the prices of most stocks rise or fall on these tides. When investors become uncertain about the outlook for business in general, they pull back from buying stocks and look more closely at alternatives, such as bonds or short-term securities.

Corporations borrow

Most money that corporations attract from investors comes through borrowing—by selling notes and bonds. When a corporation borrows money by selling bonds, it promises to pay a specified amount of money (the face value of the bond) at a specified time (maturity date). It also promises to pay a certain rate of interest until the bond matures.

The face value of a bond should not be confused with its price. Once a corporation sells a bond, all other trading of that bond is done between individuals, and the price fluctuates with market conditions. Bond prices fluctuate mostly in response to interest rates. If a $1,000 bond is sold to pay an interest rate of eight percent a year, its price will fall below $1,000 whenever investors find new bonds that are equally good and that pay, say nine percent.

In short, a rise in available yields means a drop in bond price and vice versa. Potential bondholders want to earn the best possible rate of return (interest rate) on their investment. The corporation is only

1 XYZ Chair Company, seeing strong sales forecasts, finances construction of second factory by issuing $10 million of 20-year bonds.

2 Project stimulates local economy by creating new jobs for architects, engineers, construction workers and, upon completion, furniture designers, machine operators, upholsterers, bookkeepers and janitors.

3 To make more chairs, XYZ buys additional lumber, hardware, varnish and fabrics. To meet this added demand, suppliers expand their capacities and, in turn, create still more new jobs.

4 Interest paid to XYZ's bondholders is spent or reinvested in the bond market—and the process begins anew.

Investment Capital It Goes a Long Way

USN&WR

responsible to make interest payments and pay the bond's $1,000 face value at the maturity date.

While many persons invest some savings in bonds, most are bought by big pension funds, banks and insurance firms, which value these securities for their safe income. Typically, bonds are sold in minimum denominations of $1,000. The average price of a share of stock traded on the New York Stock Exchange is about $30. Bonds are more secure than stocks. If a corporation is strapped for funds, it must pay interest due on its bonds before it pays any dividends on its stock. If a company goes broke, bondholders are among the first in line and stockholders last when the firm's assets are divided up. This lower risk makes bonds appealing to many investors and explains why the bond market is steadier than the stock market.

The commodities market

There's another market that is much riskier than the bond or stock markets—the *commodities market* where raw materials are traded. Transactions are mainly in *futures*—contracts to buy or sell a commodity at a later date.

Heavy traders, or *speculators,* of grains like corn or wheat realize that if a crop is harvested in the fall, there will be a glut on the market and prices will be down. The speculator purchases the grain with the aim of selling it at a profit in the spring when the harvest has dwindled. In doing this, speculators perform a valuable service: By buying in the fall, they bid the low prices up, then, in the spring, their sale of grain increases the supply on the market and pushes the price down. The action of speculators tends to even out the potentially huge seasonal fluctuations of commodities and, ultimately, food prices on grocers' shelves.

Using commodities markets, big firms that process and store large quantities of raw goods like wheat, soybeans, cotton or copper can protect themselves against unforeseen price changes in the market. They do this by *hedging*—balancing their cash purchases with future sales contracts. For example, say a warehouse pays $1.00 a bushel to a Midwestern farmer for grain in November and stores the grain until May. The company doesn't want to be surprised by a lower price in the spring, so it finds a buyer (through a commodities exchange, such as the Chicago Board of Trade) for future grain. The May futures price is higher than the current price, say $1.10 a bushel. And the 10-cent a bushel difference is a fair return for the cost of storing grain over the winter.

In the spring, when the warehouse firm is ready to deliver its grain, it need not worry about the price per bushel. Even if the market price has dropped to $.90 a bushel, and it stands to lose $.10 on the fall purchase, it has a contract to sell at $1.10. The firm can buy any extra grain it needs at the $.90 market price, recovering the $.10 per bushel it lost on the sale of the original November purchase, along with the $.10 profit it made by selling futures, to cover the costs of running the storage business.

For that to work, there must be traders, speculators and others, who will buy future contracts when others want to sell. Generally, these people never hold the commodities represented by the contracts they buy and sell. A vast amount of paper is shuffled around, and fortunes are won and lost, with relatively few commodities actually changing hands.

That's one reason many people wonder if trading in all these markets—in stocks and bonds as well as commodities—isn't merely an elaborate form of gambling. True, many investors and traders have the gambler's urge to increase their wealth with minimum effort. But the markets provide an important service in bringing together investors who are willing to take a risk in business activities, thus providing necessary capital for growth and development.

The law of diminishing returns

The size of maximum growth for a company is usually determined by the economic principle of the *law of diminishing returns*. This principle means that with additional inputs of one or more of the factors of production (land, labor or capital) production will increase, but only for a time. At a certain point productivity will level off, then it will decrease. A farmer's task of loading hay may illustrate this principle.

Say a farmer working by himself can bring in approximately a load of hay each day. This is a hard job for one person. He must bale the hay, pick it up off the ground, stack it on the wagon, unload it in the barn, and, finally, climb up to the haymow to stack the hay. If the farmer hires another worker to help, the two of them together could bring in three loads per day—an increase of two loads. It isn't that the second worker is stronger or more energetic. It is simply that working together, they can produce more efficiently.

If a third worker is added to the operation, it is possible that six loads of hay can be brought in each day—an increase of three loads. Up to this point, economists would say that the farmer's operation was in the stage of *increasing returns*. Each additional person increases productivity.

However, the addition of yet another worker changes the situation. With a fourth worker added to the operation, the farmer could bring in eight loads of hay each day—an increase of two loads. Total output has increased again, but not as much as before. The increased output is down from three loads to two loads. The operation is now in the stage of *diminishing returns*. Add more workers, and the output schedule might be similar to that shown in the table below. In bailing hay, or any other production operation, *decreasing returns* may eventually set in. Total production decreases with the addition of an extra person.

The farmer is confronted with a phenomenon known in economics as the *law of diminishing returns*. All businesses must deal with this situation. The manager or entrepreneur must decide how to use the three other factors of production—land, labor, and capital—to get the best results.

The factors of production are also known as *inputs* and the products are known as *outputs*. The rate at which outputs are produced is called *productivity*. The manager always wants to achieve the highest possible level of productivity. Sometimes he needs to hire another person (labor); sometimes he needs to buy more equipment (capital) or employ more resources (land). With any increase or decrease in the factors of production, efficiency will change, and the manager must be aware of the changes in order to make a profit and stay in business.

In the case of the farm example, the field of hay (land), as well as the tractor, haybaler and hay wagon (capital) were *fixed* inputs. They did not change. Labor was the *variable* input because the farmer added workers to help him.

It doesn't mean that an entrepreneur facing diminishing returns will not add more of an input during this stage. If the additonal output produced by extra input is worth more than the cost of that input, it would be worth it to add another unit. However no business would want to reach the point of decreasing returns.

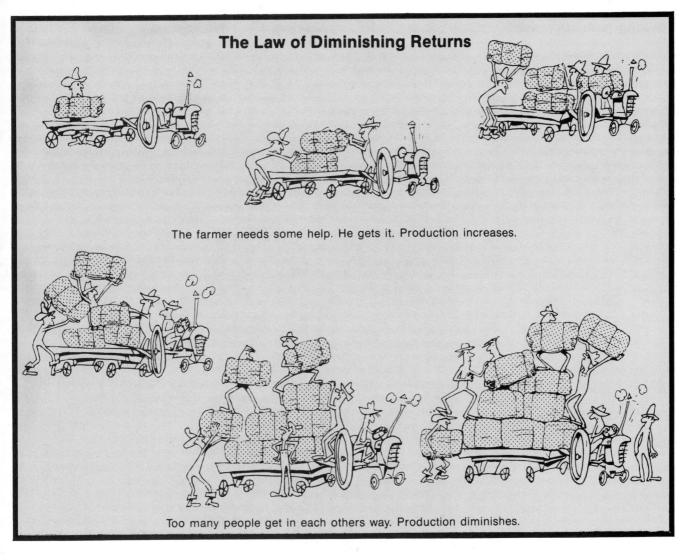

The Law of Diminishing Returns

The farmer needs some help. He gets it. Production increases.

Too many people get in each others way. Production diminishes.

The Sebastiani family samples the fruits of their labor during lunch at their winery.

The Silent Strength Of Family Businesses

Unlike many public firms, decisions come faster—and more sacrifices are made— for long-term success.

What do Snickers candy bars, Estée Lauder cosmetics, Stroh's beer and Sebastiani wines have in common?

All four of these well-known brand names are produced by companies where business is a family affair, with virtually all company stock held by members of one family.

Meetings of the board of directors can start out with kissing and hugging among brothers, sisters and cousins, while a patriarch, matriarch or a descendant of one runs the day-to-day operations.

It's a setup that, some experts say, helped many family businesses ride out the past recession much more successfully than publicly owned companies.

Wide range. Experts estimate that 12.1 million to 14.4 million of the nation's 15 million businesses are family owned, ranging in size from the corner grocery or local car dealership to such giants as Cargill, the international grain company; Bechtel, the construction kingpin, and Estée Lauder, Inc., known worldwide for cosmetics and fragrances.

While many family-owned concerns are reluctant to reveal sales and earnings, economists figure that they account for nearly 50 percent of the nation's gross national product. Nearly half of the nation's nonfarm, private-sector employment—now 72.5 million —is provided by family-owned firms.

Unencumbered by stockholders demanding big dividends each quarter, these businesses often succeed against larger and more established companies by being willing to sacrifice short-term profit for long-range gain and responding quickly to market opportunities.

That strategy helped the Stroh Brewery Company to vault from being the nation's seventh-largest beer brewer to the third biggest last year by acquiring the larger Joseph Schlitz Brewing Company, a publicly traded corporation. Stroh's could borrow funds for the half-billion-dollar takeover—which gave the Detroit-based concern a national distri-

Magazine publisher John H. Johnson is grooming daughter Linda to take over his business.

bution base—because 27 family members were willing to accept the lower dividends required to finance the deal.

"Family sacrifice is one reason we operate successfully," says Peter Stroh, president. The company had 1.3 billion dollars in sales last year, more than 2½ times the 1981 figure.

Similarly, Lennox Industries of Dallas credits its family-owned structure for beating competitors to the market with a new energy-efficient furnace. The heating-and-air-conditioning concern developed this "pulse combustion furnace" at a cost of 4 million dollars in 4½ years—nearly twice as fast as industry experts had thought possible.

In another example of quick action— in which family members accepted a cut in earnings—Lennox decided to move in 1978 and then shifted its headquarters and 800 people from Marshalltown, Iowa, to Dallas in less than five months.

"We can move faster when the opportunities arise," says President John W. Norris, Jr. "We don't have much red tape. There are no political duchies in the company that fight each other." Behind such quick decisions is the unanimity possible in family ownership. Eight of Lennox's 11 directors are related to Norris.

All in the family. In other companies, the whole board is the immediate family. The directors of Sebastiani Vineyards of Sonoma, Calif., are President Sam J. Sebastiani, his mother, his brother and his sister.

Family members can also be called on to do the less desirable jobs. Refugee Le Thi Hang uses seven of her nine children as busboys and cashiers in the prosperous Atlanta restaurant she established on the strength of her ability to turn out delicious Vietnamese-style egg rolls.

Another ingredient in the success of family-run businesses is pride. Leonard A. Lauder, president of Estée Lauder, explains: "You can't separate the fact that our name is on every package from the drive to succeed and the drive to produce a high-quality product."

Some family-owned businesses are the leaders in their fields, such as Hallmark Cards, two thirds owned by the three children, and their families, of founder Joyce C. Hall, and Mars, Inc., the maker of Snickers and Milky Way candy bars, now run by grandsons of Frank C. Mars. Loews Corporation, the family-run hotel chain, operates a casino in Monte Carlo that is so successful that a famous, 100-year-old

Family sacrifice enabled the Strohs to make their brewery the third largest in the United States.

French establishment keeps asking how they do it.

The drive and expertise that a family can bring to a business can prevail even in a recession. The Phillips Harborplace Restaurants in Baltimore did 14.2 million dollars' worth of business last year. That's 10 percent more than in 1981. The Phillips clan is opening a new restaurant in Norfolk, Va., and already operates three in Ocean City, Md.

Houston builder W. J. Dimitt had a tougher time during the long economic slump and had to take a painful step last year: Laying off two sons. At such times, Dimitt says, "family and business tend to clash. You will carry your children longer than anyone else." One son has since been put back on the payroll because of an upswing in construction.

Succession worries. On the whole, only a third of family-owned companies survive into the second generation because founders often are too busy to plan ahead or because they lack confidence in their young.

To buck that trend, heads of more family-owned companies are seeking novel ways to keep the family in the business and the business in the family.

Sutherland Lumber Company of Kansas City, sixth-largest cash-and-carry lumber chain in the nation with sales of 400 million dollars, divides ownership of its lumber yards and various subsidiaries among family members to open up as many business opportunities for them as possible. Only 20 of its 75 lumber yards are owned in common by the 4 sons, 1 daughter and 21 grandchildren of founder Robert Sutherland.

Keeping a business in the family once generally meant passing it along to a son, but that is no longer the case. "Increasingly, daughters by choice are entering family businesses and wrestling with their brothers for control and a place at the top," says Leon A. Danco, president of the Center for Family Business, a Cleveland-based consulting firm.

John H. Johnson, chairman and president of Johnson Publishing in Chicago, second-largest black-owned business in the U.S., is preparing his daughter Linda, 24, "with the idea that she will some day inherit and run this business."

She is a vice president now, and Johnson says that within five years he expects to shift to her the major responsibility for running the communications-and-cosmetics empire, which had earnings of 102 million dollars in 1982 and publishes magazines such as *Ebony* and *Jet*.

Not that offspring are guaranteed to be heirs to family enterprises. Charles W. Smith II and his wife never encouraged their two sons to take over his Allied Supply Company, a California-based supplier to the oil and chemical industries. Instead, Smith established two prerequisites for the sons' joining the company: "First, they had to work for somebody else and get the spots knocked off of them. Second, they had to come and ask us."

Today, Smith remains chairman, but Charles W. Smith III is president and Stephen L. Smith vice president and secretary after working 10 years for other businesses.

Other concerns keep family control of the board but look outside for management. "One of the things that kills a family company is nepotism—Junior becomes a member of management because he's Junior and not because he is capable," says Lennox chief Norris.

Norris, grandson of the founder, and a cousin are the only family members still involved in day-to-day management of the company, with estimated sales of 600 million dollars. Norris thinks he may be succeeded by an outsider.

Tax problems. Preparing a successor is only one obstacle to keeping a business in family hands. An even bigger one can be the liability imposed on heirs by tax laws. The business community abounds with horror stories of family businesses being wiped out by astronomical estate taxes.

The Wrigley family of Chicago, maker of gum and other confections, was forced to sell the Chicago Cubs in part because of heavy estate taxes following the deaths of two family members.

When Adolph Coors, Jr., died in 1969 and his wife died in 1970, the brewery had to take out a loan to pay estate taxes. The company then had to sell stock for the first time in 1975 to pay off the loan.

To soften the tax bite and guard against the unexpected, more family members are giving stock away before their deaths and setting up other plans to protect capital.

Allied's Smith reports that he and his sons "have written buy-sell agreements so that death or divorce and remarriage would not bring any outsider in as a part owner."

The late T. A. Pelsue, founder of the Denver company bearing his name that manufactures construction equipment, came up with a way to cover the taxes after his death. He left stock in a trust for the family and an insurance policy on his life payable to his corporation. The corporation used the insurance money to buy stock from the trust, and the trust used that money to pay estate taxes.

To insure a smooth transition, the elder Pelsue also stepped aside to let his son become president. Says Bradley A. Pelsue: "He watched and guided me and kicked me in the appropriate places when necessary." ☐

By STEVE HUNTLEY with JEANNYE THORNTON and the magazine's domestic bureaus

The Phillips restaurants in Maryland managed to prosper even during the recession.

Definitions of key terms used in business

Securities trading at a brokerage firm.

JOHN T. BLEDSOE—USN&WR

Annual report: A publication that tells how a business is performing. It shows assets, liabilities, earnings and prospects for the coming year.

Assets: The total value of everything owned by or owed to a company, including plant and equipment, accounts receivable, cash, other investments.

Balance of payments: An itemized record of all financial transactions during a period of time, usually one year, between one nation and the rest of the world. Included are gold movements, trade, capital transactions, investments, services, tourist spending and military sales.

Balance sheet: A financial statement that shows, in dollar amounts, a company's total assets, liabilities and stockholders' equity at a given day, usually December 31.

Big board: A widely used name for the New York Stock Exchange.

Bond: A promissory note to repay a loan, generally with interest, within a specified period of time.

Capital: Money and other assets needed by a company to operate a business and provide facilities for production and distribution of a product or service.

Commodity exchange: An organization of traders who buy and sell contracts for future delivery of such things as grain, cotton, hogs, sugar, coffee, gold and mortgages.

Common stock: Securities that represent an ownership interest in a company and generally entitle the owner to dividends and voting rights on matters such as choice of company directors.

Credit: A promise to pay in the future in order to buy or borrow in the present.

Currency devaluation: Action by the government or by the marketplace to reduce the value of a currency in relation to the currencies of other nations.

Deficit: The money a government or business pays out in excess of what it takes in over a given period.

Depreciation: The accounting cost to a firm of using up machinery and other assets due to wear, decay, obsolescence.

Depression: A prolonged period of sharply reduced business activity characterized by widespread unemployment, low production, a contraction of credit and a drop in consumer buying.

Discount rate: The interest Federal Reserve Banks charge on funds borrowed by commercial banks that are members of the Federal Reserve System.

Disposable personal income: Income of individuals after taxes are paid.

Dividend: A periodic payment that a company distributes to its stockholders as their share of profits.

Eurodollars: Deposits of U.S. dollars at banks and other financial institutions outside the U.S.

Exchange rates: The price of one currency stated in terms of another currency by bankers, dealers and the financial markets.

Fiscal policy: Goverment strategy on taxes, spending and borrowing aimed at influencing economic activity.

Foreign-exchange transaction: Purchase or sale of the currency of one nation for that of another.

Gross national product: The market value of a nation's total output of goods and services.

Inflation: A protracted rise in the general price level of goods and services.

Interest: Money paid to a lender in return for use of lender's money.

Labor force: All persons at least 16 years of age employed as civilians, the unemployed and those in the armed forces. Does not include people not looking for work, those engaged in housework in their own homes, full-time students and unpaid family workers laboring fewer than 15 hours a week.

Liabilities: The amount of money that a business, government or individual owes to others. Includes amounts owed for mortgages, supplies, wages, salaries, accrued taxes and other debts.

Preferred stock: Shares of stock usually entitled to receive a fixed dividend before any dividends are allocated to common stock.

Price-earnings ratio: The market price of a stock divided by earnings per share for the previous 12 months. For example, a stock selling at $20 and earning $2 per share has a price-earnings ratio of 10.

Productivity: The relationship between "output" or the quantity of goods and services produced, and "inputs" or the amounts of labor, material and capital needed to produce the goods and service. Usually measured in terms of output per worker per hour.

Profit: Money remaining after all costs of operating a business are paid.

Recession: An economic downturn accompanied by layoffs, lagging sales and reduced corporate profits. Usually defined as two or more consecutive quarters in which the gross national product declines, after adjustment for inflation.

Retained earnings: Profits added to a company's capital after dividends and taxes are paid.

Return on investment: The amount of pretax profit from an investment stated as a percentage of the original outlay or purchase price.

Revaluation: Adjusting the value of a currency upward relative to other currencies.

Unemployed person: Described by the government as a civilian who, during a given week, had no employment but was available for work and had sought a job during prior four weeks or was waiting to be called back to work or to a new position within 30 days.

Yield: The annual return on a financial investment expressed as a percentage of its cost or its current market value. A $1,000 investment in common stocks or bonds that pays $80 in annual dividends or interest yields 8 percent. □

Chapter 8

Supply and demand

- *Price determines how much of a product will be produced.*

- *Some products are "inelastic"—we must purchase them even at a high price; others are "elastic"—we buy them only if the price is right.*

Choices made in the economy involve a continuous tug of war between the consumer and the producer.

If many businesses offer the same product—making it plentiful enough to satisfy the needs of every consumer—a producer will have to sell his goods at a price not far above costs because of the competition of other producers. That is why, when produce is abundant in summer, the prices of fresh fruits and vegetables drop.

A low price—especially if it falls below what it costs a seller to produce his goods—will discourage production. A low price can drive high-cost producers out of business.

Other factors affect supply. The supply of a particular agricultural product, for example, may be reduced if poor weather ruins a vegetable crop, or if farmers plant less wheat or raise fewer cattle. The price of these products to consumers will increase.

If there is great demand for a product and supplies are low, producers are in a position to raise prices. When profits increase, they may invest in new equipment to increase output. Other firms may be attracted by the prospects of high profits to produce the same item, thus adding new competition.

This is the way the law of supply and demand operates in a free-market economy. *Price* becomes the guidepost, telling producers what to produce. At the same time, prices determine what and how much of something the consumer can have.

The economist's model

The rule of the marketplace is to "buy cheap and sell dear." Out of self-interest, the consumer tries to buy as cheaply as possible, while the seller tries to sell his goods for as much as possible, or for "what the market will bear."

The law of demand states that the higher the price of a product, the less of that product people will be willing to buy; the lower the price, the more people will be willing to buy. The relationshp between price and demand is shown in the first table.

At $.85 per pound, the demand for tomatoes in a particular city or area is 200 pounds. As the price decreases, the demand increases. Any point along the demand curve represents tomato buyers. A few buyers are willing and able to pay the

Demand Schedule for Tomatoes

Price per pound	Number of pounds demanded
$.85	200
.75	300
.65	400
.55	500
.45	650
.35	850
.25	1050
.15	1200

higher prices for tomatoes; at lower prices, more will purchase the product.

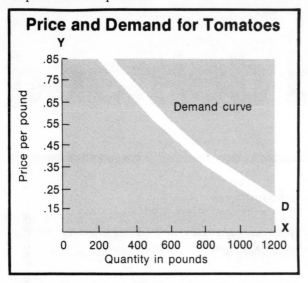

Price and Demand for Tomatoes

One reason low prices increase demand is that when the price of a product is lowered, new buyers can afford the product. Economists refer to this phenomenon as the *new buyer effect*.

A second reason a lower price brings an increase in demand is that when prices are low, consumers find that their *real income* has increased. They don't actually have more money (*money income*), but the lower price has increased their *purchasing power*. Economists call this the *income effect*.

A final reason consumers tend to buy more when the price goes down is that they can increase their total satisfaction by purchasing a lower-priced good. If tomatoes decrease in price in relation to cucumbers or other vegetables, consumers will tend to purchase more tomatoes and fewer other vegetables. They substitute the cheaper tomatoes for higher-priced produce, thereby increasing their total satisfaction. This is called *substitution effect*.

The law of supply states that an increase in the price of a product generates an increased supply of that product. Likewise, a decrease in price will reduce supply.

The supply schedule shows the seller's view of the market: the amount he would offer for sale at a given price. As prices go up, new sellers are tempted to use their resources (factors of production) to produce tomatoes. The *cost of production* for any good or service is a producer's major consideration. At low prices, only the most efficient producers can provide a product at a profit. At higher prices, a larger number of producers can profit from the production and sale of (in this case) tomatoes. The supply curve below depicts how many producers would supply tomatoes at different market prices.

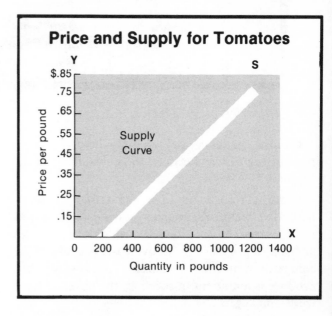

Price and Supply for Tomatoes

A price is stabilized at the point where demand equals the supply. At any other point, there will either be a shortage (fewer goods supplied than demanded) or a surplus (more goods supplied than demanded). Returning to our example of tomatoes, supply and demand are compared at the following prices:

Supply Schedule for Tomatoes

Price per pound	Number of pounds supplied
$.85	1350
.75	1150
.65	950
.55	800
.45	650
.35	450
.25	300
.15	200

Supply and Demand for Tomatoes

Price	Supply	Demand	
$.85	1350	200	surplus
.75	1150	300	surplus
.65	950	400	surplus
.55	800	500	surplus
.45	650	650	*equilibrium*
.35	450	850	shortage
.25	300	1050	shortage
.15	200	1200	shortage

At $.85 per pound for tomatoes, producers attracted to the market will find that their product cannot be sold. This surplus will force the price down and encourage more buyers. The surplus and decreasing price also will be a signal for producers to decrease the production of tomatoes.

Similarly, at $.15 a pound, buyers will find a shortage of tomatoes. This excess of demand will drive the price up, which will encourage the production of more tomatoes as new producers profit at the higher price. The *equilibrium price* eventually established in the market for tomatoes—or any product—is the point at which supply equals demand.

The market in movement

Market conditions are normally in a state of continuous change. Consumer preferences may change, altering the demand for various products. Likewise, producers may be in a position to bring either more or fewer products to the marketplace, shifting the supply of goods.

Changes in demand. A change in demand can occur for many reasons. Suppose consumer eating habits (tastes) shift from meats to vegetables, increasing the demand for tomatoes. The immediate effect of this *change in demand* is an increased price for tomatoes; more consumer purchases raise the price of tomatoes because they have become

relatively scarce. This change in demand can be illustrated—as an upward shift in the entire demand—in the movement from D1 to D2.

Changes in people's incomes, too, affect demand. When incomes increase, demand for most products tends to increase also. The opposite is true for a few products, like beans. Economy-minded families often eat beans. When their incomes increase, they may shift to other foods.

A change in the demand for one product can alter the demand for related products, either those that can be substituted for another good or those that are complementary. If the price of cabbage were to increase while the price of lettuce remained the same, consumers would shift from cabbage (and cole slaw) to lettuce (and salads). The demand for lettuce would increase, because cabbage and lettuce are *substitute goods*.

Likewise, the increase in demand for lettuce could result in a boost for tomatoes. Since lettuce and tomatoes often are used together in salads and sandwiches, the demand for tomatoes also increases. Lettuce and tomatoes are *complementary goods*.

Anything that adds or subtracts to the number of customers will shift the demand curve. Advertising, for example, attempts to change consumer demand, shifting the curve forward by enlarging the base of potential customers.

To sum up: a shift in the demand curve can result from changes in consumer wants (tastes,

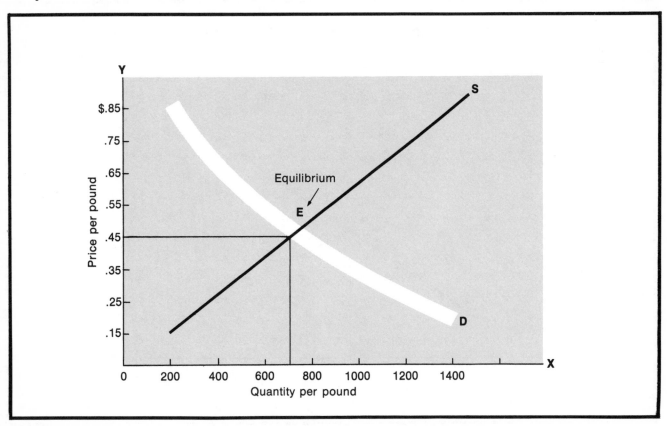

fashions, attitudes), changes in the price of substitute or complementary goods, and changes in consumer spending power (incomes.)

Changes in supply. Poor weather may ruin crops; workers may go on strike, shutting down an industry; producers may not be able to obtain vital materials from foreign suppliers—any event can result in a reduction in the supply of products on the market. This *change in supply* is illustrated by a shift in the supply curve backward from S1 to S2. The effect of this change is to both decrease the supply and increase the price of a product.

A change in the *cost of production* is the major reason for shifts in supply. An increase in production costs (of labor, land, capital, or management expenses) will decrease supply and increase prices; a decrease in costs will tend to have the opposite effect. How does this happen?

Looking at it from the producer's viewpoint, if the cost of any factor of production increases, the producer will have to charge a higher price for his product. *Marginal producers* (less efficient) will drop out of business and the supply curve will shift backward. As a result, the price of the product will be higher, while the quantity sold decreases.

Technological advances which can both decrease prices and create new mass markets for a product are perhaps the major cause of an increase in supply. The new markets, however, can lead to an increase in demand. So, over time, prices seldom fall. One exception has been electronic products like watches and computers. In recent years, their price has drastically declined, due to technological efficiency.

Elasticity of demand

The law of demand states that as the price of a good increases, the quantity demanded will decrease (and vice versa). How much the quantity will change is measured by its *elasticity*.

If a relatively small change in price results in a relatively large change in demand, the demand for the product is "elastic." That is, the demand is very responsive to price changes. If a change in price results in a relatively small change in demand, the product has an "inelastic demand."

A good example of a product with an elastic demand is steak. If the price of a steak were to increase from $2.00 per pound to $3.00, it is likely that the demand would decrease substantially. Steak is not a diet necessity. We could stop eating steaks and still get protein from other foods.

To measure elasticity, let's take, for example, the owner of a small coffee shop who is trying to decide if she should raise the price of the breakfast special (two eggs, homefries, toast and coffee) from $1.50 to $2.00. She could play a hunch, but the only sure way to determine the elasticity for

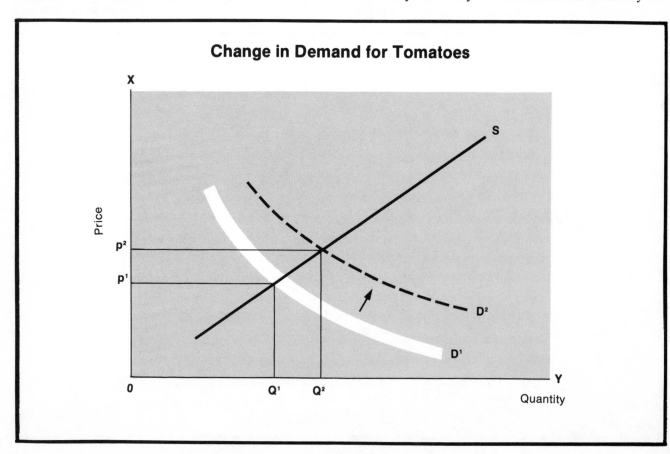

Change in Demand for Tomatoes

this breakfast special is to try it and see what happens to total revenue.

When she increased the price to $2.00, the quantity of breakfasts sold each week decreased from 300 to 250. As result, the total sales (revenue) went from $450 to $500 per week, despite the decrease in quantity. Total revenue (TR) is equal to the price (P) of a product times the quantity (Q) sold or

$$TR = P \times Q:$$

Old Price: TR = $1.50 \times 300
TR = $450

New Price: TR = $2.00 \times 250
TR = $500

TR also is shown by the two rectangular areas in the graph.

The demand for the breakfast special is inelastic. The quantity sold decreased somewhat, but the decrease (as a percentage of the total quantity sold) was not as great as the price increase (as a percentage of the selling price). The coffee shop owner was able to make more money and work less.

Total Revenue

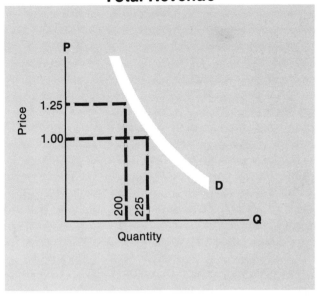

Products with *elastic* demands are ones that are: 1) unnecessary (caviar, champagne, diamond necklaces); 2) a large part of one's budget (automobile, piano, color television, carpeting for the house); or 3) easily substituted (butter, apples, steak).

Products with *inelastic* demands include 1) necessary goods (gasoline, telephone, shoes); 2) a small part of one's budget (pencil, toothbrush); or 3) items not easily substituted (light bulbs, gasoline, a ticket to a concert).

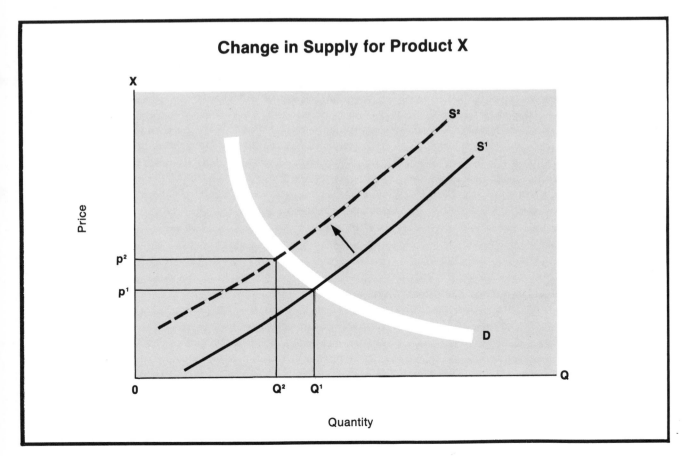

Change in Supply for Product X

Elasticity of Demand

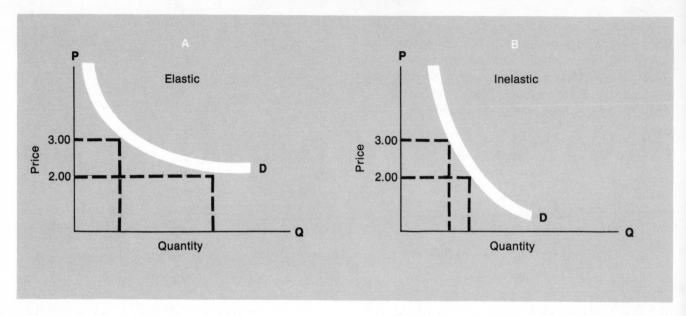

Figures A & B illustrate the difference between an elastic and an inelastic demand curve. Most businesses would prefer to have a demand curve for their product such as that of curve B. An increase in the price of the good would result in only a small decrease in the quantity demanded. In fact, many businesses make an effort to make the demand for their product inelastic. The purpose of advertising is to convince buyers that they need the product, that it is not too expensive, and that there are few, if any, other products similar to it.

Factors Determining the Price of a Commodity

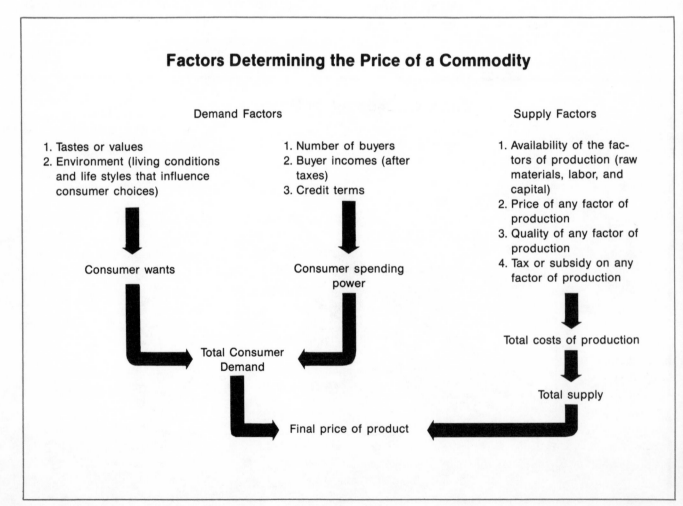

Chapter 9

Oligopoly

- *While competition is considered the cornerstone of capitalism, most industries in the U.S. are controlled by a few large corporations.*

- *Some industries can operate efficiently only if they are large.*

Steel companies announce a five percent price increase. General Motors informs the public that the price of one of its new models will go up by $475. These prices are set by big corporations. It often seems that the law of supply and demand does not work when big business gets into the act.

Prices and big business

Suspicions are sometimes aroused by prices for goods like automobiles, cigarettes, gasoline, drugs and meats—items produced by a small number of companies, or an oligopoly. These firms are dependent on other industries that supply metals, chemicals, plastics and many other ingredients. These supplies, in turn, come from a few producers. The question arises whether these corporations maintain artificially high prices, even when demand is weak.

In markets dominated by a few large firms, prices do not move up and down in response to changes in supply and demand. Instead, these firms administer prices and appear to be somewhat exempt from the law of supply and demand.

The administered prices for the products of large firms go up more often than they go down. When demand is weak, these companies can take several courses of action. One is to let prices drop to the point where profits would vanish. They are more likely to:

- cut production and sell less; this maintains profit margins but is hard on workers who are laid off and on secondary suppliers who have less business.
- try to maintain sales by stepping up advertising or initiating promotion campaigns.

- try to maintain sales by offering special discounts to their biggest customers, while adhering to the basic list price.

Eventually, if the demand stays low and list prices become too unrealistic, prices will be reduced.

Perfect competition

Pure, or perfect competition, is rare in the modern capitalist economy. The best example of perfect competition is the agricultural industry, because there are still many farmers who compete for their share of the buying market. Although farms today are consolidating into large corporate enterprises, any single farm's share of the market for a particular product is relatively small. No one farmer can have an appreciable effect on the total market supply and, therefore, on prices.

Another characteristic of perfect competition is the production of an identical product: Wheat is wheat and corn is corn, and a farmer doesn't do anything to make his product different from another farmer's. When products are different, this adds enough "imperfection" to give the seller some price control.

Monopoly

Likewise, true monopolies are rare. Perfect competition in our economy broke down in the late nineteenth century with the rise of huge companies. Single firms began to dominate certain industries—oil, railroads, and steel. In order to preserve competition, the government broke up these monopolies, or trusts. The chart shows the history of antimonopoly legislation. The monopolies that exist today are either public monopolies operated by the government (water and public electrical utilities), or those closely regulated by the government but which are privately owned (ConEdison, Southern Bell).

People who live in small American towns or villages might argue that the one hardware store, grocery store, barber, or doctor in town constitutes a monopoly within their communities. They would be correct. But local pressure and good fellowship in the small community often keep these businesses from being as unresponsive as a monopoly could be.

Oligopoly

The United States has an oligopolistic economy. An oligopoly exists when a few large firms dominate an industry. When the American consumer makes major purchases—food, automobiles, washing machines, airline tickets and beer—he or she is doing business with an oligopoly.

Some oligopolies in basic industries, such as steel and aluminum, produce identical, or almost identical products. Other industries, with a few large sellers, market *differentiated* products—automobiles, televisions, machinery.

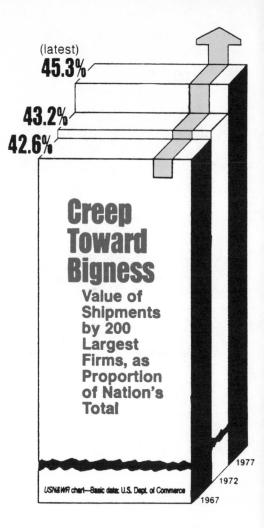

(latest)
45.3%
43.2%
42.6%

Creep Toward Bigness
Value of Shipments by 200 Largest Firms, as Proportion of Nation's Total

1977
1972
1967

USN&WR chart—Basic data: U.S. Dept. of Commerce

Anti-monopoly Legislation

1887 Interstate Commerce Act	Established Interstate Commerce Commission to regulate shipping rates of railroads. Later this applied to other forms of transportation. Made *pooling agreements* (companies agree to divide the market and share profits) illegal.
1890 Sherman Antitrust Act	Prohibits any contracts which would be in restraint of trade, and any attempts to establish a monopoly.
1914 Clayton Antitrust Act	Designed to strengthen the Sherman Act by outlawing price discrimination (charging different customers different prices for the same product), and outlawing *holding companies (one corporation runs several others in related fields).*
1914 Federal Trade Commission Act	Established Federal Trade Commission (FTC) to regulate unfair methods of competition in interstate commerce.
1936 Robinson-Patman Act	Strengthened the price discrimination provisions of Clayton Act. Specifically, forbade lower rates to chain stores or larger buyers, unless available to all buyers.

There can be healthy competition within oligopolies, which leads to better products for the consumer. A good case in point is the automobile industry. When foreign oligopolists, such as Volkswagen, Datsun, and Fiat offered American consumers smaller and more gasoline-efficient cars, American companies responded by producing their own small cars.

The oligopolist has significant control of the market, and establishes prices. Oligopolists affect supply by:

● controlling a significant amount of an industry's production; any substantial increase in supply that would decrease price can be prevented.

● making it difficult, if not impossible, for new firms to enter and compete in the market; the cost of starting a company large enough to produce and compete is prohibitive.

Oligopolists also affect the *demand* for products through sophisticated advertising in the mass media—advertising that could be supported only by large firms. Oligopolies that market differentiated products, such as automobile companies and toothpaste manufacturers rely on advertising to attract and condition buyers. Sellers in differentiated markets excel at establishing brand-names, trademarks, and other forms of distinction. Producers of services, including hair-cutters, local grocers, and dentists, also strive to develop a distinctive product or service to attract and hold customers, and they make up a significant part of this type of market.

Changing patterns

Recent economic developments, declining corporate profits and foreign competition, are changing the face of America's oligopolistic corporate structure. A trend toward bigness in business is clearly established and appears to be speeding up. The recent surge of corporate takeovers promises to be just the first phase of a new consolidation campaign among U.S. companies. The number of giant mergers in recent years has renewed public debate on a controversial issue: Whether a few large firms or many smaller ones can better satisfy the needs of the consumer.

Many firms view acquisitions of other companies as profitable investments. The total price tag for mergers announced in one six-month period in 1981 was $35.7 billion—nearly 60 percent more than the previous six months—and the trend continues. The advantages to acquiring firms are primarily twofold. First, mergers represent expansion, which is essential in a corporate setting if profits are to expand. Often, existing corporate giants have reached a limit in their original product line, and the acquisition of new companies in unrelated fields adds to their product line and opens new markets for expansion.

Second, buying a company whose stock value on the market is greatly undervalued because of a recession or other weakening factors allows the buying firm to gain valuable equipment and assets at a much lower price than would be paid on the open market. For example, when Conoco was a target for acquisition by a few large firms, its stock was valued at $60 a share, although oil industry analysts estimated the real value of Conoco's assets at $150 per share. Recently, an airline was purchased by another at a price reflecting a very low market value of its stock . The buyer acquired the other airline's fleet of airplanes at a price significantly below the market price for such equipment.

Whether this is good for the consumer is not clear. Assuming that an acquired firm was about to collapse, its acquisition may strengthen other

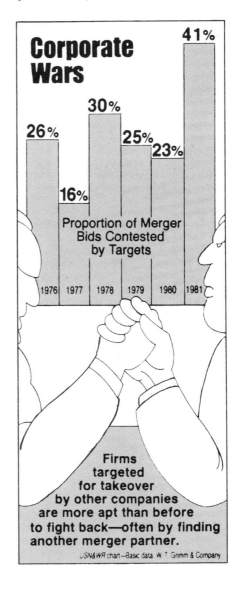

Corporate Wars

41%

30%

26%

25%

23%

16%

Proportion of Merger Bids Contested by Targets

1976 1977 1978 1979 1980 1981

Firms targeted for takeover by other companies are more apt than before to fight back—often by finding another merger partner.

USN&WR chart—Basic data: W. T. Grimm & Company

companies in the industry and provide competition that will lower prices and improve services. On the other hand, the acquisition of healthy companies may lead to so much concentration that it would end competition, to the detriment of consumers.

Despite the move toward mergers, a few actions in the other direction have been forced by the government, and their ultimate effects upon the consumer are still in doubt. Notable of deconsolidation efforts was the order by the Supreme Court in February 1983 that required the break-up of American Telephone and Telegraph Company (AT&T), the nation's most asset-rich corporation. AT&T revenues of $65 billion in 1982 provided services to 75 percent of the 80 million U.S. residential telephone customers at that time. The company was forced to divest itself of its ownership of 22 local Bell System phone companies and its control over equipment sales. Although this move is expected to eventually lower long-distance phone rates through competition with other firms and reduce costs to consumers who can buy and install their own phones, the impact in the near future is for sharp increases in local phone rates. Analysts predict that the break-up of AT&T will force local phone companies to raise rates to recover money that formerly came from the Bell parent company. Some 56 firms already have sought and are seeking rate hikes totalling more than $5 billion a year.

Corporate subsidy

One of the ironic phenomena of our oligopolistic economic system is that it has increased the government's role in subsidizing American business. When American industries in any one field consisted of countless small companies, the failure of one or of several had little impact on the national economy. As an industry becomes dominated by a few giant corporations, the loss of any one creates a gigantic impact upon our society in the loss of thousands of jobs, lost tax revenues and the economic ruin of whole communities, if not regions. The government's propping up of sick giant industries has been termed by some as "corporate socialism." Surely, it is a far cry from the free capitalism of Adam Smith.

The Chrysler Corporation, a major auto industry, was on the verge of bankruptcy in 1980. After much debate, it was decided by the government to extend $1.2 billion of loan guarantees to Chrysler. Employees agreed to work at below industry level wages. A major bankruptcy was thus avoided and Chrysler became profitable by 1983.

The major question remains: Should the Federal Government support an oligopolistic firm if it means saving jobs, or should it allow the free-enterprise competitive struggle to take its natural course, which might mean the death of the company?

Where Corporate Concentration Is High...

Proportion of Shipments by 4 Largest Companies in Each Industry

Motor vehicles	93%
Light bulbs	90%
Breakfast cereal	89%
Turbines, generators	86%
Primary aluminum	76%
Chocolate, cocoa	73%
Photo equipment, supplies	72%
Brewing	64%
Guided missiles, spacecraft	64%
Roasted coffee	61%

...And Where It's Low

Proportion of Shipments by 20 Largest Companies in Each Industry

Newspapers	45%
Wooden furniture	39%
Valves, pipe fittings	37%
Bottled, canned soft drinks	36%
Sawmills	36%
Precious-metal jewelry	35%
Sheet-metal work	28%
Fabricated structural metal	23%
Women's dresses	19%
Ready-mix concrete	14%

Note: Data are from 1977 Census of Manufactures—latest available.

USN&WR chart—Basic data: U.S. Dept of Commerce

Chapter 10

Labor and unions

- *Child labor performed much of the work in the U.S. economy until this century.*

- *Union struggles succeeded in decreasing the workweek, raising wages, and improving working conditions.*

In 1776, most workers in the newly formed United States were little concerned with management, the length of the workweek or wages. Ninety percent of Americans were farmers on small, family-owned farms.

Independence from England brought an end to a farm-dominated America. As an English colony, America produced farm products which were traded for goods produced abroad. The newly liberated citizens of the U.S. wanted freedom in every sense of the word—including independence from the factories of foreign nations. Textile mills and factories blossomed across the New England countryside as workers began producing clothes, tools, and rifles formerly imported from abroad.

By 1870, two-thirds of all workers were working for someone else, as farm laborers or in small mills and factories. For the first time, a majority of the labor force had their wages, workday, and work conditions determined by an employer. Inevitably, problems ensued.

Workers strained at back-breaking tasks. If they could make a dollar a day, they considered themselves lucky. The average workday was from daylight to dark, six days a week. Children of all ages put in twelve-to fourteen-hour shifts under miserable and often dangerous work conditions. A visitor to a spinning mill in Providence, Rhode Island, in 1800, found all of the labor being done by children from four to ten years of age.

As more and more workers became employes, a public awareness of the problems in the employer-worker relationship developed. By the early twen-

tieth century, reform movements were started to aid and protect workers.

"Statistics cannot express the withering of child lips in the poisoned air of factories; the tired, strained look of child eyes that never dance to the glad music of souls tuned to Nature's symphonies . . . who shall tally the deaths of childhood's hopes, ambitions and dreams?" These words were written in 1906 in the journalistic style of the day in a typical attack on businesses that abused children by hiring them for wearying, dangerous jobs.

Many adults began to resent both the businesses and the children involved in child labor. Jobs that could have been held by heads of households were filled by children for a fraction of the pay.

These factors, plus an increasing emphasis on compulsory education in the early twentieth century, led to the passage of the first national *child labor law* in 1917.

Child labor laws were expanded by the **Fair Labor Standards Act** of 1938. The passage of the FLSA was also the culmination of a long and bitter fight to establish a federal *minimum wage*.

The minimum wage set by the 1938 law was $.25 an hour. The ensuing four decades have seen Congress raise that wage fifteen times to $3.35 an hour. In terms of actual purchasing power, however, the minimum wage has less than doubled since 1946, when it was $.40 an hour.

Shorter workweek

As the minimum wage grew, the *workweek* shrank. Throughout the nineteenth and early

49

twentieth centuries, labor unions, led by aggressive and idealistic organizers, worked to shorten the daylight-to-dark working hours in many industries. Many strikes, sometimes violent, led to a decrease in the workweek. By 1910, the workweek was about fifty hours long.

By World War II, the forty-hour workweek was standard. As of the early 1980s, the average number of hours worked per week was thirty-five. Workers today have more paid holidays and vacations than ever before. People work less over the course of the year, but the "nine-to-five" job is still standard for most workers.

There are various reasons for the shrinking workweek. One is that the *productivity* of the American worker has increased, due mostly to the use of more efficient and sophisticated equipment. A second reason is that new inventions have led to *automation*, where machines perform tasks formerly done by people. A third reason for the shorter workweek is that people want more *leisure time* as their standards of living increase. Fourth, unions and many job experts call for a thirty-two hour workweek to *spread scarce jobs* more evenly among those who need and want to work.

Not only have the physical requirements of work—length of day, type of job, amount of wages—changed over the years, attitudes on the job also have changed. There has been a loosening of the authoritarian relationship between boss and worker. Respect for the dignity of the worker is valued highly.

Enough jobs for everyone

The task of providing enough jobs for everyone who wants to work is one of the greatest economic challenges facing the United States. Increased efficiency due to automation means that some industries require fewer workers. At the same time, a growing number of young people are entering the job market.

Economists suggest a number of ways that new jobs can be created:

1) One option would give financial incentives to businesses and industry to create jobs. Investment tax credits might provide businesses with enough extra capital to expand. A Vice-President of U.S. Steel said, "If you are not going to have money invested in tools of production, you're not going to provide new jobs."

2) Another idea is to give government subsidies to the unemployed for job training. This would support potential workers while they train.

3) Many labor union officials prefer a program of public service jobs. One plan would make the federal government "the employer of last resort." Unemployed people would be hired by the government at some percentage below the minimum wage. Critics wonder what jobs these employes would fill, without taking jobs from other workers.

4) Use of government-owned computers could create a nationwide service to match workers to

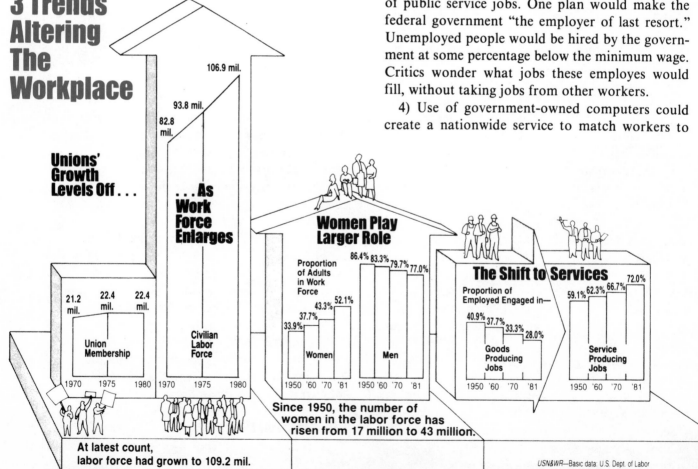

3 Trends Altering The Workplace

Unions' Growth Levels Off . . .

21.2 mil. 22.4 mil. 22.4 mil.

Union Membership

1970 1975 1980

. . . As Work Force Enlarges

106.9 mil.
93.8 mil.
82.8 mil.

Civilian Labor Force

1970 1975 1980

At latest count, labor force had grown to 109.2 mil.

Women Play Larger Role

Proportion of Adults in Work Force

33.9% 37.7% 43.3% 52.1%   86.4% 83.3% 79.7% 77.0%

Women   Men

1950 '60 '70 '81   1950 '60 '70 '81

Since 1950, the number of women in the labor force has risen from 17 million to 43 million.

The Shift to Services

Proportion of Employed Engaged in—

40.9% 37.7% 33.3% 28.0%   59.1% 62.3% 66.7% 72.0%

Goods Producing Jobs   Service Producing Jobs

1950 '60 '70 '81   1950 '60 '70 '81

USN&WR—Basic data: U.S. Dept. of Labor

jobs. Government funds would also be necessary to help workers relocate where the jobs are.

5) Another possibility is to share the available work. Many experts predict that the thirty-two hour workweek will become a reality in the near future.

6) A traditional method of creating jobs is to spend tax money on highways, dams, sewers, and post offices. A major problem is timing. The impact of public works on employment and inflation is difficult to control. The typical project takes years to plan and, once started, must be completed even though its job-producing function may have become outdated. A half-finished dam is useless.

7) Another way to create jobs is to stimulate a demand for goods. This can be done by cutting income taxes and increasing government spending so that consumers have more money to spend, thus creating demand for more products.

Fitting work into life

Much work in our economy is tedious and always has been. Management can rearrange work procedures or break the routine by shifting jobs around, but many jobs are just dull. Up to 90 percent of the work in our economy is of this nature. Even aspects of so-called status jobs, such as a professor grading papers, a doctor performing routine examinations, and a writer laboring over an uninteresting story, can be irksome.

Over ten percent of the non-farm, salaried work force participates in some form of flexible work schedule. This figure is larger if you consider that many self-employed people, such as lawyers, insurance agents, writers, and sales representatives, build flexibility into their work day. While *flextime* has grown in recent years, its popularity may be limited. Many companies have found that supervising the staggered schedules of workers involves added costs and presents new problems.

Modern workers also benefit from the widespread attitude that it is always possible to change jobs— even careers. With greater educational training and access to efficient transportation, today's worker is free to take whatever opportunities present themselves. This may mean a new job in the same city or moving cross-country.

People also change careers when they grow bored or disenchanted with their work, even when they have spent many years in training for a career. A career change for some people means giving up a lucrative job for work with less pay. However, a growing number of workers feel that money is not necessarily the most important aspect of a job.

Adam Smith, the eighteenth-century architect of capitalist economics, remarked that there is no prospect in trying to make everybody happy in work; it can't be done. For many, work ought to be viewed for exactly what it is: a way to pay for necessities and to help enjoy leisure time. It may not be possible for everyone to enjoy his or her work. Eli Ginzberg says "It's not whether people like their jobs, but whether they are happy with the total structure of their lives: whether work and leisure together make for a satisfactory life."

Labor markets

According to traditional economic theory, workers' wages should follow the rules of supply and demand in the marketplace. Workers should attempt to find as high a salary as possible, and employers should pay as little as they have to.

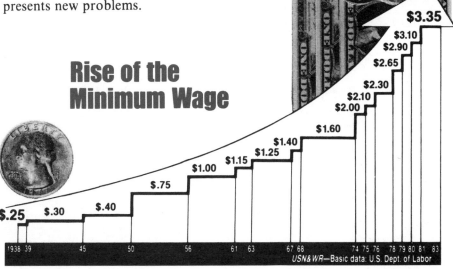

Rise of the Minimum Wage

$.25 $.30 $.40 $.75 $1.00 $1.15 $1.25 $1.40 $1.60 $2.00 $2.10 $2.30 $2.65 $2.90 $3.10 $3.35

1938 39   45   50   56   61 63   67 68   74 75 76 78 79 80 81 83

USN&WR—Basic data: U.S. Dept. of Labor

Where there is a large supply of unskilled labor, as was once the case for factory workers, wages are kept low. In the modern American economy, however, wages are not determined by the pure competitive market, but are generally negotiated or set.

The wages paid to a grocery store clerk and a professional athlete, despite the huge differences between them, most closely follow supply and demand conditions. Because there are many people who can fill a clerk's job, the salary is kept low. Because there are few workers with the talent to perform as a basketball superstar, the salary is high. Nevertheless, minimum wage laws (for unskilled workers), and minimum salary agreements (for professional athletes), set floors under which these salaries cannot fall.

The salaries paid workers such as corporate managers, administrators, and salespeople vary not so much with the relative supply or demand for the skills of these workers as with the economic position of the company. A well-established, prosperous firm can pay more for the same worker than its less affluent counterpart.

The wages of auto assemblers, electricians, bricklayers, and other skilled workers are often the result of *union negotiations* with employers. The fees of physicians, dentists, and lawyers are set under the guidelines of their professional organizations.

Labor unions

In the process known as *collective bargaining*—workers, through a union, negotiate with employers about wages and working conditions. Collective bargaining has a long history in the United States. As early as 1791, carpenters, shoemakers, and printers banded together to meet with their employers to discuss and resist wage cuts.

Nearly one of every four people in the work force belongs to a union. Although the proportion of union members has fallen, from 26 percent of civilian workers in 1968 down to about 21 percent in the early 1980s, unions have a major impact on the U.S. economy.

At union-management bargaining tables, unions negotiate wages, work hours, working conditions, vacation periods, sick pay, medical insurance, retirement benefits, and other work issues. But union influence goes far beyond the bargaining table. For example, when blue-collar, unionized automobile workers get wage increases, identical new benefits are granted by the auto companies to their nonunion, white-collar workers. Non-union companies often raise wages in line with rising union scales to maintain morale and keep workers from joining a union or seeking employment elsewhere.

Union representatives lobby heavily in Congress and state legislatures to further the welfare of their

Government Labor Legislation

Clayton Antitrust Act (1914):	Stated that unions were not the same as business monopolies and labor was not a commodity. With this, unionization was declared legal, as were peaceful union assemblies, strikes, picketing, boycotts, and strike pay to workers.
Norris-LaGuardia Act (1932):	Declared that workers had the right to organize or join a labor organization of their own choosing; prohibited the yellow-dog contract; and limited federal courts' use of injunctions against union strikes.
National Labor Relations Act (1935):	Required employees to bargain collectively with union representatives, and forbade employers from interfering with the organization of unions.
Taft-Hartley Act (1947):	Outlawed 1) the jurisdictional strike, 2) the secondary boycott, and 3) the closed shop. States also were given the right to prohibit union shops ("right-to-work" laws). The act also placed various restrictions on union activities, while requiring a sixty-day "cooling off" period before a strike and permitting the President to invoke an eighty-day injunction prohibiting strikes that seriously affected the national welfare.
Landrum-Griffin Act (1959):	Requires unions to file financial reports with the Secretary of Labor, and to conduct business-elections and member disciplinary action—according to democratic procedures.

workers. Presidents and governors rely on unions for support and advice, as do various interest groups including civil rights, women's rights, and environmental organizations.

The labor movement

Early unions were *craft guilds*. An employer—a "master craftsman"—worked with employes—"journeymen" and "apprentices." The goal of an apprentice was to become a journeyman, while the journeyman worked to become a master craftsman. The craft guild served primarily to control the supply of workers in trades. This they did by limiting the number of young men accepted as apprentices and by establishing examination standards for journeymen and masters.

With the industrial revolution, factories grew, and work arrangements became less personal. Often, company owners were not directly involved in the operation of their plants. They were stockholders, and managers ran the business. The major goals of these companies were efficient production and high profits; workers were paid wages no higher than absolutely necessary.

Efforts were made by workers to form national *unions*. Employers opposed unions, arguing that they should have the right to bargain with workers individually. To prevent union development, employers used various tactics. *Yellow-dog contracts* required job applicants to sign a pledge that they would not join a labor organization, or participate in any strike. *Blacklisting* was practiced—employers collected and circulated lists of workers who were considered undesirable employees because they held opinions or engaged in activities considered contrary to management's interests. Employers established *company unions* to control their workers who were thus kept from joining independent unions.

In violation of the **Sherman Antitrust Act** of 1890, the courts also supported the companies by interpreting the formation of unions as "combinations in restraint of trade." The Act, designed by Congress to curb the monopolistic practices of large corporations, was redefined by the courts to find that unions were in violation of the law.

The first national unions were formed in the late 1800s. *The National Labor Union* (1866) and the *Noble Order of the Knights of Labor* (1869) attempted to organize all workers—skilled and unskilled alike. Although the Knights of Labor developed a sizable membership, neither organization was long-lived. Particularly to the skilled workers, it seemed that the interests of skilled and unskilled workers were too different for one organization to represent both. There were other reasons

Types of Unions	
Closed shop:	Employers are only permitted to hire union members. The Taft-Hartley Act forbids the closed shop for firms that engage in interstate commerce.
Union shop:	An employer may hire anyone he or she chooses, but all employees must join the union within a stated period (usually within thirty to sixty days.)
Agency shop:	Workers may choose to join a union or not, but all must pay dues to the union.
Open shop:	Both union and nonunion members work side by side.

these unions failed. Both anti-union company practices and court decisions against unions impeded their development. In addition, the National Labor Union showed an interest in social reform through political action, which brought charges of socialism. This, together with the economic hard times caused by the panic of 1873, led to its collapse.

The Knights of Labor were caught up in another national tragedy, the Haymarket Square riot (1886) in Chicago, where several strikers and one policeman were killed. Although there was no proof of its involvement, the union, in the public's eye, was associated with the anarchists who were accused of inciting the riot.

In 1881, the **American Federation of Labor** (AFL)—an organization of a group of various existing craft unions—was formed. The AFL, under the leadership of Samuel Gompers for more than thirty years, grew steadily during the late 1800s and early 1900s.

A *craft union* is composed of workers in one trade. For example, machinists, electricians, plumbers, or carpenters have separate craft unions. Gompers reasoned that the American worker was more interested in wages, hours, and working conditions within his or her own occupation than he was in general social reform or in one big union. Within the AFL, however, the separate craft unions could come together to wield more economic and political clout.

A movement for industry-wide unions gained

strength in the 1930s, the era of the Great Depression. Union organizers, like John L. Lewis of the coal miners and Sidney Hillman of the clothing industry, attempted to organize the unskilled industrial workers within the AFL. When this failed, due to craft union opposition, they formed the Committee for Industrial Organizations in 1935. In 1938, the AFL expelled unions that belonged to the committee; these unions formed the *Congress of Industrial Organizations* (CIO), whose membership grew rapidly over the next ten years.

An *industrial union* is made up of many different kinds of workers in an industry. For example, the CIO organized an Automobile Workers Union and a Building Trades Workers Union. All of the workers within the industry—machinists, electricians, plumbers, carpenters, and unskilled assembly workers—became members of the union.

Aided by pro-labor legislation—the *Norris-LaGuardia Act* (1932) and the *National Labor Relations Act* (1935)—union membership in both the AFL and CIO expanded significantly during the 1930s and 1940s. Union strikes during World War II brought a strong reaction which led to the passage of the *Taft-Hartley Act* (1947) which forbade certain types of strikes and, in other ways, attempted to restrain the power of unions.

A heated battle for new members was resolved by the merger of the AFL and CIO in 1955. Total union membership in the United States, of which

Union Weapons

Strike:	Labor's most powerful weapon. Workers refuse to work. Strikers lose wages, but union funds often offset some of the losses. Workers eventually gain more through higher wages and other benefits.
Picketing:	Workers form barriers in front of the store or plant in an attempt to discourage other workers from going to work and the public from doing business with the company.
Boycott:	A refusal to buy goods and services from a company or employer.
Slowdown:	Workers deliberately reduce their output or refuse to do part of their usual work.

Other union weapons that have been declared illegal:

Sit-down strike:	Workers "sit down," or refuse to leave the plant preventing new workers from taking their place.
Jurisdictional strike:	A strike between two or more unions over which one will represent the workers on a particular job.
Secondary boycott:	A boycott against a company which is doing business with a company whose workers are on strike.

Settling Labor-Management Disputes

Collective bargaining:	The employer deals with workers as a whole through a labor representative to produce a contract acceptable to both labor and management.
Mediation:	A neutral third person or persons enters the collective bargaining arrangement and tries to find a solution acceptable to both labor and management. The parties in the dispute then make their own settlement, either accepting or rejecting the mediator's solution.
Voluntary arbitration:	A third person or persons enters the dispute only after labor and management have agreed to accept the decision of the arbitrators as final and binding.
Fact-finding:	Labor and management agree to the appointment of a board to investigate a dispute and recommend a possible settlement. Neither party is obligated to accept the board's recommendations as final.
Presidential influence:	The President makes public appeals to both labor and management to reach an early agreement. This is usually used only in industries that affect the national interest.
Injunction:	A court order is issued against a union or a company preventing it from acting in any way. It maintains the current situation until some settlement can be made.
Seizure:	The government takes over the management of a firm and can, during this period, negotiate with union representatives to find new terms of employment.
Compulsory arbitration:	A third person or persons enters the dispute and makes a decision which labor and management must accept as final and binding.

over 90 percent is now affiliated with the AFL-CIO, continued to grow. Union membership reached a peak of 22.8 million members in 1974. It has since declined somewhat.

This decline has been brought about by several economic developments. First, there has been a shift in the work force toward white-collar occupations—professional, managerial, administrative, and sales—in which unionization is not as common as among blue-collar workers. Second, as union demands become accepted by business, management is likely to give similar benefits to nonunion workers. This lessens the desire of workers to join unions. Third, scandal surrounds some unions.

During their formative years, American unions were predominantly national in scope, supporting programs that fostered social goals. The unions were in the forefront of social reform for education, welfare, women's rights, tax reform, health care programs and social security. In the last few decades, union battles have been waged mostly for workers benefits—including wages, shorter work hours, and pension funds. Today major objectives of unions are for lowering the unemployment rate and obtaining national health insurance programs.

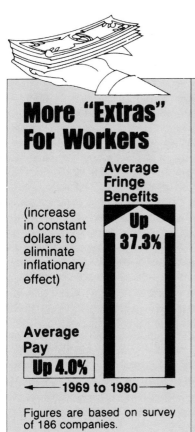

More "Extras" For Workers

Average Fringe Benefits

Up 37.3%

(increase in constant dollars to eliminate inflationary effect)

Average Pay

Up 4.0%

◄— 1969 to 1980 —►

Figures are based on survey of 186 companies.

How Industries Compare in Fringes

Average cost per worker in 1980—

Manufacturing
Petroleum	$10,578
Chemicals, allied products	$7,490
Primary metals	$7,474
Transportation equipment	$7,399
Fabricated metals	$6,612
Electrical machinery	$6,293
Printing, publishing	$5,954
Food, beverages, tobacco	$5,808
Stone, clay, glass	$5,769
Rubber, leather, plastics	$5,562
Pulp, paper, lumber, furniture	$5,427
Textiles, apparel	$3,534

Nonmanufacturing
Public utilities	$8,238
Banks, finance	$5,828
Insurance	$5,555
Trade	$4,210
Hospitals	$3,855
Department stores	$3,656

Where Benefits Go

Of the $6,084 in average fringes per worker in 1980—

Social Security (employer's share)	$954
Life, health insurance	$950
Pensions	$888
Paid vacations	$808
Paid rest periods	$577
Paid holidays	$550
Workers' compensation	$261
Unemployment compensation	$223
Sick leave	$215
Profit sharing	$202
Other benefits	$456

USN&WR charts—Basic data: Chamber of Commerce of the U.S., from survey of 983 companies

Chapter 11

Money and banking

> - *Money is of value only if you can exchange it for something else.*
>
> - *Money has value because it is scarce.*

How great it would be to have a million dollars! But suppose the million dollars were offered with just one restriction: You'd have to take it to the moon. A million dollars on the moon isn't so appealing. There is nothing on the moon to buy. Money is of value only if it can be exchanged for goods and services.

Money

Money has three functions. Anything that performs these functions can be considered money. 1) It is a *medium of exchange,* generally acceptable in exchange for goods and services. 2) It is a *measure of value,* the yardstick by which the value of other things is measured. 3) It is a *store of value,* a convenient form in which purchasing power can be saved to be used at a future time.

Consider how you would get along without money. If you are one of the relatively few people who make or grow things, you might barter your products for what you need. A farmer might trade some steers for a new car, but how, without a common denominator of values, could he judge the relative worth of steers and cars? And how could he buy a pair of shoes with a steer, or save the proceeds, if they were in a form other than money, when he sells an entire herd? Industrial society could not function without money.

Kinds of money

In the past, many items were accepted as money—Indian wampum, clam shells, furs, lumps of metal,

tobacco. Gold and silver, valued for their scarcity, durability, and wide appeal, served most commonly.

Today, money consists mainly of currency (coins and paper money) and demand deposits (bank checking accounts).

Checkbook money makes up three-fourths of the active money supply. Much money is transferred without any checks or currency changing hands. A person may use a bank "debit" card for purchases. The card signals an electronic funds transfer (EFT) from a person's bank account to a store's account. But it's still checking-account money that's being spent.

Money has value because it is scarce and useful. Money is useful because it can be exchanged for goods and services. It is wanted not for its own sake, but for the things it will buy, either today or in the future. As long as money serves its three basic functions, it has value.

The stock of money

Under the Constitution, the federal government has sole authority to mint coins and to determine their value. Among the first coins put out by the U.S. Mint were silver dollars and $10 gold "eagles." Until the Civil War, the government issued no paper currency, although private banks did, often freely and with disastrous results because there was no way to guarantee its value.

In 1862, the government issued paper notes and silver certificates in order to finance the Civil War. For a while, this money was backed up by silver or gold. For example, the silver certificates could be redeemed for silver. Both gold and silver have *intrinsic value,* as a resource apart from their use as money. Paper money has little intrinsic value; its value is *extrinsic,* or placed on it from outside, usually by the government. The money issued by a government has value only as long as people have confidence in it.

People began to hoard the currency that was backed by precious metals. The metals were scarce, and the money supply was limited. It could not easily be expanded to meet the needs of a growing economy. Gradually, the government stopped backing the money supply with precious metals. It declared coins produced by U.S. Mints in Philadelphia, Denver, and San Francisco, and paper money, printed by the U.S. Treasury and the Federal Reserve Banks, to be the only legal tender of the United States. This means that any U.S. bill or coin offered in settlement of a debt must be accepted as legal money. Failure to accept legal tender money in settlement of any obligation means the debt is cancelled.

The money supply

M1, the basic money supply, has become a magic term. Several years ago, few people would have cared about the size of M1, or would even have heard of it. Today, not only bankers, but farmers, labor leaders, business managers, and many other people take an interest in the ups and downs of M1. The **Federal Reserve Bank** (FED) controls the supply of M1.

M1 is the amount of money people have to spend, including currency, checking accounts at banks, NOW (negotiable order of withdrawal) accounts, share draft accounts at credit unions, and other checking-type deposits. Changes in M1 affect prices, business sales, employment opportunities, and the general economic climate. Most M1 money is in checkbook and other demand deposits.

Savings accounts are included in *M2,* a second money category used by the FED to distinguish spending money from savings money. However, this distinction has become blurred: The FED decided to include interest-bearing checking(NOW) accounts as M1, even though they are partly used for savings. And the FED includes money-market funds in M2, even though they have checking account features. These and other innovations by banking institutions keep FED officials busy trying to control the money supply.

Since the early 1970s, the money stock has been growing as the economy has grown—and often faster. During most years, M1 increases about 5-6 percent, while the nation's output of goods and services has gone up approximately 2 percent. During some periods, changes in the money supply have been very erratic. Some government officials and business leaders feel that extra money places inflationary pressure on the economy, leading to higher prices.

Banking

Banks are so important in every community that it's difficult to think of getting along without them. The roots of modern banking go back many years.

Goldsmiths often stored gold and other valuables for people in exchange for a small fee. The person would deposit his gold and receive a receipt. When the depositor claimed his gold, he was given back the exact piece that he had deposited. The goldsmith soon found that it wasn't necessary to return the same piece of gold to the depositor because gold is interchangeable. One piece of the same size and weight has exactly the same value as another piece. Soon, holding gold for people in exchange for a small fee became a worthwhile business. After a time, the goldsmith no longer smithed gold, but became a holder of other people's gold. He might then have been called a banker.

He began to realize that at any given time he had far more gold sitting in his warehouse than he had demand for, because few people withdrew gold. Most just left it there for safekeeping. Being a wise man, he began to lend the gold reserves and charged a fee for doing so. This fee is called

---

HOW BIG A MONEY SUPPLY?

Here are four ways the Federal Reserve defines and computes the money supply—

M₁ =	Basically, checking accounts at commercial banks plus currency in circulation
M₂ = M₁	plus amounts credited by the commercial banks to savings accounts, time deposits and certificates of deposit (C.D.'s) of less than $100,000 apiece
M₃ = M₂	plus deposits held by mutual savings banks, savings and loan associations and credit unions
M₄ = M₂	plus negotiable C.D.'s of $100,000 and up

Source: Federal Reserve Board data

---

interest. On any particular day, only about 2 percent of the gold was actually called for, so he had a lot of it available to lend to borrowers.

This is the principle of banking: Hold money for many people, and lend a good proportion of that money to other people. This is so successful an idea that, today, people do not have to pay a fee for placing money in a bank for safekeeping. They even receive money in return for doing so. They receive interest on their savings accounts. Financial institutions have an important job. They transfer buying power from people who have more money than they need—the *lenders* or *depositors*—to people who have less money than they need—the *borrowers.*

Banks have a long history—much of it very violent. Bank robberies occurred frequently when large reserves of precious metals were kept in storerooms. Bank runs also occurred whenever people feared that bad times were coming, and they all wanted their money at the same time. These runs were known as *panics.* In order to make banks safer and avoid panics, Congress set up the **Federal Reserve System** in 1913 and gave it the responsibility of controlling the banking system.

Communities have banks of several different kinds: commercial banks, savings banks, and savings and loan associations. Most bank accounts are insured by the federal government, and people are confident that their money is safe. Thus, banks provide two major services: they keep money safe and they lend it to people who need it.

The Federal Reserve System

The Federal Reserve System coordinates the money and banking functions of the nation. There are 12 regional Federal Reserve banks whose policies are set forth by a Board of Governors. Each district also has one or more branch reserve banks. There is a total of 36 reserve banks and branches. The Reserve Board consists of seven members, appointed by the President of the United States for terms of 14 years, subject to confirmation by the Senate. All commercial banks whose charters are approved by the federal government are members of the Federal Reserve System.

A banker's bank

The Federal Reserve system is the *banker's bank.* It performs services for member banks in the same way that commercial banks perform services for their depositors.

All member commercial banks are required to keep a cash reserve of about 12-18 percent (depending on the size of the bank) against all the "demand deposits" (checking accounts) of their customers, and a much smaller reserve, 4-6 percent, against "time deposits" (savings accounts) with the Federal Reserve bank in their district. The Federal Reserve banks, by holding cash reserves for many commercial banks, have more than enough cash in the vaults to keep any member bank from failing, should there be a run on its deposits. This banker's bank, then, is able to prevent a widespread run on a bank by providing funds if a large number of depositors choose to withdraw at the same time. The Federal Reserve can thus prevent panics. The following are functions of the Federal Reserve banks:

● 1) They lend funds to member banks as needed. Just as individuals or businesses can borrow from commercial banks, so, too, can commercial banks borrow from Reserve banks. The interest that the member banks pay to the Federal Reserve is known as the *discount rate.* When a Federal Reserve bank raises or lowers the discount rate to member banks it has a great effect on the entire economy.

● 2) They collect and clear checks. Any check you write, unless the receiver uses the same bank you do, is sent to an appropriate Federal Reserve bank that *credits* (adds to) the account of the other person's bank while it *debits* (takes out of) the account of your bank. In turn, the Reserve bank forwards the check to your bank which then debits your account.

● 3) They provide currency for commercial banks when they are short. (In effect, the member bank draws on its account with the Federal Reserve bank.) Old, worn out bills also are traded with the Federal Reserve for crisp new bills.

In fact, almost all of the services your local bank renders to you are also available to your bank through the Federal Reserve banks.

The government's bank. Reserve banks also do an enormous amount of work as the financial agent for the federal government. The Treasury Department deposits funds in Federal Reserve banks and writes checks against these deposits.

Reserve banks also buy and sell government securities, provide loans, and perform other useful functions for the government.

Federal Reserve notes, the major kind of paper money in our economy, are issued by Reserve banks. They are held in the Reserve banks until the commercial banks buy them for use by their customers. This paper money is no longer backed by gold, silver, or other precious metals—only the vast assets of the Reserve system. Since those assets are largely government securities, the backing is ultimately the taxing power of the federal government.

Banks create money. Perhaps the most important function of the Federal Reserve System is to control the money supply. To understand how it does this, one must first understand how commercial banks create money. They do not issue currency; that is the function of the U.S. Treasury. Only 10 percent of the money supply (or M1) is currency. The rest is made up of *demand deposits* such as checking accounts.

Recall that commercial banks are required to hold some of their money (reserves) with the Federal Reserve bank. Just as a customer maintains a checking account in a commercial bank, the commercial bank has an account with one of the Federal Reserve banks.

Assume that you wrote a check for $1,000 (borrowed from bank A) to an automobile dealer for a car that you just purchased. Your bank (bank A) was able to make the loan because it had at least $1,000 in excess reserves available. In making the loan, bank A reduced its reserves with the Federal Reserve by $1,000 and added $1,000 to the money supply. The automobile dealer then deposited the check in his bank, bank B.

Bank B now has excess reserves. If we assume that the reserve requirment is 15 percent, this bank must keep $150 of this new $1,000 on reserve with the Federal Reserve. Just as bank A could lend excess reserves, bank B now has $850 that it can lend to customers. In other words, the $1,000 lent by bank A enables bank B to create an additional $850.

When bank B makes loans of $850, this money might be deposited in bank C. Bank C now has excess reserves of $850 from which it can lend $722 (85 percent of its new deposits, maintaining 15 percent on reserve). Now, bank C will be creating an additional $722 in the economy.

When new loans of this $722 are made, they could be deposited in yet another bank, Bank D. Bank D must keep 15 percent of the deposit on reserve, but this leaves $614 that can be lent to new customers. More money is thus created by the banking system. This process continues on and on as shown in the chart. Eventually, the supply of checkbook money, demand deposits, is increased $6,667, or 6 2/3 times the original deposit.

This expansion of the money supply is created by the banking system as a whole. No single bank could do it alone; it would be too risky for one bank to lend out 6 2/3 times more than it has

reserves on hand. There is no guarantee, and very little chance, that the money would be deposited back in the original bank. All the banks in total, however, are able to expand the money supply by creating new demand deposits.

The extent to which the money supply is expanded depends on how much the banks lend. In other words, the money-creating potential of banks depends on the Federal Reserve's reserve requirements. If the reserve requirement were only 10 percent, banks would have more money to lend— 90 percent of new deposits. Total expansion of the money supply, if we were to work through the same creation process, would be ten times the initial demand deposits. If the reserve requirement were 20 percent, the expansion potential would be only five times the original deposits.

Creating Money in the Banking System

	Amount added to demand deposits	Amount required as legal reserve	Excess which can be loaned out
Bank A			$1,000
Bank B	$1,000	$ 150	850
Bank C	850	128	722
Bank D	722	108	614
Bank E	614	92	522
Bank F	522	78	444
Bank G	444	67	377
Bank H	377	57	320
Bank I	320	48	272
Bank J	272	41	231
All banks	$6,667	$1,000	$6,667

The FED loses members

In 1969, the Federal Reserve System had over 400 more banks than it did in the early 1980s. The number defecting from the system is expected to grow. More and more banks are deciding that the cost of keeping non-interest-earning reserves at their district Reserve bank is not worth the advantage of borrowing money from the FED at a discount.

Not all banks are members of the Federal Reserve System; neither savings and loan associations nor credit unions are members, and only banks with charters from the federal government are required to join. Approximately 50 per cent of state-chartered banks are members—but the number is declining. In total, there are approximately 5,500 commercial banks in the Federal Reserve System. These banks account for fewer than 40 percent of the commercial banks in the United States, but control about 70 percent of all bank assets.

The exodus of banks creates problems for the FED. Changing the reserve requirements of member banks is a major tool with which the FED can influence the money supply. With fewer banks in the system, more banks can carry on business without regard to the FED's reserve requirements.

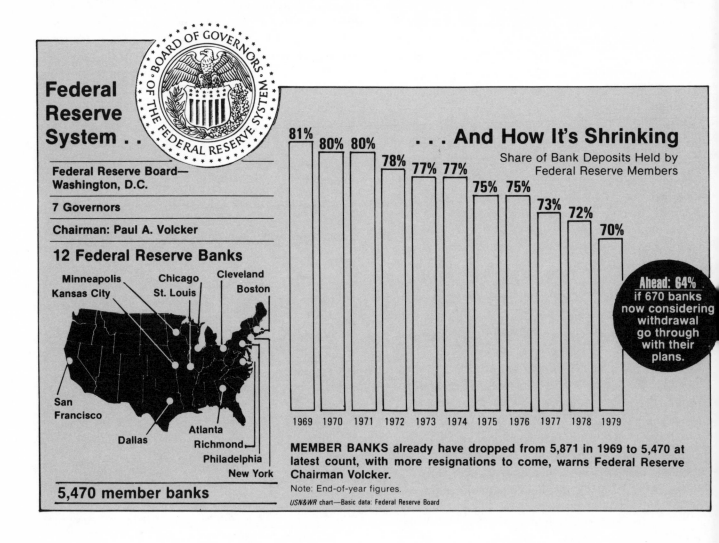

Federal Reserve System . . .

Federal Reserve Board— Washington, D.C.

7 Governors

Chairman: Paul A. Volcker

12 Federal Reserve Banks

Minneapolis
Kansas City
Chicago
St. Louis
Cleveland
Boston

San Francisco

Dallas
Atlanta
Richmond
Philadelphia
New York

5,470 member banks

. . . And How It's Shrinking

Share of Bank Deposits Held by Federal Reserve Members

81% 80% 80% 78% 77% 77% 75% 75% 73% 72% 70%

1969 1970 1971 1972 1973 1974 1975 1976 1977 1978 1979

Ahead: 64% if 670 banks now considering withdrawal go through with their plans.

MEMBER BANKS already have dropped from 5,871 in 1969 to 5,470 at latest count, with more resignations to come, warns Federal Reserve Chairman Volcker.

Note: End-of-year figures.

USN&WR chart—Basic data: Federal Reserve Board

Chapter 12

Government

> - *The federal government buys more goods and services than any other institution.*
>
> - *Millions of people benefit from government programs.*

The federal government is America's biggest business. It buys more typewriters, constructs more buildings, employs more people, spends more for scientific research, and handles more money than any other entity in America.

Add state and local governments, and you have an immense machine that not only creates massive economic effects in its own right, but sets the rules under which all businesses operate.

Services performed by local governments

The largest portion of taxes paid to local governments is used to build, maintain, and operate public schools. Most of the revenue for local governments comes from the property tax. Because of the importance given public education in our country, more tax funds have gone for this purpose each year. When local governments need more money, they must often rely on voters to pass a *bond issue.*

The building and repair of highways, roads, and streets is the next largest item in the budgets of local governments. Public welfare, for care of the aged and others who are unable to care for themselves, is generally the third largest expense.

Services performed by state governments

State governments garner funds through sales taxes and, in many cases, state income taxes. An increasing amount of money is going to state (and local) governments from the federal government in the process known as *revenue sharing.* The federal government collects tax money and then provides it to states for specific expenses. In this way, taxes from wealthier states help provide services for less wealthy states.

As with local government, the largest expenditure of state governments is education. The major share of this goes to support state colleges, universities, and training schools; some is used to help local public schools. The next largest expense of state governments is highway construction and maintenance. States provide funds for many other services: welfare programs, unemployment compensation, public health, state police, parks, recreation areas, forest preserves, and prisons.

Total expenditures for all local and state governments are still considerably less than the expenditures of the federal government. State and local governments spend about one-third of all tax dollars. This leaves two-thirds of public expenditures carried out by the federal government. The major source of revenue for the federal government is income tax on individuals and corporations.

The federal government's role in the economy

The founders of the American Republic envisioned a limited role for government in the economy: to coin money, regulate trade, and provide a few basic services, such as police protection, roads, public education, and defense—only because these were services that could not efficiently be provided by private firms. But the functions of the federal government soon expanded enormously, even during the early years of the Republic.

Federal investments in roads, canals, and railroads in the 1800s, for example, made it easier to transport products to faraway markets and people to new homes on the frontier. Federal grants of land to homesteaders encouraged families to settle and farm western territories. At the same time, the federal government found it increasingly necessary to regulate banks, credit and the circulation of paper money.

The Preamble to the Constitution states that the basic purposes of the national government are to "establish justice, insure domestic tranquility, provide for the common defense, promote the general welfare, and secure the blessings of liberty."

Basic government functions

A major expenditure of the federal government is national defense. Defense money goes toward the purchase of military equipment and supplies, salaries to millions of men and women in the armed forces, the maintenance of military bases in the United States and abroad, research and development, operation of the national military colleges, veterans' benefits, and pensions.

Other large expenditures of the federal government are for various welfare programs. Many people receive funds from the Social Security programs. The unemployed receive financial assistance, employment services, and job training programs. Other needy people are provided income supplements and health care benefits. The federal government provides funds for educational programs and research, as well as for public health facilities and research. The federal government also incurs expenses in areas of agricultural research, natural resource development, commerce, and transportation.

There has been a rapid growth in government activities. At the turn of the century, one of every twenty-five workers was on a public payroll. In 1982, the ratio was one to seven. Before World War I, federal, state, and local government outlays amounted to little more than $3 billion, about 8 percent of the gross national product. In the early 1980s, government costs represented about 33 percent of the GNP.

There are many reasons for the increase. A larger military budget has resulted from the development of more sophisticated and expensive weapons. Rising expectations have led to demands for more public services, such as Social Security, welfare, aid to education, superhighways, and airports.

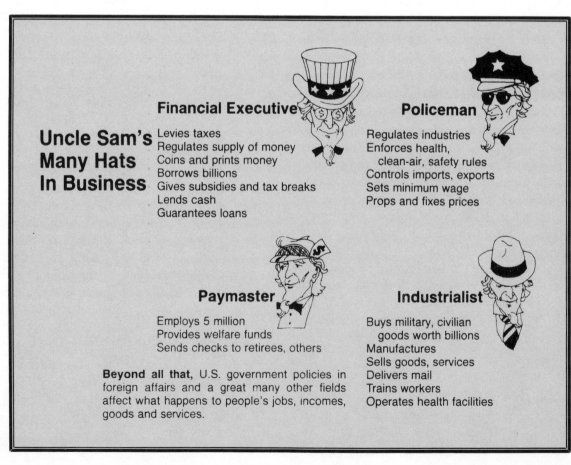

Uncle Sam's Many Hats In Business

Financial Executive
Levies taxes
Regulates supply of money
Coins and prints money
Borrows billions
Gives subsidies and tax breaks
Lends cash
Guarantees loans

Policeman
Regulates industries
Enforces health,
    clean-air, safety rules
Controls imports, exports
Sets minimum wage
Props and fixes prices

Paymaster
Employs 5 million
Provides welfare funds
Sends checks to retirees, others

Industrialist
Buys military, civilian
    goods worth billions
Manufactures
Sells goods, services
Delivers mail
Trains workers
Operates health facilities

Beyond all that, U.S. government policies in foreign affairs and a great many other fields affect what happens to people's jobs, incomes, goods and services.

THE MAKING OF A BUDGET—STEP BY STEP

Spending and taxing plans drawn up year-round affect the outlook for families and businesses. Far more than dollars and cents are at stake, too.

Creating the federal budget, by most accounts, is the single most important activity performed by Congress and the White House each year.

The budget is no mere tally sheet of outlays and revenues. It is a blueprint of the Government's pervasive impact on millions of Americans.

Primarily, the budget is a spending plan for the Government, indicating just where national problems such as poverty, energy or national defense rank in terms of priority when it comes to earmarking hard cash.

It is also a signal to Congress to raise needed revenues, thus setting the stage for debates over which groups of consumers and businesses should benefit from tax cuts, or pay the tab for new programs.

The size of the budget and its deficit also are crucial instruments of federal economic policy. Bigger deficits can shove the economy out of recession in slack times, or cause rampaging inflation during a boom.

In each of these roles, the budget is at the heart of sensitive political decisions that both shape the course of the American economy and offer solutions to problems that face the nation.

So the federal budget is immensely important. But just who determines what goes into the budget, and how is it created?

In essence, the federal budget is a spending and taxing plan for the 12-month period stretching from October 1 in one year to September 30 of the next—the so-called fiscal year. It contains details of every revenue and spending program for every single activity of the Federal Government.

The report that follows sketches the broadest outlines of the budget-making process. The timetable traces, month by month, the work behind the scenes leading up to the start of a new fiscal year on October 1.

18 Months Ahead: An Outline

Work on the budget starts in the Office of Management and Budget more than a year and a half before the fiscal year actually gets under way.

In April or May, OMB reports give the President his first look at how much new spending and taxation are likely to be needed in the year starting some 18 months hence, and how much stimulation or restraint business will need.

These reports confront the President with his first two decisions:

• He must set the size of the budget and offer general spending targets for the departments and agencies.

• He must also decide whether the economy 18 months ahead will be strong, requiring smaller deficits or a surplus to restrain the private economy, or weak and in need of some stimulus. That decision will determine whether a tax increase or cut is needed, or whether spending should be increased or slowed down to meet these broad goals.

Once those decisions are made, the process of building the President's budget gets under way.

15 Months Ahead: Agencies Plan

With the President's guidelines in hand, the various agencies of the executive branch—ranging from huge departments such as Health, Education and Welfare to the smallest regional economic commissions of the Commerce Department—begin planning their requests for funding in the budget year ahead.

This process begins at the lowest levels, with the many subdivisions of each agency deciding how much money they would need to run their programs efficiently. Each separate division of the Justice Department, for instance, evaluates its needs for the year and requests that sum from senior Justice officials.

Top officers will cut some requests, add to others and pass their final funding plans on to OMB.

13 Months Ahead: Budget Season

When the agencies and departments present their requests to OMB, the budget season begins. Stretching from September through early November of the year before the fiscal year starts, OMB sits down with individual agency officials to knock out final budget plans to submit to the President.

When OMB has settled on its plans for the budget of each department or agency, the Director of OMB presents that plan to the President, who makes the final decision on the agency's spending.

If agency heads still are not satisfied with their budgets, they may make an

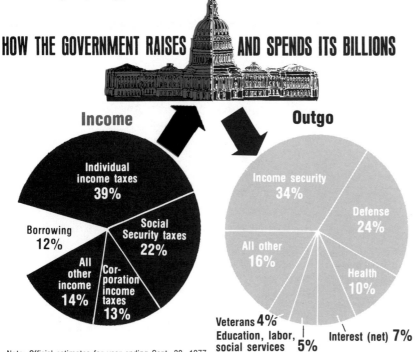

HOW THE GOVERNMENT RAISES AND SPENDS ITS BILLIONS

Income
- Individual income taxes **39%**
- Social Security taxes **22%**
- Borrowing **12%**
- All other income **14%**
- Corporation income taxes **13%**

Outgo
- Income security **34%**
- Defense **24%**
- All other **16%**
- Health **10%**
- Interest (net) **7%**
- Education, labor, social services **5%**
- Veterans **4%**

Note: Official estimates for year ending Sept. 30, 1977.
Source: U.S. Office of Management and Budget

appeal to the President and the OMB Director. After these appeals, however, the President's decision stands as the amount to be requested.

9 Months Ahead: Executive Budget

Within 15 days after the Congress convenes in January, the President presents his budget plans in a message to lawmakers. Specifics of his proposals are contained in a series of budget books numbering more than 1,000 pages.

The budget lays out in detail the President's plans for spending on all types of programs, and his proposals for changes in taxes. And it indicates the plans of off-budget agencies, such as those that guarantee loans to home-owners or farmers, whose borrowing and outlays are not counted with other federal spending.

9 Months Ahead: Congress Gears Up

Even before the President's budget is released, Congress is busy preparing for its part in the budget-making process. There are several groups on Capitol Hill that work on the budget.

The Congressional Budget Office, created by a 1974 law that established new procedures for budget making, helps the House and Senate evaluate the cost to taxpayers and the economic impact of budget proposals.

The CBO also reviews various programs to evaluate alternative ways to address issues ranging from poverty to defense, and keeps track of tax and spending bills to make sure that Congress follows its own rules for making the budget.

Both the House and Senate also have budget committees that are assigned to set broad spending and taxing goals—much as the President does for federal agencies—and to oversee the process of budget building in each chamber of Congress.

Finally, there are the tax-writing and appropriations committees in each house that review specific bills to authorize taxes and spending.

These committees have the option to rewrite considerably the budget proposals of the President, and they often do just that.

6 Months Ahead: First Resolution

By April 15 of the year in which the fiscal year begins, the budget committee in each house must settle its plans for spending and revenue, and may set specific targets for tax changes and for spending in several broad categories.

The two houses of Congress must, by May 15, approve the first "concurrent resolution" on the budget for the approaching fiscal year.

In that resolution, the lawmakers specify their over-all budget targets, which often differ from those set by the President.

5 Months Ahead: Appropriations

The targets in the first resolution are used by the appropriations and tax-law-writing and other committees of Congress as a guide to how much they can spend and tax.

The appropriations process stretches from May to September, with commit-

tees considering bills to raise or lower taxes, to spend money on new programs or to authorize existing ones for another year or more.

Those bills, as with all legislation, must pass both houses of Congress and be signed into law by the President.

1 Month Ahead: Second Resolution

By the seventh day after Labor Day each year, Congress is obliged under law to finish all appropriations for the fiscal year that is to begin on October 1.

Congress then evaluates whether it has stayed within the targets of the first resolution, and checks the state of the economy to make sure that the spending and taxing program approved in May still offers the right amount of stimulus or restraint to the economy.

On September 15, at the latest, Congress must pass a second concurrent resolution. This resolution sets binding limits on spending and revenue to which Congress must adhere. If spending or tax bills passed before September 15 do not conform to the second resolution, they must be passed again to conform.

Zero Hour: The Fiscal Year Starts

If all goes well, the passage of the second concurrent resolution completes the process of constructing the budget. Once October 1 rolls around, the departments and agencies of the Federal Government begin committing the money appropriated to them under the laws passed by Congress, while the White House and Congress focus their attention on the next year's budget.

The government—through programs like defense, health, and atomic energy—now pays for much of the nation's research and development.

Modern technology has resulted in new problems. Some complex chemicals and drugs are a danger to human health, and industrial processes pollute the environment. A market system that gives businesses incentives to hold down costs does not deal effectively with these problems, and government has had to intervene with regulations.

Government regulates

Today, government regulations attempt to protect consumers and competitors from deceptive business practices, insure the quality and safety of goods and drugs, establish safety standards for mines, factories, and other places of work, regulate airlines, railroads, and buses, and assure people equal access to housing, jobs and education.

Americans also have turned to public agencies to solve social problems. Government is involved

in helping to rebuild run-down neighborhoods, providing housing for poor people, creating jobs in depressed areas, feeding poverty-stricken families, aiding minority businesses, and providing medical care for the aged and poor.

Through these activities, the federal government has become a major source of income for millions of people. About half the population relies on pay, pensions, welfare aid or other forms of income from federal, state or local governments.

When markets are weak, Washington establishes price floors for important commodities to bolster the incomes of farmers. It sets minimum wages that must be paid to most workers. It regulates interstate commerce. State commissions usually establish the rates for electricity and natural gas. Local boards set fares for buses and taxis.

Government, a business

Finally, government is involved in business as an owner and operator. It provides most of the mail service. It makes all the enriched uranium to fuel nuclear power plants. It's in the lending business, dispensing billions of dollars in loans to railroads, rural telephone and electric cooperatives, farmers, small companies, and foreign buyers of American exports.

The government also sells timber. In the process, it has a major role in deciding how much lumber will be produced for home building each year. It leases federal lands and offshore areas to private companies for mineral exploration, thus influencing supplies of oil, gas, and coal. It generates and sells electricity.

The federal government fills many roles in the economy—as a regulator of business practices, an employer for millions of workers, the sponsor of many social projects and programs, and the financial agent for the functioning of the total economy.

The federal budget will soon reach $848 billion. How much is that?

If 1 million dollars had been spent each day since the birth of Christ, about 127 billion would still remain.

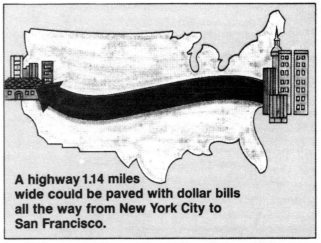

A highway 1.14 miles wide could be paved with dollar bills all the way from New York City to San Francisco.

At current spot-market prices, the budget would pay for almost 20 years of America's oil imports.

You could drop a $1 bill on each square foot of Los Angeles every 10 seconds and make that money storm last 11 minutes before spending the budget.

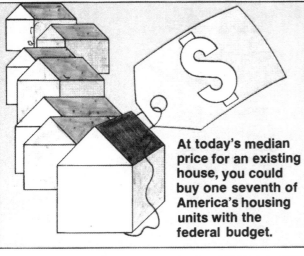

At today's median price for an existing house, you could buy one seventh of America's housing units with the federal budget.

Laid end to end, 848 billion $1 bills would soar 82 million miles into the sky—almost to the sun.

USN&WR chart by Richard Gage

65

Putting the Budge

Fewer and Fewer Years to Pass $100 Billion Milestones

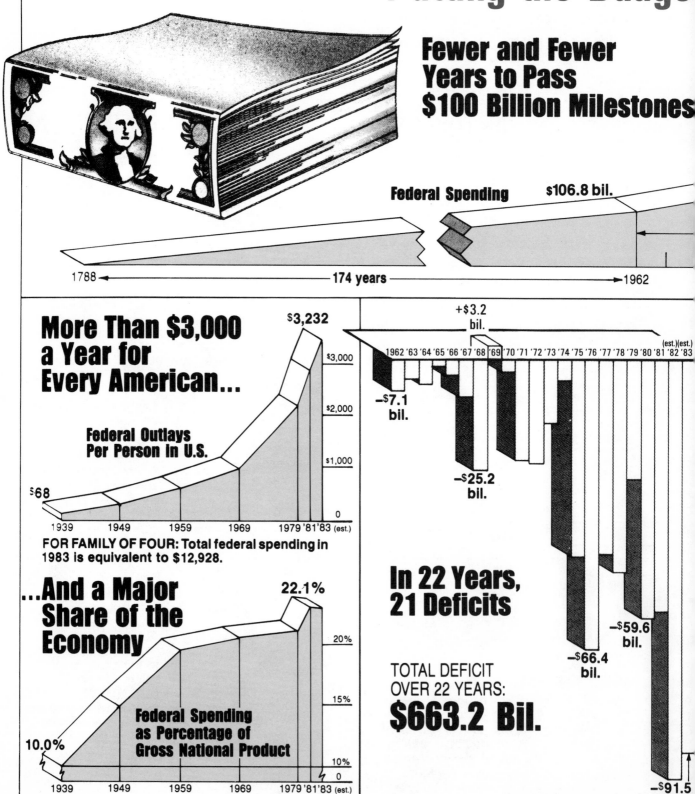

Federal Spending $106.8 bil.

1788 ←———————— 174 years ————————→ 1962

More Than $3,000 a Year for Every American...

$3,232

Federal Outlays Per Person in U.S.

$3,000

$2,000

$1,000

$68

0

1939   1949   1959   1969   1979 '81 '83 (est.)

FOR FAMILY OF FOUR: Total federal spending in 1983 is equivalent to $12,928.

...And a Major Share of the Economy

22.1%

20%

Federal Spending as Percentage of Gross National Product

15%

10.0%

10%

0

1939   1949   1959   1969   1979 '81 '83 (est.)

+$3.2 bil.

1962 '63 '64 '65 '66 '67 '68 '69 '70 '71 '72 '73 '74 '75 '76 '77 '78 '79 '80 '81 '82 '83   (est.)(est.)

−$7.1 bil.

−$25.2 bil.

In 22 Years, 21 Deficits

−$59.6 bil.

−$66.4 bil.

TOTAL DEFICIT OVER 22 YEARS:

$663.2 Bil.

−$91.5 bil.

Note: Years through 1976 end June 30; those starting with 1977 end September 30.

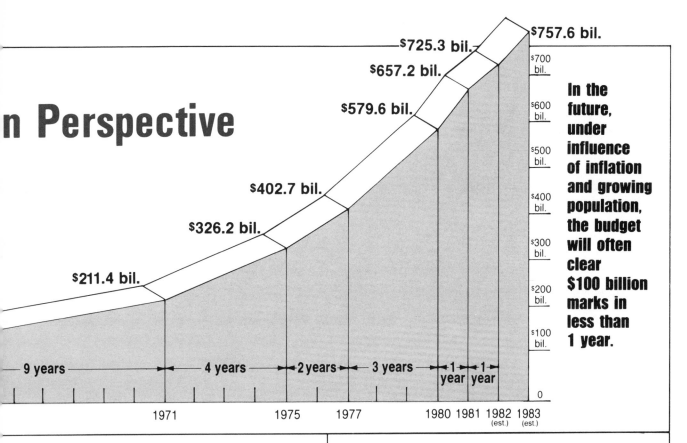

n Perspective

$757.6 bil.

$725.3 bil.

$657.2 bil.

$579.6 bil.

$402.7 bil.

$326.2 bil.

$211.4 bil.

$700 bil.
$600 bil.
$500 bil.
$400 bil.
$300 bil.
$200 bil.
$100 bil.
0

In the future, under influence of inflation and growing population, the budget will often clear $100 billion marks in less than 1 year.

9 years — 4 years — 2 years — 3 years — 1 year 1 year

1971   1975   1977   1980 1981 1982 1983
                                          (est.) (est.)

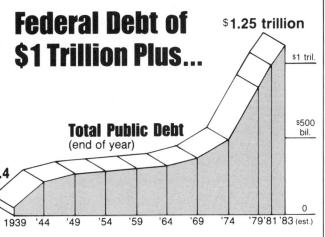

Federal Debt of $1 Trillion Plus...

$1.25 trillion

$1 tril.

Total Public Debt
(end of year)

$500 bil.

0

1939 '44 '49 '54 '59 '64 '69 '74 '79 '81 '83 (est.)

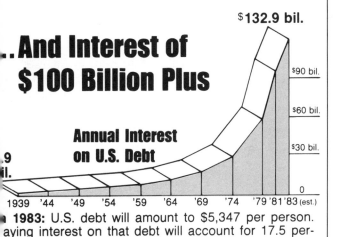

...And Interest of $100 Billion Plus

$132.9 bil.

$90 bil.

$60 bil.

Annual Interest on U.S. Debt

$30 bil.

0

1939 '44 '49 '54 '59 '64 '69 '74 '79 '81 '83 (est.)

1983: U.S. debt will amount to $5,347 per person. aying interest on that debt will account for 17.5 percent of all federal spending.

Nearly Everybody Has a Share of U.S. Budget

Some of the millions who benefited directly from federal spending programs in 1983.

People collecting Social Security   **36,900,000**
Medicaid beneficiaries   **22,400,000**
People receiving food stamps   **21,400,000**
People helped under medicare   **28,900,000**
Children in school-lunch programs   **23,200,000**
Railroad-retirement beneficiaries   **974,000**
Members of families receiving Aid to Families
   With Dependent Children   **11,000,000**
Workers on unemployment compensation   **3,600,000**
Disabled coal miners   **440,000**
Civil-service retirees   **1,400,000**
Military personnel   **2,100,000**
Military retirees   **1,400,000**
Aged, blind, disabled receiving aid   **3,600,000**
Government workers   **2,700,000**
Veterans or survivors collecting
   pensions or compensation   **5,400,000**

What's more: Millions of Americans are helped by other programs, such as federalized housing, small-business loans, farm-price supports, college-student loans.

Note: Figures cannot add to a total because many people receive government help under more than one program.

USN&WR chart—Basic data: U.S. Office of Management and Budget; U.S. Depts. of Treasury and Commerce

Chapter 13

Taxes

- *Taxes are the way to pay for government services.*

- *It is difficult to tax all people fairly.*

Some government agencies sell goods and services. That is, they receive funds from various kinds of fees, licenses, and fines. The revenue received from these sources, however, is small in comparison to total government expenditures. State, local, and federal governments also borrow money to finance some operations for specific projects. The borrowing is usually done by selling government bonds to financial institutions or the general public. At the local level, such borrowing often requires approval by voters. But most of government's money comes from taxes.

Criteria for a good tax

To most people a good tax is a low tax. But in addition to imposing taxes at a rate as low as possible, governments must tax high enough to generate enough revenue. Each level of government—state, local, and federal—uses a variety of different taxes. There are some specific criteria for judging a "good" tax:

1) **Adequate.** A tax should provide enough money to pay for the services it must finance.

2) **Easy to administer.** A tax should be easy and inexpensive to collect.

3) **Easy to understand.** The nature of the tax should be clearly understandable to both the taxpayer and tax collector.

4) **Flexible.** A tax should vary with economic conditions: When the economy is booming, tax payments should be higher; when economic activity is slow, a tax should automatically adjust to lessen the tax burden.

5) **Neutral.** A tax should interfere as little as possible with the production of income and wealth.

6) **Fair.** A tax should pose an equal hardship on all taxpayers, yet those who benefit the most from a government service should be taxed accordingly.

This final criterion is the most difficult to meet because it often poses contradictory objectives. There are two basic, but very different, principles for judging how fair a tax is. One is called the *benefits received* principle, the other is called the *ability to pay* principle.

Proponents of the benefits received principle argue that an individual's taxes should bear a close relationship to the benefits or services he or she receives. A good example of this principle is the gasoline tax. Motorists, when they purchase gas, usually pay both a federal and state tax. The revenues from this are used to build and repair streets and highways. People who buy more gas—either because they drive more or drive bigger cars which consume more road space—pay a higher tax.

On the face of it, this appears to be a sound principle. It does have shortcomings. The benefits of most government services are difficult, if not impossible, to measure. Public education, for example, is paid for by all taxpayers, not just by families who have children in school. If the benefits principle prevailed, many families could not afford to send their children to school. Besides, families with children are not the only ones who benefit from good schools; society as a whole is clearly better off when everyone receives an education.

The ability to pay principle is based on the idea that the higher people's incomes, the more taxes they should pay. Most taxes, particularly personal and corporate income taxes, are based largely on the ability principle. This principle is sound, to a point. When the benefits of government services fall generally on the public, those with more money should pay higher taxes. The argument is often extended to say that not only should higher-income people pay more in simple dollar terms, but they also should pay higher tax rates. This is called *progressive* taxation. A progressive tax is based on the idea that an extra dollar is less valuable to a wealthy person than a poor one.

Types of taxes

Taxes are classified as *progressive, regressive,* or *proportional.* As described above, a *progressive* tax is one that imposes a higher rate of taxation on people with higher incomes. In contrast, a *regressive* tax imposes a higher tax rate on lower income groups. With a *proportional* tax the "rate of taxation" is the same for everyone.

The best example of a progressive tax is the personal income tax. In 1977, a person who earned $2,200, the lowest income level subject to taxes, paid a tax of 14 percent of his or her taxable income. At the other extreme, anyone with a taxable income above $102,000 paid a tax of 52 percent on the first $102,200, then 70 percent on all income above this amount.

In practice, the income tax is much less progressive than it appears to be. This is because taxpayers are permitted to take exemptions and deductions from their taxable income for expenses such as interest payments, charitable contributions, and depreciation on property. On the average, high-income earners obtain proportionally more tax deductions, or receive money in ways (other than wages, salaries, and fees) that are taxed at a lower rate. The result is what economists call a *lower effective rate of tax* for higher-income groups, than the theoretical rate.

A good example of a regressive tax is the *sales tax* that most people pay on most goods, and everyone pays on some goods. The sales tax appears

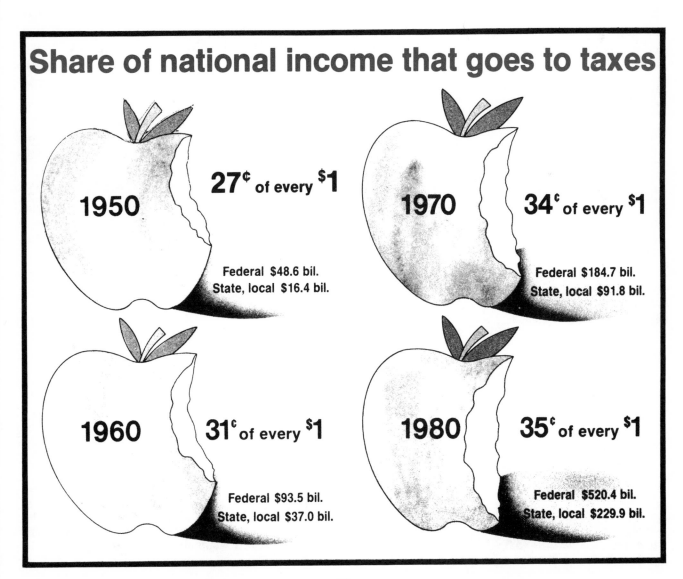

Share of national income that goes to taxes

1950 — **27¢** of every **$1**
Federal $48.6 bil.
State, local $16.4 bil.

1970 — **34¢** of every **$1**
Federal $184.7 bil.
State, local $91.8 bil.

1960 — **31¢** of every **$1**
Federal $93.5 bil.
State, local $37.0 bil.

1980 — **35¢** of every **$1**
Federal $520.4 bil.
State, local $229.9 bil.

Impact of Progressive Taxation

Adjusted Gross Income	Tax Rate People Pay
$ 10,000	3.0%
$ 20,000	9.2%
$ 25,000	11.3%
$ 30,000	13.4%
$ 40,000	17.3%
$ 50,000	20.8%
$ 75,000	27.8%
$100,000	32.3%
$200,000	41.0%

Note: Figures assume family of four filing jointly, with one wage earner and no itemized deductions, at 1983 tax rates. *USN&WR*

to be a proportional tax: Individuals pay a fixed rate, usually around 4 or 5 percent, on goods they purchase. The exact tax rate and type of goods taxed varies from state to state. However, people tend to spend different amounts of their income on goods and services. Generally, higher-income people spend a smaller proportion of their income on taxable goods and services, and are able to save or invest more money. The basis for determining whether a tax is progressive or regressive is the percentage of an individual's income spent on that tax.

Because the personal income tax dominates our federal tax system, it is basically progressive. However, there are some criticisms:

1) The progressive income tax is unfair because it "soaks the rich." This discourages people in higher tax brackets from working as hard as they might otherwise work.

2) The present income tax is unfair because it permits too many loopholes for wealthy people, thereby lessening the impact of its progressive quality.

State and local taxes are generally regressive. States and cities rely heavily on sales and property taxes because they are easy to collect. State and local governments also rely heavily on these taxes because the income tax has been preempted by the federal government. With a tax that claims nearly one-fourth of the average person's income, there is not much left for state and local tax collectors to take. Despite this, nearly all states have some form of income tax (a drastic change from twenty years ago), and a growing number of cities now have this tax.

Revenue sharing

Governments get some of their money from other governments. The federal government, with the income tax, has the best, most flexible source of revenue. Local and state governments have relatively inflexible tax sources, but their needs for funds are rapidly growing. As a result, the federal government shares some of its tax receipts with states and localities.

Similarly, within the states there are "grants-in-aid" from state governments to local governments—primarily for schools, highways, and public assistance. In this way, poorer areas of a state are better able to maintain minimum standards of schooling, roads, and living. Despite revenue sharing there remain sizable differences in the financial capabilities from state to state and from city to city.

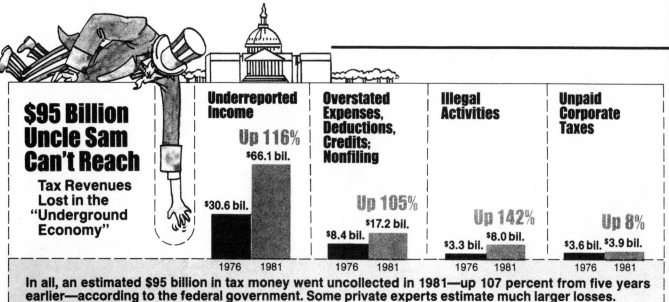

$95 Billion Uncle Sam Can't Reach

Tax Revenues Lost in the "Underground Economy"

Underreported Income — Up 116% — $66.1 bil. / $30.6 bil. — 1976 1981

Overstated Expenses, Deductions, Credits; Nonfiling — Up 105% — $17.2 bil. / $8.4 bil. — 1976 1981

Illegal Activities — Up 142% — $8.0 bil. / $3.3 bil. — 1976 1981

Unpaid Corporate Taxes — Up 8% — $3.9 bil. / $3.6 bil. — 1976 1981

In all, an estimated $95 billion in tax money went uncollected in 1981—up 107 percent from five years earlier—according to the federal government. Some private experts estimate much larger losses.

USN&WR—Basic data: U.S. Dept. of the Treasury

Few people claim to like taxes. As long as they have been collected, taxes have been considered a burden. As Englishman Edmund Burke wrote, when America was still a British colony, "To tax and to please, no more than to love and be wise, is not given to men."

But taxes are not only a burden to the average individual, they are also a benefit—in the form of government services. Without taxes, highway systems, military forces, police and fire protection, research and development facilities, and public parks would not exist.

Are taxes too high? Do they "rob" the average taxpayer and sap the vitality of the U.S. economy?

Compared with other nations, taxes in the United States are not high. Most industrialized countries have higher rates than the United States. Figures vary slightly from year to year, but Sweden tops the list with tax revenues amounting to over 50 percent of their economy's total domestic product. France, West Germany, Italy, and Great Britain all have higher taxes than the United States. Of the major industrial countries, only Japan has lower taxes.

Growth of the Income Tax

Underground Economy: $100 Billion in Lost Taxes

As millions of Americans dig deeper into their pockets to pay their taxes, millions of others are scheming to pull the wool over the tax collector's eyes.

Talk with the tax dodgers and federal and state tax agents across the country and you find workers moonlighting at off-the-record jobs. Homeowners report maids and repair people who want only cash payments. It is not unusual for investors to conceal their holdings. Homemakers and retirees bring in free-and-clear cash by doing informal chores for others. Small-business owners frequently keep two sets of books.

All are part of a vast and growing *underground economy* where income goes untaxed and much business activity is unmeasured. Some are hood-winking Washington out of only a few dollars. But others routinely avoid thousands of dollars in tax.

All told, the Internal Revenue Service estimates that it is losing close to a billion dollars a year. Others say that is only part of the loss.

Economists gauge the underground economy's size in the hundreds of billions of dollars a year as measured in sales of goods and services. That's a total that exceeds the entire gross national product of many countries. Subterranean deals are estimated to equal 14 to 30 percent of the above-ground U.S. GNP.

As many as 30 million people may be involved, at least in part, says Peter

Many repair workers take only cash.

Butmann, a professor at Baruch College in New York City. Gutmann, a close observer of the trend toward unreported income, forecasts that underground transactions could total 450 to 470 billion dollars a year, causing many economic indicators to understate the health of the economy. For example, unemployment figures may be too high and productivity statistics too low.

The bottom line: Almost 1 of every 5 dollars in taxes that the government should be collecting is slipping through its fingers, federal officials estimate.

For many people, fudging on their tax returns also means covering their financial tracks—on what they earn as well as what they spend. "I know lots of people who deal strictly in cash," says a Los Angeles attorney. "Words like check, Visa and Mastercard are not in their vocabularies."

A maid in Chicago asks that the $35 she charges for cleaning a high-rise apartment be in cash. A laborer in Washington, D.C. offers to haul away a truckload of basement trash for $40, but adds: "You'll pay in cash, right?" In Atlanta, an auto-repair firm that doesn't report all its income offers customers a 2 percent discount for cash. It's not that they are afraid of the checks bouncing. Rather, they don't want any record of the income.

A San Francisco waiter pays tax on his tips and salary at a posh restaurant where he works nights. But the cash he gets from working during lunch at a small bistro goes unreported and is kept out of his bank account.

"I want no records," he says, adding: "I don't feel like I'm cheating anyone. I'm earning that money."

Some people are even avoiding cash. They're bartering one service or product for another. A motorcycle mechanic in Georgia says he traded a $200 engine for a plumbing job at his home. Now he's considering trading a frame and engine for some ceiling material. Though no cash changes hands, the IRS says the value of the property that is received should be treated in the same way as cash for tax purposes. Organized bartering groups regularly advise members of the need to pay tax. Still, many who barter ignore this.

Most comply, but—. Workers whose wages or salaries are subject to withholding don't have much opportunity to hide that pay, though under-the-table wage payments are sometimes made. The government says it fails to collect tax on only 2 or 3 percent of such income. There is no such barrier for people who are self-

Some maids want their wages unreported.

employed, do casual jobs or earn income on which withholding is not mandatory.

A Detroit free-lance writer, for instance, supplements his earnings by doing painting and carpentry work for homeowners. He does not keep records of the income or pay tax on it. His justification: "I don't want to provide the government with extra money for bombs and bullets." A private-duty nurse in New York City who cares for hospitalized patients pockets all she gets. Her reasoning: "How will the IRS ever know about it?"

Some complain that the government wants too much. Explains a factory worker in Los Angeles, who does not report the $4 an hour he charges for household jobs on weekends: "I'm already paying too much in taxes for what I earn on my regular job."

Others use their employers as a way to line up untaxed income. A Maryland electrician told a homeowner that a wiring job would cost $125 if done through his firm but then offered to come back at night on his own and do it informally for half the price.

Not reporting tip income appears to be the rule rather than the exception. The government estimates that less than 20 percent of tips are disclosed on tax returns—a tax loss of about 2.3 billion dollars in 1981. In 1982, Congress passed a law requiring restaurants to withhold estimated tips from workers' wages as a percentage of daily receipts. Under the

Drug pushers cover up their deals.

new law, one waitress got a paycheck for $0. She and others are organizing to get the law changed.

One Midwestern waitress accepts a lower-than-average salary but also gets an unreported rent-free apartment in a building owned by her boss.

Other pockets of unreported income include homemakers who run businesses out of their houses. A Los Angeles-area woman has turned garage sales into a profitable venture by buying items at swap meets and then reselling them. "Who reports income they earn from a garage sale?" she asks.

Not all feel they are hiding anything. Says a Cleveland woman who doesn't report her income from sewing: "This isn't a job; it's something I do for friends and neighbors to make a little extra money."

A retired San Francisco-area construction worker makes $200 to $300 a month in unreported income hauling yard debris and doing odd jobs. He recalls: "I didn't set out to cheat the government. People would hand me cash, and I'd put it in my pocket. I didn't think of it as formal income."

Beyond the law? Also puffing up the underground economy are illegal aliens, drug pushers, loan sharks and others who normally would not come forward and file returns in any case. The IRS says narcotics dealers alone evade up to $8 billion a year in taxes.

Some people say they are forced into being accomplices in tax evasion. "I went through five different maids in three months before finding one who would even let me pay what was supposed to be her contribution to Social Security," says a suburban New Yorker. "Getting one who would pay her own contribution to Social Security was simply out of the question. You can assume they're not

paying income tax."

A couple in New York's Westchester County pay their once-a-week maid $60 in cash because she is on welfare, and recording her wages or paying Social Security could destroy her eligibility. Says the husband: "She's very capable, and we need her and like her. I see no reason to ruin the situation."

It is clear from reports by *U.S. News & World Report* bureaus that the temptation to deal in the underground economy infects business executives and investors, as well as wage earners.

Many investors in securities, real estate, artwork, livestock and other assets routinely conceal their profits. One of the attractions of investing in stamps and coins is the ease with which they can be bought and sold without the tax collector's knowing about it, admits a stamp dealer who tries to drum up clients by exhibiting at conventions attended by executives.

A New Jersey man who built up a large collection of baseball cards as a youth proudly recalls selling them for several thousand dollars, adding matter-of-factly: "Of course, I didn't pay any tax on it, either."

Tallying losses. An estimated 9.1 billion dollars in capital-gains tax escaped collection in 1981, about half of what should have been collected.

Contributing to that total are families who defer tax on the profit from the sale of a home by replacing it with a new one but do not keep track of the deferral for future taxation.

Many dividends and interest receipts are going undeclared, too. The Treasury says about 20 billion dollars in such payments are being hidden. Some investors put their money to work outside the U.S.

as a way to escape tax. Two popular havens: Mexico and the Cayman Islands in the Caribbean.

The biggest tax loss in the underground economy is accounted for by unincorporated small businesses, according to the IRS. These include retail shops, street vendors, door-to-door salesmen, building contractors and professionals, such as doctors and lawyers. The estimated tax evaded in 1981 by such groups: Close to 21 billion dollars, says the IRS.

Some small-business operators claim they have to keep two sets of books to survive. "If small businesses reported all their income they couldn't stay in business," says an Atlanta auto mechanic. The owner of a small Chicago advertising firm, which does some work "off the record," explains that high interest rates make it hard to make ends meet.

For many people, not hiding income seems foolish. Says an auto mechanic: "Ninety-nine percent of the American people do not report all their income. I'm no exception."

Louis Ferman, a sociologist at the University of Michigan's Institute of Labor and Industrial Relations, explains that some people feel they have to hide some of their income from tax "to get by," but others do it to spite the government.

Says a department-store clerk who supplements his $900-a-month income with unreported earnings from playing the piano three nights a week in Northern California bars: "It's the difference between brown-bagging it and going out to lunch or affording a concert ticket every now and then."

Still, millions of Americans apparently pay all they owe. For them, the burden of carrying the income hiders and tax evaders is an increasingly heavy one.

Waiters sometimes pocket tips without paying tax.

Definitions of key terms used in taxation

Adjusted gross income: On tax returns, the amount of income subject to tax after subtracting such things as moving expenses, business costs and payments to individual retirement plans.

Ad valorem tax: A tax, import duty or other levy computed on the value of the property involved.

Audit: Examination of a taxpayer's return by the Internal Revenue Service to verify accuracy. Audits may be conducted by correspondence, at home, at your office. Taxpayers have the right under law to have their tax cases kept confidential.

Capital-gains tax: A levy on the profit made on sales of assets or capital. That includes stocks, bonds, art and real estate. Net gain on an asset held more than one year is called long term and is taxed at a maximum effective rate of 20 percent. Other—short term—gains are taxed as ordinary income.

Consumption tax: A tax on the purchase or consumption of a product or service. The two main consumption taxes are the sales tax and the excise tax.

Corporate income tax: Amount levied on a company's income remaining after expenses and other deductions are subtracted from sales and revenues.

Depletion allowance: A deduction from income for exhaustion of resources such as minerals, oil, gas and timber.

Depreciation allowance: A tax deduction covering the exhaustion, wear, tear and obsolescence of property used for business or investment purposes.

Estate tax: An assessment on the value, after certain deductions, of a deceased person's land, securities and other assets. It is paid by the estate, before assets are divided among heirs.

Excise tax: A tax on consumption or purchase of items such as tires, airplane tickets, gasoline, beer, liquor and cigarettes. Sometimes called a luxury tax, it is used at all levels of government.

Flat tax: Plan that would apply a uniform rate to all income above a certain tax-free allowance. In pure form, all credits, exemptions, deductions, exclusions and the like would be eliminated.

Gift tax: A levy on the gift of property. The giver pays the tax.

Income averaging: An income-tax computation that permits a part of an unusually large increase in the amount of taxable income for any one year to be taxed as if it were income over a number of years, thus being taxed at a lower rate.

Individual income tax: A direct tax on the income of individuals, imposed by the federal and some state and local governments. The federal tax is progressive: As income rises, so does the tax rate.

Individual retirement account (IRA): A way to set aside money for retirement. Contributions are tax-deductible and are taxed only when withdrawn.

Itemized deductions: Items that can be subtracted from adjusted gross income for income-tax purposes. These expenses include medical and dental costs, taxes, interest, charitable contributions and casualty and theft losses.

License taxes: Fees, usually at a flat rate, for the exercise of a privilege, such as use of motor vehicles or on amusements, hunting, fishing or business.

Payroll tax: A direct tax on an employer's payroll and the employe's pay to help cover costs of Social Security, medicare and unemployment compensation.

Personal exemption: A reduction of $1,000 at present in taxable income for self, dependents, blindness or age.

Personal property: Autos, boats and other possessions taxed by state and local governments. Taxes are generally paid annually on the goods' values.

Property tax: A state or local tax on the value of land and buildings. This is the main source of income for local governments.

Sales tax: A charge by states—45 at latest count—and localities on retail sales of goods and services. Rates are flat and usually between 4 and 8 percent.

Severance taxes: Levies on removal from the land of natural products such as oil, gas, minerals and timber.

Tax credits: A direct reduction of income-tax liability. Credits are allowed for such things as political contributions, child care, energy conservation, foreign taxes and investments.

Tax shelter: A tax-favored investment, usually in the form of a partnership or joint venture. These investments frequently involve much capital and a high degree of risk. They can result in large tax deductions for investors.

Taxable income: The amount remaining on an individual's Form 1040 after subtracting from adjusted gross income such items as deductions and personal exemptions. This is the total on which taxes due are computed.

Taxable year: The 12-month period—usually the calendar year—on which taxable income is computed.

Value-added tax: Also called VAT and widely used in Europe, it puts a levy on the value added to goods at each stage of production and distribution.

"Windfall profits" tax: A temporary federal excise tax on the production of crude oil. It is imposed at the wellhead as each barrel is extracted and sold.

Zero-bracket amount: The lowest bracket of the federal income-tax-rate schedule. The zero-bracket amount—not subject to taxation—is $3,400 for married taxpayers filing jointly and surviving spouses, $2,300 for single persons and heads of households and $1,700 for married taxpayers filing separately. □

Chapter 14

GNP

> - *The GNP is the best indicator of the nation's economic health.*
>
> - *A rise or decline in GNP makes headline news.*

Our economic yardstick

Just as families keep track of household income and expenses and businesses maintain careful financial records, economists record the production, spending, savings, and investing of the American economy. This is known as *national income accounting,* and is at the heart of *macroeconomics*—the study of the total economy. National income accounting enables economists to measure the level of production in the economy. It provides information for many federal government policy decisions.

Gross national product

To most economists, the best indicator of the nation's economic health is the total annual output of goods and services. This total output is the gross national product, or GNP, computed from the vast data gathered by the Department of Commerce.

Only products that have a market value are computed in the GNP. Work done by a housewife—raising children, cooking, and cleaning in the family home—is not counted, although services performed by a housekeeper are part of GNP. Excluded is the work of millions of volunteers, who donate time to the Red Cross, churches, the Boy Scouts or Girl Scouts, or thousands of other organizations that contribute to the quality of life in America.

The GNP does include food that people grow for their own use. There is an allowance in the GNP for rent that homeowners would pay if they did not own their own houses.

The only products included are those that reach a final user. A machine for shaping bicycle parts is included, but not the steel and other metals that went into making the machine. A bicycle is counted, but not the raw materials and parts the manufacturer bought and used to make the bicycle.

These products are left out to avoid duplication. Otherwise, coal and iron ore would be counted once when used to produce steel, again when the steel was purchased by the machinery manufacturer, and a third time when the bicycle company bought the machine and the metal shapes to process that machine. They would be counted yet again when the finished bicycles were sold. The result would greatly overstate the nation's actual output.

Other items in GNP. New plants and the equipment to run them are counted as final products. So are new houses. Changes in business inventories also enter into the GNP. If businessmen accumulate supplies faster than they use them, this tends to increase the GNP.

Government spending figures into the calculation to the extent that the money is used to buy goods and services. Checks sent out to people living on pensions, for instance, are not counted. The purchases made by retirees with their pension checks are called *transfer payments* and are not expenditures for goods or services. Welfare payments and interest paid on the government debt are also transfer payments. So is the Social Security Administration's purchase of a computer used to pay government workers.

How accurate is GNP? No one claims that every final purchase or sale is included. But the grand total is less important than the changes that show up from one quarter to the next. These indicate the direction of business movement, whether a recession is getting worse or a recovery is getting stronger.

Over time, however, the basic data become outdated. People's spending patterns change. They may spend more for travel, health care, and housing, and less for cars and clothing. Industries gain and lose importance as a result. Periodically, the GNP inputs are revised to reflect more current data.

A recent change in computing GNP is the shift in the status of mobile homes, formerly considered personal consumption expenditures on the basis that they were vehicles, reclassed as residential structures. Another change classifies trucks bought by consumers as personal outlays rather than business investments.

How meaningful is GNP? GNP is not necessarily a good guide to the quality of life. Many things economists would like to measure elude the GNP. Is life becoming safer—more pleasant? Is government more efficient and just? Are the goods and services produced of high quality? Are natural resources becoming depleted?

No one has figured out how to include such vital data in the GNP, which is merely the best gauge available for a limited purpose—to show how productive the economy is in a commercial sense, and the extent to which the economic machinery is speeding up or slowing down. These are important things to know in making investment plans, framing government policies, or sizing up the chances for full employment.

National Income measurements

Economists, financial experts and government officials use measures other than GNP to analyze the nation's economic position.

The gross national product (GNP), is the estimated final total dollar value of all goods and services produced annually in the economy. A more accurate figure of the real value of the nation's productivity, although one much less used than GNP, is the *net national product (NNP)*. NNP is GNP minus the value of goods (capital) used up or worn out in the production process. NNP takes into consideration the depreciation of machinery and equipment that occurs in producing new goods and services.

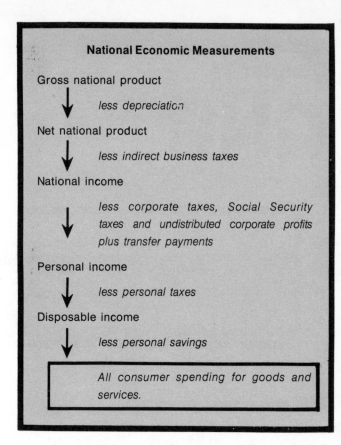

National Economic Measurements

Gross national product

↓ *less depreciation*

Net national product

↓ *less indirect business taxes*

National income

↓ *less corporate taxes, Social Security taxes and undistributed corporate profits plus transfer payments*

Personal income

↓ *less personal taxes*

Disposable income

↓ *less personal savings*

All consumer spending for goods and services.

Another measure of economic activity is *national income (NI)*. NI is NNP minus indirect business taxes, which include gasoline and sales taxes, but not corporate and personal income taxes or Social Security payments. NI, then, is the total before-tax income earned by individuals, business firms, and government agencies—the factors of production.

NI minus corporate taxes, Social Security taxes, and undistributed corporate profits, plus government transfer payments (Social Security retirement benefits, unemployment compensation, welfare) and interest payments (on government bonds) is another income measurement called *personal income (PI)*. This figure is the total before-tax income of individuals.

The final national income measure is *disposable income (DI)*, or PI minus all personal taxes. This is the after-tax income that individuals and families have at their disposal to spend or save.

Stock and flow

Economists are also interested in *stock* and *flow* in measuring the wealth of a nation.

Stock is the quantity of economic productivity that exists at some given point in time. This is also known as *wealth*. Wealth consists of land and its resources, factories and their equipment, office buildings, and homes and home furnishings, as well as other producer and consumer goods.

Wealth is an important economic measurement in that it can lead to *income*. But the two are different. Wealth is much greater than income. Although it is impossible to measure accurately, the wealth of our nation is estimated to be more than $7 trillion dollars—over $30,000 for every person in the country.

Flow measures the rate of economic activity over a certain period of time. GNP and the other national income measures are flows. The principle of flow is important in understanding the interrelationships among various aspects of the total economy.

Flow of production and spending

GNP is a measure of the final value of goods and services produced in the economy. It is also equal to the total *expenditures* in the economy, which, in turn, are the same as the total *income* people and businesses receive as payments.

Expenditures and income are opposite sides of the same coin. The *circular flow of money* principle holds that every monetary expenditure (by individuals, business, government agencies) for consumption or investment is a monetary income to someone else. What one person spends, another receives.

In other words, goods and services are produced in response to expenditures by consumers, businesses and government. In turn, this production leads to income payments, which are used again as expenditures. The circular flow below illustrates this interaction of money and production.

Flow of Money and Production

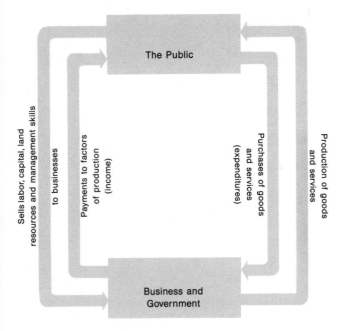

Three views of national income and GNP

The flow of national economic activity provides a way of analyzing the nation's economic health. Gross national product can be viewed in the following three ways:

1) Expenditures. Gross national production is a total of all the spending in the economy by consumers, businesses, and government. Economists also express it this way:

$$\text{GNP} = \text{C (consumption)} + \text{I (investment)} + \text{G (government)}$$

2) Incomes. Total expenditures by different sectors in the economy represent income to various factors of production—labor (wages), land resources (rents), capital (interests), and management (profits). But not all income earnings go for the consumption of goods and services; some must be given up for taxes and some are saved. To account for taxes and saving, GNP can be expressed as:

$$\text{GNP} = \text{C (consumption)} + \text{S (savings)} + \text{T (taxes)}$$

The flow diagram below shows how income earned by the different factors of production can become some form of expenditure—either as consumption (C), investment (I), or government (G).

The smooth functioning of the flow from *income* to *expenditures* is crucial to the well-being of the economy. Money that is earned as income must be spent as purchases in some form, or the economy will slow down and possibly even stagnate. The money that families spend on necessities is regarded as consumption (C), while savings (S) and taxes (T) are used to make purchases by business (I) and government (G).

The critical and least dependable flow is from income saved as business investment expenditures. If savings are not used for investments, the flow is broken and total expenditures in the economy are not sufficient to support full employment. If savings are used for investments, the flow is completed and economic activity continues at a steady pace.

3) Production. The third view of GNP (previously discussed) is the total dollar value of all goods and services produced.

The interrelationship of these three views is shown in the comprehensive national income chart on the next page.

At the top of the chart is a box representing gross national product—indicating the final total of the nation's production and income. As you move clockwise around the main flow, GNP breaks down into net national product, then national income, personal income and disposable income. At each stage, the chart shows how income is distributed to the savings and investment sector, and back to the GNP in the form of expenditures—consumption, government, and investment.

In this examination of the nation's macroeconomic picture, foreign transactions—*exports* and *im-* ports—have been ignored. The production of goods and services for markets in other countries is part of the gross national product. Relative to other components, this sector is small. But, to be completely accurate, gross national product is the sum of consumption goods and services, investment, government purchases, and exports. In abbreviated form:

$$\mathbf{GNP} = C + I + G + E$$

National Income as Expenditures and Income

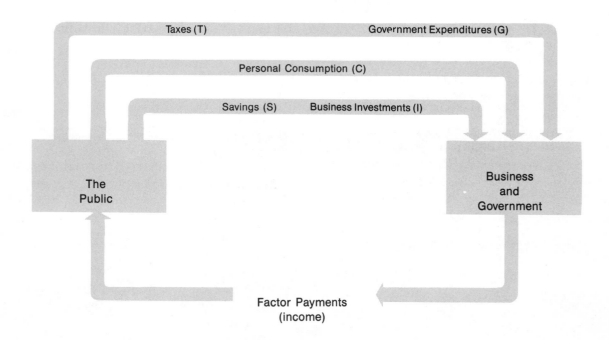

Flow of National Income

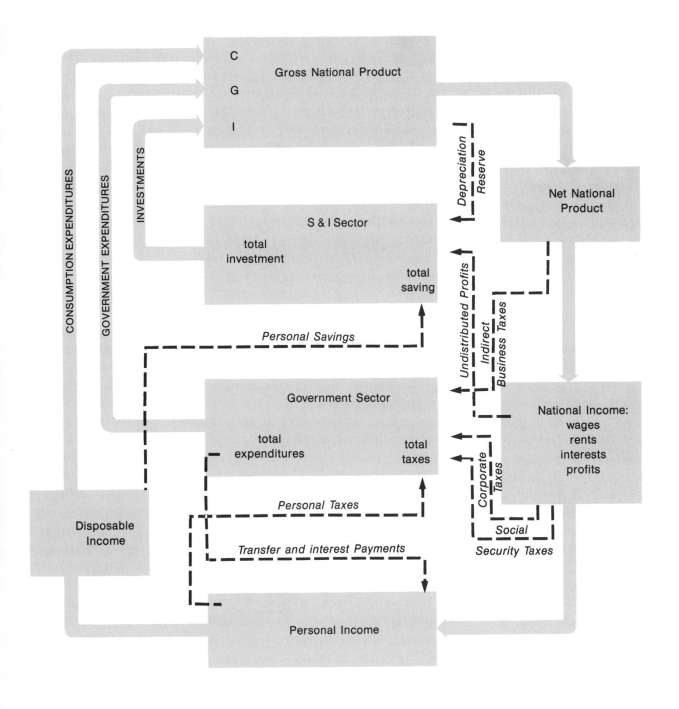

Growth of the GNP

in current dollars

Milestones Along the Way

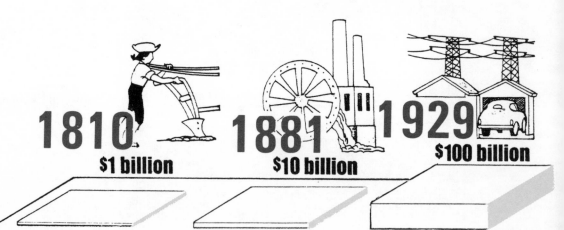

1810 $1 billion

1881 $10 billion

1929 $100 billion

America's young economy was still primitive when total output crossed the $1 billion level. Three fourths of its workers farmed; most manufactured goods came from Europe. This was a nation of 7 million people in 17 states east of the Mississippi—but poised to expand west.

The Industrial Revolution was in full flower. Manufacturing had overtaken farming in output by the time the U.S. crossed the $10 billion threshold. New railroads were opening up parts of the West, bringing prosperity to other regions. Immigrants poured to these shores to meet industry's needs for workers. Population: 52 million.

The economy took off in the Roaring Twenties. After a brief post-World War I slump, auto making, home and office construction and the growing electrical industry all helped spark a decade-long expansion that pushed output to $100 billion. Then came the Great Depression, and the U.S. would not see another $100 billion year until the onset of World War II.

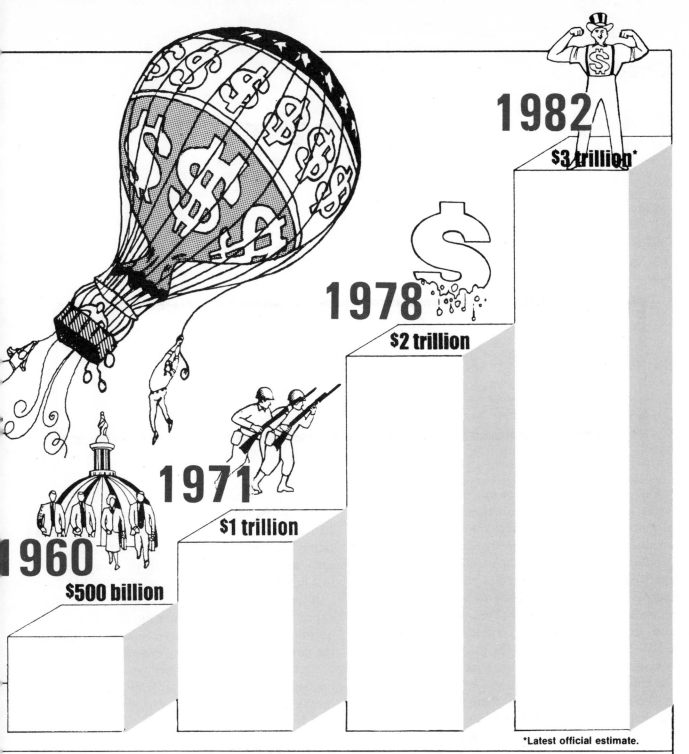

1960
$500 billion

1971
$1 trillion

1978
$2 trillion

1982
$3 trillion*

*Latest official estimate.

Despite deep recession in 1957-58, output passed $500 billion. Demands of the Korean War helped, as did the accelerating transformation of the U.S. into a service rather than a goods-producing economy. In 1960, another recession set in, and federal-government policy was aimed at speeding growth.

The longest boom in history, aided by the Vietnam War and lasting until 1969, pushed output to the $1-trillion milestone. By then, a new factor was fueling the growth in dollar volume: Inflation, which accounted for about half of the increase since 1960. The nation entered a period of rapidly rising prices and slower actual growth of the economy.

Despite the 1973-75 recession—the worst economic downturn since 1929—it took only 7½ years for the gross national product to double. But real growth accounted for just one fourth of the jump from $1 trillion to $2 trillion—inflation did the rest. Increasingly, economists used a new term to describe the phenomenon: Stagflation.

The U.S. began 1982 with a $3 trillion economy. That's six times as great as in 1960 in dollar terms, but only twice as much after higher prices are taken into account. Still, the nation's economic muscle remains awesome. Output of goods and services exceeds the combined output of the next four largest Western powers—Japan, West Germany, France and Britain.

USN&WR chart by Carl Vansag—Basic data: U.S. Dept. of Commerce, U.S. Office of Management and Budget, Conference Board, National Bureau of Economic Research.

Chapter 15

Our growing economy

> - *Economic growth is a sought-after goal.*
>
> - *Too much growth leads to high prices and inflation.*

One of the major goals of our economic system is the growth of total production. Gross national product is the yardstick used to measure the nation's productivity. Economic growth is the gain in that productivity—a comparison of GNP at different specified times. While there has been a substantial increase in GNP from 1929 to the present, the climb has not been steady. Periods of prosperity and growth have been interrupted by declines in GNP. Much of the 1930s, the post-World War II period and the early 1980s are striking examples of these downturns.

The economy grows when there is an increase in the output of goods and services. GNP must be adjusted for changes in the value of the dollar which occur due to inflation or recession. This adjusted figure is in real dollars.

It is important to consider changes in the price level, particularly since inflation has become a constant companion to most modern economies. Consider the Brown family of four in 1973, who were just making a decent living on an income of $13,000 a year. They believed that an income of $20,000 in a few years would make life very comfortable. In 1983, the Browns had an annual income of $25,000, but they were no better off than they were in 1973. Rising prices for food, clothing, housing, medical care, and other needs had com-

pletely offset their gain in income.

The Brown's situation is not distorted. The U.S. Labor Department estimated that the average urban family of four in 1982 had to earn $25,600 to maintain an average standard of living. In 1968, this figure was $9,200 and in 1978 it was $17,000.

It is frequently useful and more accurate to express GNP as a per capita figure. The total real output of the economy may be increasing, but if the population is increasing even more rapidly, the productivity and income per person may be decreasing. Real per capita GNP gives a better measure of the average individual's material well-being.

Affluent America

In absolute terms, material well-being in the United States is impressive. Americans can buy more of most goods and services—cars, shoes, clothing, televisions, food, education—than can people of most other countries. Our growth rate, however, is surpassed by some nations. The American economy is the giant of world economic systems, but several nations are closing the gap.

Economic growth in the United States has been a much-cherished goal. This goal has been unchallenged by economists, business leaders, politicians, and public policy makers. To many people,

An Economy That Speaks In Trillions

This nation's economic system is climbing into a dizzying range of big numbers that few individuals are likely to encounter in their daily lives. But statistics that go into trillions boggle the mind and defy most conventional measures. For an idea of how these astronomical numbers can be translated into everyday terms—

3 Trillion Dollars
Total National Output

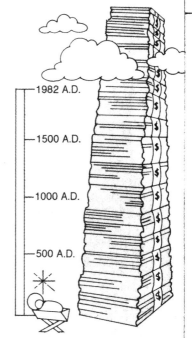

— 1982 A.D.

— 1500 A.D.

— 1000 A.D.

— 500 A.D.

If given away at the rate of 4 million dollars a day since the birth of Christ, would not yet all be gone.

2 Trillion Dollars
Total After-Tax Personal Income

Would rain a $1 bill on each square foot of the city of Boston every 10 seconds for 4 hours and 20 minutes.

Would buy a $444 color-TV set for each of this planet's 4.5 billion people.

1 Trillion Dollars
The Federal Government's Debt

If gathered in a single stack of $1 bills, would reach farther than 67,700 miles into the sky—more than one fourth the distance to the moon.

Would buy 172.8 million two-door subcompact cars costing $5,788—enough for every adult American, with 3 million cars left over.

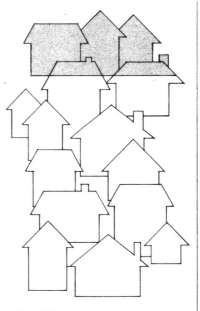

Would buy more than three fourths of the nation's 54 million single-family houses, which now are worth an average of $79,000 apiece.

our national reputation is dependent on the Department of Commerce's GNP reports.

Rising GNP, however, is no guarantee that we are materially better off. Rising prices and increasing population may offset gains from the vantage point of the individual. Aside from this, the production of more goods and an increase in personal income and wealth is little indication that the quality of life has improved. What's missing are more specific indicators related to the quality of the environment, which might include: recreation facilities, traffic conditions, pollution indexes, health and educational resources and political participation.

In recent years, the unquestioned belief in economic growth has come under scrutiny. Economic growth, many people have come to realize, doesn't solve all of our problems. It even creates a few. Still, economic growth is important to our nation's well-being.

Importance of growth

There are several benefits of economic growth. With an increase in per capita real output, people enjoy a higher standard of living. In addition, increasing productivity makes it possible for most people to work fewer hours and have more leisure time. Over the past century, the American worker has been rewarded with a gradually decreasing work week and work year.

Economic growth makes it possible to allocate more resources to government services. These resources can be used to combat social problems, among them: poverty, unemployment, alcohol and drug abuse, pollution, and crime.

Finally, economic growth makes it possible to continue and expand American aid to less-developed nations. These countries are dependent upon the developed nations not only for food but also for capital equipment, research, and technical know-how.

Determinants of growth

The United States is a wealthy nation for a variety of reasons. It has abundant *natural resources,* including fertile land, and raw materials for energy and other industrial uses. To accompany our natural resources, the United States has had a plentiful, skilled, and energetic *labor force.* The "work ethic" as one of our basic social values has been an important factor in developing our economic might.

Added to this has been the ability and desire to provide resources for *scientific research* and *technological development.*

The level of growth

Any level of production (GNP level) represents incomes earned by workers, managers, entrepreneurs and others. When all of this income is spent to purchase the total production of goods and services, the economy is in *equilibrium* or state of balance. Economists call this total spending *aggregate demand.* It is the total of all spending by consumers, businesses, government, and foreign buyers—C + I + G + E.

But the economy also can contract (stagnate) or expand (grow). At these times, it is in a state of *disequilibrium.* When all the incomes earned in the production process are not flowing back as expenditures, the level of GNP will contract. In other words, businesses spend more than they receive. When there is more than enough aggregate demand, the level of GNP will increase. Economic growth is stimulated.

Why would total spending not be enough to purchase the total output of consumer goods, capital goods and services? As noted in the previous chapter, the problem is that savings are not making their way into investments.

Why the reverse? How can there be more aggregate demand than incomes earned? Excess savings are spent when prices are low or when money has been made easy to borrow through lower interest rates. The banking system may also create more money for people to borrow and spend. When forces in the economy (among businesses, households and government) stimulate production and incomes or spending, economic growth results.

GNP and full employment

A steady GNP does not necessarily mean full employment. The economy can be in equilibrium at a level where resources are not fully utilized, some workers are unemployed and some capital goods are standing idle. When aggregate demand increases, the GNP increases and with it the use of resources increases. This can happen when consumers step up their rate of spending or businesses find reasons to invest, or foreigners buy more of our goods, or the government stimulates the economy with more spending.

If aggregate demand rises, stimulating the GNP past the level of full employment, a different problem arises. The economy cannot expand its output of goods and services beyond the productive capacity of its resources (factors of production). When aggregate demand is too high, competition for limited products drives prices up. At equilibrium GNP, any increase in aggregate demand must be

Anatomy of Nation's Output—

Origin, by industry average, of each $1 in goods or services produced—

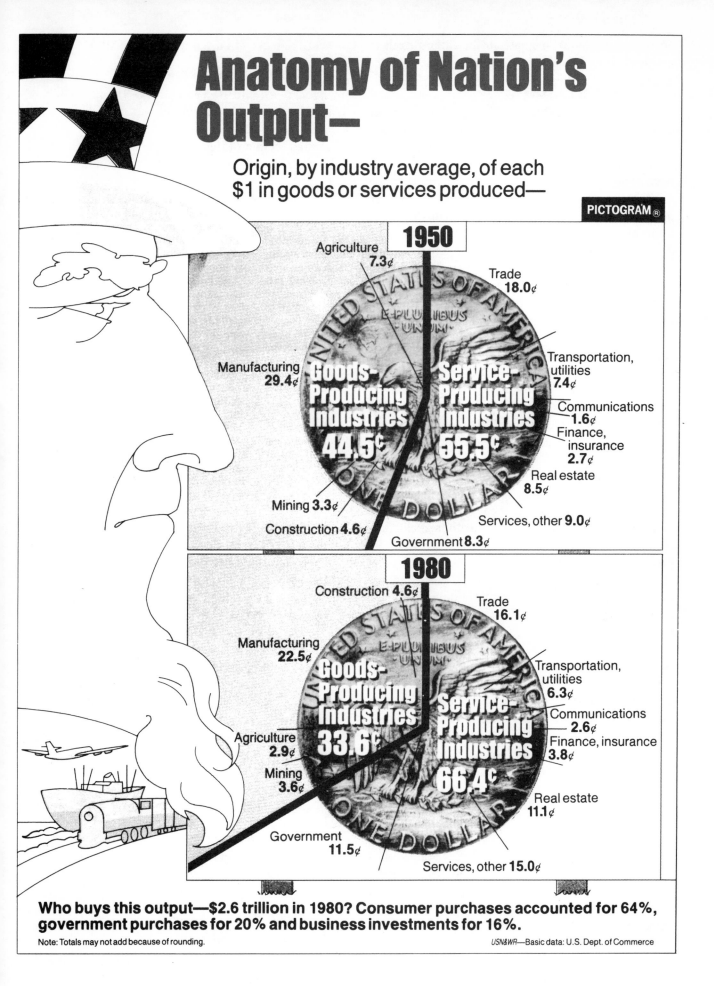

1950

Agriculture **7.3¢**

Trade **18.0¢**

Manufacturing **29.4¢**

Goods-Producing Industries 44.5¢

Service-Producing Industries 55.5¢

Transportation, utilities **7.4¢**

Communications **1.6¢**

Finance, insurance **2.7¢**

Real estate **8.5¢**

Mining **3.3¢**

Construction **4.6¢**

Services, other **9.0¢**

Government **8.3¢**

1980

Construction **4.6¢**

Trade **16.1¢**

Manufacturing **22.5¢**

Goods-Producing Industries 33.6¢

Service-Producing Industries 66.4¢

Transportation, utilities **6.3¢**

Communications **2.6¢**

Agriculture **2.9¢**

Finance, insurance **3.8¢**

Mining **3.6¢**

Real estate **11.1¢**

Government **11.5¢**

Services, other **15.0¢**

Who buys this output—$2.6 trillion in 1980? Consumer purchases accounted for 64%, government purchases for 20% and business investments for 16%.

Note: Totals may not add because of rounding.

USN&WR—Basic data: U.S. Dept. of Commerce

85

accompanied by an increase in the total output of goods and services. Otherwise, inflation sets in.

Problems of growth

Economic growth isn't automatically a desirable goal. There are problems—environmental, economic, and social—that can result from growth.

Economic growth can take a heavy toll on the environment. Superhighway systems cut through fertile farm lands and use up valuable urban property in our cities. Construction of high-rise buildings blocks panoramic views, while housing divisions spoil scenic prairie land. Strip mining shears away soil and vegetation, while animals that live on the land are driven off. In addition, industrial and other wastes in waterways threaten the existence of marine life, and water that once was free and abundant has become expensive in some areas. Air pollution presents health hazards for all living creatures.

In the pursuit of growth, *forced obsolescence* has been built in to some major consumer goods: automobiles, washing machines, and air conditioners. This means the products are designed to wear out. Prematurely used-up goods create the need for more production. This results in economic growth, but it can be hard on the family budget.

Another major convenience for consumers is disposable goods—paper bags, cardboard cartons, plastic containers, throwaway bottles, even disposable clothing. This has made life easier for the consumer, and has stimulated GNP. However, for every bag of groceries brought home from the market, we also bring nearly a bagful of trash in the form of wrappers, containers, papers, plastics.

Along with these environmental and economic problems, growth has created a materialistic mentality in most Americans. We have come to depend on, or to psychologically need, an increasing number of goods and services. Color televisions, automobiles, stylish clothing, items that were once luxuries to Americans—and still are to most people in the world—are needs for many of us today.

Decisions about where, when and how to limit growth are not easy ones. Most often these decisions involve a conflict between different benefits to society. Thousands of acres of cut timberland may destroy the habitat for wildlife, but it creates new homes for people. Likewise, strip mining of lovely hillsides fuels homes through cold winters. New factories, highways, shopping centers, and housing developments also create jobs.

Often economic growth advocates and environmentalists only see the benefits of their respective policies. Simple solutions to the complexities of economic growth are not readily available.

The multiplier effect

Increases and decreases in GNP are propelled by two effects: the *multiplier* and the *accelerator*.

A large advertisement appeared in the help-wanted section of the newspaper in a small southern town. An appliance company was building a new factory. Hundreds of people were hired to work on the construction project. Later, when the plant was in operation, several thousand men and women found regular jobs there. The new investment spending created jobs and generated a flow of income into the community and surrounding area.

The incomes received by construction workers and company employees were only the initial effect of the new investment. These people saved some of their money, but most of it was spent. Area grocery stores, clothing stores, restaurants, movie theaters, bookstores, automobile dealers, and other businesses began to feel the impact of the new appliance company. The workers spent much of their earnings in the community. Within time, the grocery stores had more food shipped from various producers, and the clothing stores ordered larger supplies of dresses, shirts, and blue jeans. Businesses generally purchased new inventories, bought more equipment, and added employees. The original investment spending had an impact on a second group of businesses and workers.

The second round of food processors, clothing manufacturers, and other people spending the new earnings generated yet another round of income to more businesses and individuals. This process is known as the *multiplier effect:* Money spent by one person is income received by someone else. The person receiving this money then spends it, or part of it, and the process continues until the total expenditure is much greater than the original investment.

How much new income will this multiplier effect create? Assume that the original investment by the appliance company was $100,000, and that on the average all of those people who received new income spent 90 percent of it and saved 10 percent. This means that the area retail stores and other businessess received $90,000 in new income. If they, in turn, retained 10 percent of their new income for savings, and spent the remaining 90 percent, a new injection of $81,000 would stimulate the economy. If successive rounds of spending continued to be generated throughout the economy, as much as $1,000,000 (ten times the original investment) could be created. The multiplier in this case would be ten.

The larger the percentage of new income that people spend, the larger the multiplier effect will be. As more money "leaks out" in the form of savings, the multiplier effect is diminished.

The multiplier effect also operates in reverse to reduce economic activity. When a plant shuts down, employment, income, and spending are reduced in the same way.

The accelerator effect

Increases in spending also can have an *accelerator effect:* it takes increased investment in new equip-

The Multiplier at Work

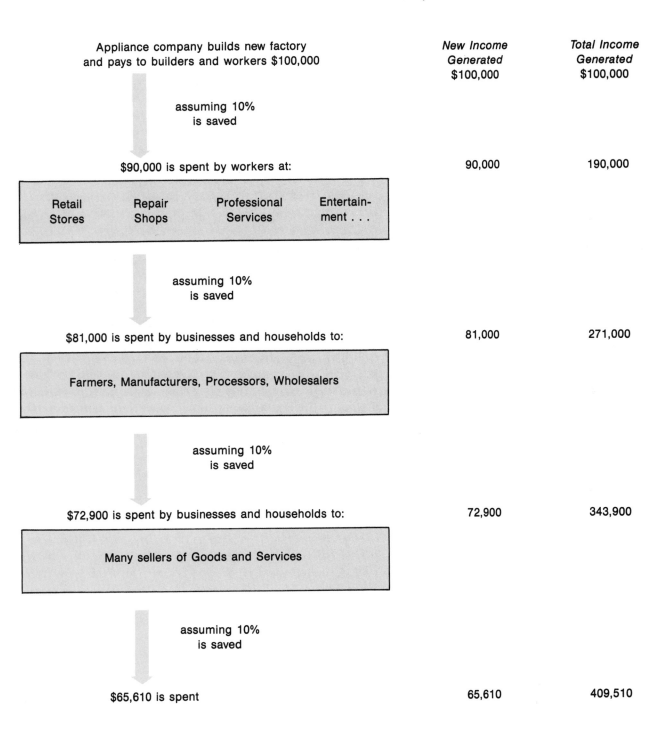

	New Income Generated	Total Income Generated
Appliance company builds new factory and pays to builders and workers $100,000	$100,000	$100,000
assuming 10% is saved		
$90,000 is spent by workers at:	90,000	190,000
Retail Stores / Repair Shops / Professional Services / Entertainment . . .		
assuming 10% is saved		
$81,000 is spent by businesses and households to:	81,000	271,000
Farmers, Manufacturers, Processors, Wholesalers		
assuming 10% is saved		
$72,900 is spent by businesses and households to:	72,900	343,900
Many sellers of Goods and Services		
assuming 10% is saved		
$65,610 is spent	65,610	409,510
Total Income Generated		$1,000,000

ment to supply increased demand created by a higher level of consumption.

The purchase of motors used in assembling refrigerators and air conditioners is one of the expenditures of an appliance company. Another local company that produces these motors becomes the chief supplier for the new appliance firm. The motor manufacturer had ten machines, each with the capability of producing 1,000 motors a year. Annual motor sales of the company were 10,000 per year. Each of these machines had a useful operating life of ten years. This means that one replacement machine had to be purchased every year.

With the arrival of the appliance company in the area, the motor manufacturer found that sales jumped to 11,000 the next year. As a result, the company had to acquire two machines, one as a replacement and one to produce the additional 1,000 motors. Investment by the motor company doubled (increased 100 percent) in order to meet the 10 percent increase in sales. This new investment represented new sales, employment, and spending for another company.

The accelerator effect means that increased spending leads to a greater percentage increase in investments. This spending can be generated by consumers and government as well as other businesses. However, if the sales of a company do not continue to increase, new annual investments will fall back to the replacement level—in this case to one machine. The accelerator, unlike the multiplier, requires a constant level of new investment.

Like the multiplier, the accelerator works in reverse. A drop in sales sets off a reduction in capital investments because worn-out equipment might not have to be replaced. Together, the multiplier and accelerator reinforce each other. Consumer spending for goods stimulates business spending for capital goods.

U.S. productivity sluggish

Annual gains in U.S. productivity have averaged only about two percent during the past 20-30 years. In contrast, Japan and West Germany have averaged about seven percent annually. America for many years earned the right to be called the world's number one economy (as the nation with the highest per capita GNP), but can no longer make this claim. At least four other nations in the industrialized world have surpassed the United States.

Through decades of hard work, American labor and capital built transportation systems (canals and railroads), cheap power (coal mining and oil wells), heavy duty machinery and plants (such as steel mills) and other factors that make up the foundation of an industrial economic system. After developing its economic base, the United States was able to mass-produce consumer goods and services. But in modern times the industrial foundation has not been maintained.

One problem has been too much consumption and too little savings and investments. If a nation is to maintain a strong industrial base, businesses and individuals must plow profits and savings back into industry. But spending for plant and equipment and on research and development, which comes out of savings, has been too low. Other nations, including Japan, Canada, and West Germany, who compete with the United States for international markets, have devoted more financial resources to capital investments.

Another problem, or solution, depending on how the situation is viewed, is to *disinvest,* or move funds out of so-called "sunset" industries and into "sunrise" industries. Some economists believe that government should not support sunset industries, such as the textile and steel industries, which can no longer compete with efficient foreign producers. Instead, they believe, government should seek ways to channel development funds into promising industries, such as semiconductors.

Business, labor, and communities will all be better off when resources are shifted from dying industries to expanding, productive industries. Subsidizing ailing businesses, these economists say, will only prolong the agony. And if the new growth industries are not helped, they may be upstaged by foreign competitors from Japan, France, and Germany.

Nothing short of *reindustrializing* the American economy may be necessary to modernize industry and boost production. Reindustrialization will involve such measures as actively pursuing tax policies that favor capital investments and discourage consumption; cooperation among government, businesses and banks to help industries build or modernize plants and equip them with efficient machinery; upgrading the nation's transportation system; increasing the level of research and development; and providing federal aid to promising industries.

TO REBUILD AMERICA—
$2.5 TRILLION JOB

Bridges, ports, roads, sewage disposal—these and other underpinnings of U.S. life and economy are eroding from long neglect. Repairs will be costly. But, say experts, more delays could be disastrous.

City Streets— Thoroughfares crumbling at record rate need rebuilding.

Cost: $600 billion

Highways— 8,000 miles of the interstate system, two thirds of other major roads need repair.

Cost: $952 billion

Bridges— Nearly 45 percent need major repairs or total replacement.

Cost: $47.6 billion

Mass Transit— About one quarter of the country's bus and subway systems should be replaced.

Cost: $40 billion

Ports, Waterways— Aging locks, congested harbors and shallow channels require major work.

Cost: $40 billion

Water Systems— Hundreds of cities need new pipes to stop heavy leakage and bursting mains.

Cost: $125 billion

Chapter 16

Inflation and recession

- *The business cycle seems to follow a pattern that is difficult to control.*

- *Experience shows that recession usually follows inflation.*

The American economy has always been on a kind of roller coaster, with relatively lengthy periods of gradual business growth punctuated by sharp, but usually shorter, declines.

Fortunately, the ups have been far larger than the downs, so the economy has grown substantially over the decades, providing more jobs and a better living for many people.

The financial interdependence of nations now means that they share economic conditions; prosperity and depression have ripple effects that spread throughout many nations of the world.

Changing conditions in the economy seem to follow a pattern known as the *business cycle*. The phases of the business cycle are: prosperity, recession, depression, recovery. In the following description we start with recovery after a recession.

Recovery. The recession is over. Businesses have idle machines and plants and are eager to get more orders. There is almost no difficulty in finding skilled workers. Costs have been cut to a minimum. Retailers have pared their inventories to the minimum needed to meet the slack demand of the slump.

Credit is easy to get. Federal taxes have been cut. The government has launched bigger spending programs to bolster demand.

Investors, sensing better times ahead, are putting more money into the stock market, where prices are going up.

Gathering speed. Business begins to expand. Consumers and companies grow more confident and are inclined to spend and borrow. They make some of the purchases they put off during the recession.

Companies are getting more orders, so they boost output, take on more workers, and lay in larger supplies of raw materials and components. Retailers find that they need bigger inventories to keep up with demand.

Builders are putting up more houses, which sell easily because mortgages are cheaper and easier to get. Government spending grows to pay for programs initiated during the downturn, and there is little worry about restraining it, because tax receipts soon will increase thanks to higher profits and larger personal incomes.

As idle facilities are put back into production, rising profits encourage businesses to invest in new plants and equipment. The multiplier effect is taking hold. That is, each new business provides impetus for many other new businesses.

Restraining the boom. At some time, problems may occur. Some companies run out of idle capacity and can't keep up with demand. Shortages develop. Prices climb rapidly. Money management becomes

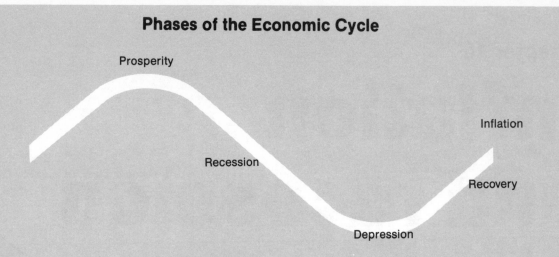

Phases of the Economic Cycle

Prosperity

Inflation

Recession

Recovery

Depression

Prosperity. Business is brisk, jobs are plentiful, and wages are high. Plants are operating at full, or near full, capacity. As a result, production is high, unemployment is at a minimum, and most wage earners have more than their usual incomes to spend on an ample supply of products. The 1920s, the war years of 1940-45, as well as much of the 1950s and 1960s were periods of prosperity.

Recession. Business is declining, some workers are laid off, and others find pay increases and over-time work difficult to obtain. As a result, less money is spent for new goods and services. This decline in spending leads to further reductions in business activity and employment. Recessions in recent years include the post-World War II years—1946-49, 1953-55, 1957-59, 1969-70, 1973-75, and 1981-83.

Depression. When business is poor for a long period of time, a recession turns into a depression. Declines in production are more severe than in a recession, and unemployment is higher. The Great Depression started in 1929 and lasted through the decade of the '30s, up to the United States' entrance in World War II (1941). Other depressions in U.S. history reached their worst periods in 1837, 1873, 1893, and 1907.

Recovery. As businesses find some profitable ventures, firms begin to hire more workers and step up production. The earnings of these new workers increase spending in the economy, which stimulates more production and more employment. During recovery, the economy is moving out of the recession or depression toward prosperity.

Inflation. There is excessive rise in prices throughout the economy and the cost of living soars. A little inflation, 2-3 percent annually, is normal and stimulating to economic growth. Too much spending by consumers and businesses during prosperity, as well as government deficits (spending more than receiving from taxes), leads to inflation. This is "too many dollars chasing too few goods." Total spending has outrun production.

more difficult for the Federal Reserve.

Demand for credit is growing and interest rates are rising. The Federal Reserve System, in trying to decide how much money to create, is torn between a desire to encourage expansion and a fear that the economy will grow so fast that inflation will begin. The Federal Reserve has to decide when to raise the discount rate in an effort to prevent a runaway boom.

Still, for a time, conditions continue to favor rising prices, inventories, and increased speculation in stocks and commodities. Skilled workers are in a seller's market. Unions are demanding bigger raises to compensate for higher living costs and to give workers their share of the prosperity.

Higher interest rates on securities now may pull money out of the mortgage market. Builders find many of their houses standing empty. Money to continue building is hard to come by. Consumers have taken care of their *pent-up demands,* and their expenditures increase less rapidly, although it is still easy for them to get loans. Merchants find they have more goods than they need, so they order less.

Downturn. Some producers are forced to reduce production and lay off employees. Workers who do not have jobs, or are putting in less time, have difficulty keeping up the payments on their debts.

Increasing costs and higher interest rates make new capital investment less attractive.

As demand falters, cuts in production and employment spread. Many people suffer a decline in income. Pessimism becomes widespread and demand shrinks further. A recession is under way.

Fighting recession. Once again, businesses work off their excess inventories. Costs are pruned. Debts are paid off. Some weak companies go under. Some plants are permanently closed. Congress, the White House, and the Federal Reserve again try to increase demand and make money plentiful.

Since boom and bust periods cause such havoc, government control over the economy becomes necessary.

WHAT A DEPRESSION IS REALLY LIKE

Failing banks were besieged by anxious depositors.

UPI

When Americans today talk about the danger of another "depression," how many realize what kind of economic disaster they're talking about?

It was a time when one fourth of the entire labor force was jobless. Savings of a lifetime were wiped out. Homes and farms were lost. Businesses and banks failed by the thousands. Millions of people went hungry. Few families escaped unscathed through the national nightmare that began with the stock-market crash of late October 1929, and cast its pall of poverty over a full decade.

The vignettes that follow highlight—in human terms—the miseries, the struggles and the occasional triumphs of the depression years.

"Destroyed my father." From a man who grew up in North Dakota, a painful memory:

"The depression destroyed my father.

"He was a successful, well-liked manager of small-town banks, lumber yards and grain elevators. As the economic situation worsened, he had to foreclose mortgages on hundreds of farmers who knew and trusted him—until then.

"When the banks failed, he and his depositors lost almost everything they had. Desperate people who had been his friends looked upon him as an ogre.

"The strain broke his health. He died at an early age."

Sheriff's sale. It was in a suburb of Philadelphia. Just as the depression hit, a father who was the town's superintendent of schools lost a battle with a politically minded school board.

Ousted because of his determination to maintain high standards of education when the board had other ideas, he could find no other job in his profession.

He tried to be a salesman, without success. His savings gradually disappeared. His son recalls: "We sold off our library, bit by bit; then we lost our car, and finally our house went at a sheriff's sale."

Stripped of possessions, the family—scrounging, scrimping and struggling—somehow survived years of hardship.

The son managed to work his way through the University of Missouri. Eventually, the father was able to return to work as a school administrator.

He worked until age 78 and lived to be 90—always frugally, and always fearful that he might again be stranded without income and without savings.

When wealth went. For many families who had enjoyed the fruits of wealth, the depression brought drastic changes in life styles.

One man looks back:

"I remember my Uncle Harry. He had a beautiful home on Long Island during the boom years—the '20s. He made his pile in the stock market. I can still see him in his chauffeured Pierce-Arrow. After the '29 crash, he lost everything. He was grateful to get a job as a waiter in a restaurant.

"The depression changed my family's life style, too. My

Migrants from Midwest went to California hunting jobs.

Free-food lines were a common sight in many towns.

father, during the '20s, built whole communities of houses. He became a millionaire at 35.

"We had a big, eight-bedroom home. Six servants—butler-chauffeur, cook, maid, governess, nurse and gardener. Trips to Europe. Box at the opera. Lavish parties at the country club.

"After the crash, the change came gradually for us. It took longer in the real-estate business than in the stock market. My father held hundreds of second-trust notes. People couldn't pay.

"One by one, our servants were dismissed. Finally, it was my mother who had to do the housework. I remember her scrubbing the kitchen floor. Then about 1939 we lost the house and sold the furniture for a pittance. Friends drifted away.

"Through it all, I don't remember my parents complaining or feeling sorry for themselves. I don't know how they did it, but they managed to send four children to college."

"A shattered man." A classic American success story—to which the depression brought a sad ending:

"My father started out in business in Indiana with a push cart, collecting junk. From that beginning, he worked his way up. He first bought a grocery store in Mishawaka. As the 1920s advanced, he invested in more real estate. Then he bought big—a large industrial tract where he set up a coal-and-junk business. We were living in clover. I remember, for instance, our big Haines car.

"Then the depression set in. One by one, the properties were sold to pay off mortgages. In a few short years there was nothing left but a dying junk business. Even the coal business collapsed. People couldn't afford to buy coal.

"The change in my father was heartbreaking. I saw him change from an optimistic, dynamic and proudly successful businessman to a shattered man overwhelmed by a sense of failure—sitting at a battered desk, scrawling entries of transactions with the stub of a pencil. Few transactions involved more than a dollar."

Lifelong effects—

"Now, 40 years later, I find myself waking at night with a nagging feeling of fear that it's all going to happen again. I own a house, have money in the bank and a good job—but all of that is not enough to dim the picture of my shattered father struggling to keep the family afloat."

The family next door. Among recollections of the depression years in a small town in Georgia:

"Next door to us lived an elderly couple. They had paid for their home and retired comfortably. They had 10 children,

all married, who had scattered throughout Georgia and Alabama with their own families, working in manufacturing plants and on other jobs.

"As the depression bit deeper, plants closed. It was impossible to get work. The children started coming back with their families to live with the old folks. To help feed them, the elderly parents mortgaged their home. Things kept getting worse, and there was no money to make the mortgage payments. The elderly couple lost their home. Within a year, both died penniless. They grieved themselves to death, my family always felt."

Making a fortune. For a few, the depression era brought riches instead of poverty.

One memory reported is that of a grandfather in Boston—an uneducated Russian immigrant tailor—who made a fortune while others were losing theirs.

The tailor became a moneylender, making loans to poor risks at high rates of interest. When loans were in default, he repossessed borrowers' property. With his profits, he kept buying houses.

To increase his liquidity, he sold some of his real estate and was safely liquid when the impact of the depression began to be felt.

So he was ready to take advantage of an opportunity to buy Florida real estate—5½ acres of Miami Beach waterfront, which cost him less than $10,000. The immigrant held that land for years. Finally, he sold it at an astronomical profit. It is now the site of one of Miami Beach's most luxurious hotels.

"I kept my mouth shut." People whose jobs were depressionproof were singularly fortunate in a period of acute deflation of the dollar. A woman whose husband was a U. S. customs inspector in Maine recalls:

"The depression hardly touched us. Of course, most of our friends were having a terrible time. I didn't dare let people know that we weren't feeling it, too. I kept my mouth shut.

"We could go to the market with a $5 bill and come out with a whole week's groceries. Steak cost 25 cents a pound. Good clothing was so cheap it wasn't even worth mending old clothes. We just gave away our used stuff and bought new things.

"We bought a brand-new Plymouth for about $800. Gasoline was cheap and abundant. There were no shortages of anything. All you needed was the cash."

In the "Dust Bowl." The depression era was a time of disastrous drought in the Midwest and Southwest. A staff member's mother, who lived in Kansas and Oklahoma in the '30s, tells what it was like.

In Kansas—

"It wasn't just the depression, it was the eternal drought and the infernal dust that every puff of wind raised. The farmers could not work the land to keep the dust from blowing because they had no fuel, the tractors were worn out, there was no seed for crops. Cattle and horses stood, ribs hanging with skin, pawing listlessly at the few tufts of sage and tumbleweed. The topsoil blew off the fields and into great hills of dust against the fences and buildings.

"The farmers had mortgaged their land, and began to see it change title to the bank. Dad saw section after section of land he had farmed for years disappear down the mortgage drain."

In Oklahoma—

The head of the family had a stroke of luck. He managed to find work running a gasoline station. But customers were few and cash was scarce. The way it was:

"Somehow, we managed on $5 a week. . . . Even so, we felt well off, seeing the many men who came by the station looking for enough work for a meal.

"They weren't bums, or hoboes, or 'hippies.' They were honest heads of families who had left home to look for a job somewhere . . . knowing there would be one less mouth to feed at home, and the wife could then apply for welfare for herself and the children, and receive the commodities doled out by the county.

"Sometimes people traded whatever they had and didn't need immediately as they started the trek westward from the ruined farms they had left in eastern Oklahoma. One time a man gave Dad a tiny diamond, with tears in his eyes. We couldn't eat it, so Dad gave it back, along with a little gasoline."

Mother's Day. Scene: Syracuse, N.Y., 1931:

A 7-year-old boy tells his father he has saved a few cents but needs more to buy a Mother's Day plant.

Father, whose income for the past several months has averaged $50 a month: "Mother will understand if she doesn't get a fancy plant this year."

Boy improvises. Finds an empty coffee can, fills it with dirt and sprigs of apple blossoms from nearby trees and adorns it with colorful crepe paper he has bought with his savings.

Now, more than 40 years later, the boy remembers the tears of gratitude in his mother's eyes for a Mother's Day gift during the Great Depression.

A bank—and a mob. One who grew up in a Mississippi town remembers the day the bank didn't open:

"It was more than just a bank failure—one of the bank officials had disappeared with the cash and negotiable contents of safe-deposit boxes. I don't believe he was ever caught. It was easy to disappear in those days.

"My memory is of a silent, sullen, despairing crowd of men in front of the bank. Later, it would become a mob. The doors were broken down, the bank's papers were thrown into the street and the alley behind. For days the wind whipped mementos of financial disaster through the town."

Ostracized. On March 6, 1933, President Roosevelt ordered the temporary closing of all banks in the U. S. So many banks had failed that FDR took that drastic step in preparation for imposition of a tough new set of rules governing bank operations. One recollection of that day:

"We lived in a small town in western Kansas and my father worked in a bank. I was in the sixth grade at school. The day the banks closed I was suddenly ostracized, just as if my father had personally ordered the closing. And the situation stayed that way until the banks reopened—which, fortunately, all of them did in my home town."

Making do without cash. In some places, money was so hard to come by that scrip came into common use as a substitute for cash.

For example, an old-timer's recollection of the way it was in San Bernardino, Calif., in 1934:

"I got part of my pay in scrip. I worked for 'The San Bernardino Sun,' and the company issued its own scrip. All our advertisers accepted it. We used it to buy groceries and other necessities.

"Other companies, such as the Pacific Electric, which operated the interurban railway system in southern California, used scrip extensively."

The Californian recalls, too: "Prices were so low that if a man had 50 cents in cash he could buy more fruit and vegetables than he could carry home alone."

"It still shocks me." In an Iowa town, many families lived on incomes totaling $10 or $15 a week.

It was a time when, with fathers unable to find work, children had to become breadwinners. Says a woman who remembers being told again and again that she was "one of the lucky ones" because her father held on to his job:

"It still shocks me that a girl in my seventh-grade class at school had to drop out to become a servant for one of the town's few wealthy families."

Tires, teeth—and a tombstone. In Phoenix, a skilled carpenter with seven children was jobless for many months. A member of his family gives some examples of what this meant:

● "We had to burn old tires in our furnace for a while. It was the only fuel we could lay our hands on."

● "With no money to pay a dentist, Dad would extract his own teeth when necessary, going into the back yard for privacy during the ordeal."

● "When two of the children died suddenly of diphtheria, there was no money for a tombstone. Dad made a suitable marker with his own hands."

Penny restaurant. Those who were among the unemployed in the nation's capital in the grim winter of 1933 remember with gratitude—if not affection—a place where a penny bought a meal.

"Penny restaurants" in Washington and elsewhere were financed by the late Bernarr Macfadden, the physical-culture advocate and health-food faddist who became a millionaire publisher. One who was compelled to be a regular customer at the penny-a-meal counter on Pennsylvania Avenue, a few blocks from the White House, recalls:

"You had to queue in a long line. When you reached the serving counter you had one choice: a generous bowl of cracked wheat, doused with milk and sprinkled with brown sugar. Macfadden claimed the bowl-for-a-penny contained all the essential vitamins.

"For all I know, he may have been right. It was boring fare, but to a man as hungry as I often was it was surely satisfying."

"Hoover Towns." All across the country, on the outskirts of cities, colonies of homeless families existed in makeshift camps. These communities of the miserable were known as "Hoover Towns" or "Hoovervilles"—a sardonic allusion to President Herbert Hoover.

A description of one such place, outside Oklahoma City:

"Nothing else I have ever seen could compare with the squalor and degradation of that place. It was cold November and children ran practically naked from hen coop to hen coop, so dirty and thin it was unbelievable. The old sat huddled around fires outside the ramshackle huts. I hope I never see such suffering again."

Stranger at the door. A Philadelphian can't forget this:

"You learned never to open the door to a stranger. He could be an agent of the landlord, come for payment of overdue rent, or even the sheriff arriving to evict you . . . or a collector for an installment owed on the furniture. He could be the grocer or the butcher. Those were the people to whom you were constantly and grindingly in debt."

Hired and fired. In New York City in 1932, a youth who had just graduated from high school was jubilant when he

At a farm foreclosure sale in Iowa in 1933, Guardsmen stood by to preserve order in the watching crowd of angry neighbors.

landed a job in a garment factory. Working 10-hour days, he was paid $8 a week.

When FDR's New Deal began launching recovery measures a year later, a raise to $12 and later to $15 became mandatory. But, to the employer, the $15 loomed so large that he brought his uncle in to handle the job and fired the young fellow.

Pay cuts. For most of those who had jobs, pay kept dwindling in the early '30s. An editor reminisces:

"I started as a reporter in a Southwestern city at 25 bucks a week in 1930, became city editor in 1931 at $27.50 and then was jumped to assistant managing editor at $35. Three pay cuts that same year put me back within pennies of the original $25.

"But a comfortable, two-bedroom apartment that rented for $65 a month in 1930 was down to $17.50 a month by 1933. You could buy a custom-made suit for $37.50 cash—if somebody would lend you the money."

Another editor:

"Twice in the early '30s the boss—editor and majority owner of a small daily newspaper in Kansas—called the staff together and announced:

"'I've either got to fire somebody or cut everybody's wages. What do you think I should do?'

"The unanimous answer: Cut.' The reason: We didn't want anybody to be thrown out of work, because there were no other jobs to be had. And there was always the fear that the one fired might be 'me.' "

Costly errors. On a Los Angeles newspaper in the '30s, pay cut followed pay cut until it seemed to the threadbare staff that management couldn't reduce wages any further.

But an efficiency expert imported from New York came up with an idea quickly approved by the publisher. It was an arbitrary system of fines imposed for errors—$5 for a misspelled name in a piece of copy, $7.50 for an incorrect street address, $10 for missing a deadline.

Nobody complained—out loud. Jobs were too hard to come by. And reporters who in the course of their work saw too many breadlines, too many soup kitchens, too many evicted families, shuddered at the thought of joining the swelling ranks of the unemployed.

Happy ending. Mid-1930s, the Bronx. It was the boy's birthday. His father had gone to Boston to take a job in a relative's grocery store for $9.50 a week. His mother planned a birthday picnic in a Westchester County park.

A trolley trip was involved. She calculated the costs—20 cents for trolley fare, a dime for an ice-cream bar and a soda. She brought 30 cents with her.

But the trolley trip, which necessitated a change of cars, cost more than she expected. There was no ice-cream bar or soda—and instead of the two dimes needed for the trip home, she had only one. She put it in the fare box and sat nervously, broke. When the mother and boy got up to leave at their stop, the conductor asked for another dime. The mother explained that she had no money left. The conductor told her to forget about it. The day had a happy ending.

"People quit smiling." Bad times in Birmingham, Ala.:

"I remember the years 1930-32 most vividly. People generally just quit smiling.

"My father was an architect-engineer. For more than two years, nobody built anything. Those were the years when I was 14 to 16 and the world to which I had become accustomed just plain vanished. The country-club membership went, along with the maids. The car was garaged by 1931.

"Walking to school, I crossed the viaduct above the Southern Railway tracks. The tracks were lined with shacks, mostly cardboard. On the way home, I would sometimes go down along the tracks to talk to the men there. That is when I learned that grown men cried—from hunger, anger, loneliness and frustration."

Red-letter day. This was in Pittsburgh. A man with no job, four children under 10 to feed and another on the way.

The family moved in with relatives. There was a daily trudge in quest of odd jobs. There was barely enough to eat—soup, stew, homemade bread. Then came a red-letter day—the day an insurance policy was cashed in.

On the way to the insurance office, the family car ran out of gasoline. So the first bit of money went for fuel. Then, a splurge—$15 worth of groceries.

Recalling that day, the mother of the family said:

"It was probably equivalent to at least $50 worth of groceries today. We didn't know what to cook first. I can recall roasting a large round of beef that had cost a dollar."

Baked beans. Food often figures in recollections of the lean and hungry years. A Midwesterner's flashback:

"We lived in a small town where my father ran a delivery

service for grocery stores—two or three trucks hauling groceries to homes of customers. Few people had cars, of course.

"Often store managers were as short of cash as most other people, so it wasn't unusual for my father to collect his pay in the form of food—a few cans or perhaps a case of some surplus item. I can recall eating baked beans for a week during one stretch. At that, we were better off than most of our neighbors."

No sale. One night in a Kansas town—

"I remember how depressed my father was that night. Unable to get a salaried job, he was trying to sell used cars for a 10 per cent commission.

"Earlier in the day he had been elated. He had made his first sale of the week, a 1926 Oldsmobile for $65. But the car's ignition system caught fire just after the new owner took delivery. He demanded his money back and Dad lost his $6.50 commission."

Well off. It was like this for one working his way through college:

"One week, after paying college expenses, my food budget was down to only enough money for one chocolate bar a day. That's all I had to eat. On Sunday, I hitchhiked 30 miles to visit my brother. The real idea was to get a square meal. My brother was well off. He was married and had a baby and a job—at $12.50 a week."

Trash basket. There were pockets of prosperity. The gold-mining region of California was one. The mines were busy, especially after FDR raised the price of gold to $35 an ounce.

So a staff member whose boyhood was spent in a gold-mining town was unaware of the hardships of the depression until he visited Sacramento one day with his parents. He remembers this episode:

"While waiting in the car for my parents, I finished a lunch I had brought from home and then dropped the bag and wrappers in a corner trash basket.

"Immediately, two or three ragged men I hadn't noticed before scrambled to the basket, tore open the bag in search of crumbs and scraped their teeth along the inside of a banana skin they found there."

Other people's jobs. Young men who graduated from college in the early '30s often discovered, if they were lucky enough to land jobs, that their good fortune resulted from the misfortunes of other people.

"What hurt us," says a man whose first employment was as a $22.50-a-week reporter on a New York newspaper, "was the realization that we were replacing experienced men—married men with children—who had been fired because the boss couldn't afford to pay the salaries they were earning—$55 to $70 a week."

Among the newsman's memories of New York in those days:

"There was tragedy on every street corner . . . decent, well-spoken men begging for handouts.

"At the back doors of restaurants there were always clusters of people waiting to claim what they could of the scrapings from plates. At soup kitchens, you'd see men carrying cans of soup to give to their wives who waited around the corner.

"Men who once lived luxuriously were glad to get menial jobs.

"The fellow who swept out McSorley's Ale House, which I frequented as a young reporter, had been a prosperous broker with a big home on Long Island, which he lost when the stock-market crash came.

"But with all the misery, there was much good humor. It's remarkable how many people were able to laugh at their troubles."

"For me it was great!" He left college in 1932 with a degree in journalism. A job? None to be found. A wise friend advised him:

"Look around the world. Somewhere there is prosperity. Go there."

It didn't take much research for him to discover that Japan was booming, producing cheap goods. But how to get there? His great-grandmother—a Civil War widow—provided a loan of $250. It was enough for passage on a Japanese freighter. He landed in Yokohama with $37 left—7,000 miles from home.

The first job he applied for, he got—on an English-language newspaper in Tokyo. The pay was low but adequate. Soon, he learned that because of the depression not a single American newspaper had a full-time correspondent in Japan. He sold his services as a "stringer." By 1934, he was Tokyo correspondent for five big U.S. dailies and a news syndicate. His income kept growing. All was well until 1940, when Japan began to make life difficult for foreign newsmen. Then he came home—first class on a luxury liner. His comment now: "The depression? For me it was great!"

Scars—and rewards. Many of those who survived the Great Depression still bear its scars. Others cherish rewarding memories, often reflecting the fundamental virtues of faith, hope and charity.

Among observations illustrating lessons learned in a decade of adversity are these:

● "The richest part of life in the depression was the fellowship with so many others, all caught up in the same problems."

● "There was no complaining because everyone suffered equally, it seemed. People just did the best they could with what they had."

● "What the depression impressed upon my generation was the necessity for a steady job, with money put away for a rainy day. For better or worse, our children do not seem to have this feeling."

● "A person who had a job—even a part-time job—felt himself lucky. The whole attitude toward work was different than now."

● "It was a period of travail softened by a spirit of faith and hope."

● "Through it all, I don't recall a sense of sacrifice or even hardship. All of my contemporaries were living the same way I was."

● "There was a great deal of sharing of what you had, no matter how little that was."

● "There was so much genuine gratitude for help given. I remember a hungry stranger in my mother's kitchen, repeating after every sip of the bowl of vegetable soup she gave him, 'Oh, God bless you!'"

● "As a boy in the '30s, I couldn't afford even the 10-cent movies. Instead, I went to the library and read the works of the greatest authors. That enriched my boyhood. It was a small but unforgettable victory over the hardships of the depression."

● "There was such a strong will to survive. I remember something I heard said by a man who was jobless and broke: 'The future sure looks bleak, but I don't want to miss a minute of it.'"

Where Inflation Is Leading Us

Imagine the day when a gallon of gas costs $5.30, an 8-ounce tube of toothpaste $4, a typical new car $18,200 and a 5-pound bag of sugar $6.70.

The year 2000? 2020? Guess again. If the costs of these goods and services continue going up at the rate of the past decade, such prices will be reality by 1991.

On this page is a sampling, based on what's happened to each item since 1971, of what may lie ahead—sooner than many people realize.

New home
(median price)

| 1981 | $69,300 |
| 1991 | $191,000 |

Week's groceries
(urban family of four)

| 1981 | $112 |
| 1991 | $260 |

Top Broadway musical
(weekend orchestra seat)

| 1981 | $35 |
| 1991 | $82 |

Beer
(six-pack)

| 1981 | $2.45 |
| 1991 | $4.30 |

Hospital room
(semiprivate, per day)

| 1981 | $170 |
| 1991 | $484 |

New auto fender installed

| 1981 | $364 |
| 1991 | $1,063 |

Carton of cigarettes

| 1981 | $6.17 |
| 1991 | $10.40 |

Coffee
(2 lb.)

| 1981 | $5.12 |
| 1991 | $14.00 |

Dry cleaning
(two-piece suit)

| 1981 | $3.96 |
| 1991 | $9.00 |

Postage
(1 oz., first class)

| 1981 | 18¢ |
| 1991 | 40¢ |

Hamburger
(Big Mac)

| 1981 | $1.15 |
| 1991 | $2.40 |

Potatoes
(5 lb.)

| 1981 | $1.38 |
| 1991 | $4.40 |

USN&WR chart by Carl Vansag—Basic data: U.S. Depts. of Labor, Commerce and Energy; U.S. Postal Service; Insurance Information Institute, McDonald's Corporation

Chapter 17

Stabilizing the economy

- *Attempts to stabilize the economy become political issues.*

- *In order to stimulate a sluggish economy, the major question is whether to promote "supply side" or "demand side" incentives.*

The basic economic goal is steady growth, coupled with full employment and stable prices.

For years, Americans lived with the notion that periodic recessions and inflations were a fact of economic life. Having established a sound currency and an organized banking system by the early 1900s, it was reasoned that a little inflation would occur from time to time, and could be lived with. As for recessions and depressions (recession and depression are really the same—a slowdown in business production and increase in unemployment—except that depression is longer and more severe), there was little that businesses and households could really be expected to do except await the upswing in the economic cycle. There was always the optimism that the economy would return to full employment and the full use of resources.

British economist John Maynard Keynes shattered this sense of well-being. In the 1920s and 1930s, Keynes wrote that there was no certainty that prosperity would return. The economy might reach equilibrium at less than full employment. It was Keynes who taught us that total spending must equal total income in an economy. Much of the theory of GNP (Gross National Product) and national income levels is referred to as *Keynesian economics*.

GNP is affected by changes in the level of *aggregate demand* (consumption plus investment plus government spending). Instability in the economy results from fluctuations in aggregate demand. If the economy is to be stabilized, then GNP must be stabilized. And if GNP is in equilibrium at a level less than full employment, then aggregate demand must be increased.

According to Keynes, business investment moves up and down much more than consumer spending. When business investments decline, the level of economic activity (GNP) declines. It is unreasonable, he wrote, to expect either businesses or consumers to voluntarily pick up the spending necessary to bring about recovery and full employment. It is neither sound business practice nor wise household management to spend during a recession. Keynes' solution was government spending.

This idea shocked traditional economists, businessmen, government leaders, and the public. In a capitalist system, the government's role was supposed to be minimal. Placing the government in a position to control the economy was a revolutionary idea. In addition, Keynes's analysis unveiled a shortcoming of capitalist economics; private enterprise, functioning naturally and as it should, could and did lead to disastrous consequences.

The United States pulled itself out of the Great Depression, but not through the deliberate use of

Keynesian policies. The government started many federal job programs in the 1930s, spending money that bolstered the economy. Then World War II followed in the early 1940s. By necessity, government spending again increased a great deal, and the economy was lifted out of the depression.

By 1946, public officials demonstrated an acceptance of Keynesian theory. In that year, Congress passed the Employment Act, making it the responsiblity of government to foster the general welfare and promote maximum employment, production, and purchasing power. There are two principal ways the federal government can attempt to fulfill the Employment Act of 1946: one is referred to as *fiscal policy* and the other as *monetary policy*. Government policy makers have several Keynesian fiscal tools to help combat instability in the economy. In addition, the Federal Reserve Board exerts control through its monetary decisions.

Fiscal policy

During the Great Depression of the 1930s, business investment in capital goods and the total production of goods decreased significantly. With this, unemployment grew to an alarming degree (a full one-third of the work force was jobless by 1932), earned incomes declined, and total spending was very low. With business investments and consumer spending down and showing no prospect of rising, the Keynesian solution was to substantially increase government spending. Federal policy makers initiated an array of new government programs and public works projects.

Where would government find the money to finance these projects? The usual sources of government revenue, personal and business taxes, was down during a time of high unemployment and low business earnings. Consequently, government funds would have to be borrowed—but from where? During wartime, governments borrow heavily from the public by selling bonds. During the depression, however, people had little money to lend. Anyway, their loans would be self-defeating: the more money people lent to the government, the less they would have to spend to help stimulate business.

The government turned to its other major source

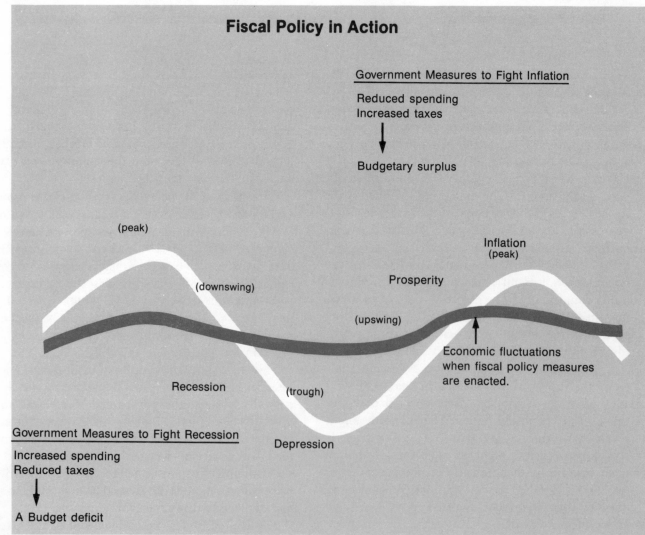

Fiscal Policy in Action

Government Measures to Fight Inflation

Reduced spending
Increased taxes

Budgetary surplus

(peak)

(downswing)

Government Measures to Fight Inflation
Inflation
(peak)

Prosperity

(upswing)

Economic fluctuations
when fiscal policy measures
are enacted.

Recession

(trough)

Depression

Government Measures to Fight Recession

Increased spending
Reduced taxes

A Budget deficit

of funds, the Federal Reserve banks. Much of the money to finance the spending programs that fuel the economy during any recession comes from the Federal Reserve. This has the added benefit of creating more money in the economy. Whether loans are made by a commercial bank or the Federal Reserve, the money creation process that starts in the banking system stimulates economic activity. Also, government spending, like consumer or business spending, sets the multiplier and accelerator effects into motion.

All this borrowing and spending by the government in the absence of income tax revenues led to a growing federal debt. This *deficit financing*, Keynesians explained, was both inevitable and necessary. But a large and growing government debt, or even a debt of any size, was alarming to most Americans. This debt, theorists explained, would be reduced when prosperity returned and the flow of tax dollars to Washington automatically increased. At the same time, government spending could be reduced.

Fiscal policy during recessionary periods calls for one or both of two courses of action. The federal government can increase aggregate demand by *increasing its own spending*, or it can stimulate consumer and business spending by *reducing taxes*—or both. Increased spending tends to be the preferred policy beacause it puts people to work right away. With a reduction in taxes, there is no guarantee that the extra disposable income will be spent on consumer goods or expanding business.

During an inflationary period, the opposite government spending and taxation policies are appropriate. Spending programs by the government should be cut back—they will only fuel the inflation—and taxes should be increased. The effect of these fiscal measures is to reduce overall demand. Consumers have less money to spend. Such policies often have to be carried out in the face of strong public opposition. As a result, they are often not enacted, or only weakly carried out. People don't like to see their favorite government programs cut back, or to be hit with higher taxes. This helps explain why government actions have been less effective in limiting inflation than in combating recessions.

Built-in stabilizers

There are some government-related measures that automatically go into effect, operating in the same fashion as fiscal policies. They are called the "built-in" or "automatic stabilizers." During a recession, aid to dependent children and other public welfare programs provide assistance to a growing number of the poor. Unemployment insurance, business severance-pay provisions, and guaranteed wage agreements also provide income payments that otherwise would not exist. In effect, these are government spending measures that need not await the approval of Congress. They are an immediate stimulus to the economy. During periods of prosperity and inflation, spending for these programs is automatically reduced as more people are able to find employment.

In addition, Social Security retirement payments and private pension plans provide a steady source of income for retired persons. These automatically buffer the hardships of recession or depression. None of these programs was designed as fiscal policy; they are a response to other needs in our society. But they help provide a constant level of income so that there will always be a minimum of spending.

Another built-in stabilizer is the progressive taxation system that affects personal and corporate income. During a time of recession, when earnings are reduced, proportionately less income is taken away as taxes. With a progressive tax system, the amount of money available for consumers and businesses to spend after taxes is more than would be available with either a proportional or regressive tax. During inflation, progressive income taxes cut proportionally more into the income of businesses and households.

Monetary policy

The *Federal Reserve System* also plays an important role in combating recession and inflation. It too affects aggregate demand in the economy, but it does so by controlling the *money supply*. The Federal Reserve, through *monetary policy*, affects the potential of the banking system—its member banks—to increase or decrease the supply of money. The Fed has three major tools at its disposal.

1. Open Market operations

The most frequently used tool of monetary policy is *open market operations*. A decision to create money in the banking system through this device is made by the *Federal Open Market Committee*, or FOMC. This committee consists of the seven Reserve Board members, the president of the Federal Reserve Bank of New York, and four other Reserve bank presidents who are chosen in rotation.

First, the Federal Reserve staff reviews the latest trends in industrial production, trade, employment, inflation, and the money supply, and calculates

How the Federal Reserve Creates Money

STEP 1

The Federal Reserve System's Open Market Committee decides to expand the money supply. It sends instructions to the open-market desk at the Federal Reserve Bank of New York.

STEP 2

Officials of the New York Federal Reserve Bank buy $100 million in Treasury bills from a securities dealer and pay with a check.

STEP 3

The dealer deposits the check in Bank A. Result: $100 million is added to the dealer's account and to the money supply.

STEP 4

Bank A puts 15 percent, or $15 million, into reserves and lends the rest to XYZ Auto Company, thus increasing the company's account and the nation's money supply by $85 million.

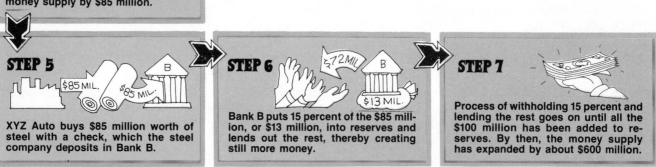

STEP 5

XYZ Auto buys $85 million worth of steel with a check, which the steel company deposits in Bank B.

STEP 6

Bank B puts 15 percent of the $85 million, or $13 million, into reserves and lends out the rest, thereby creating still more money.

STEP 7

Process of withholding 15 percent and lending the rest goes on until all the $100 million has been added to reserves. By then, the money supply has expanded by about $600 million.

Note: Under Federal Reserve rules, a bank that receives new funds must put a portion—currently averaging about 15 percent—in its district Federal Reserve Bank and can lend or invest the rest.

predictions. The committee then instructs the Federal Reserve Bank of New York to buy government bonds in the open market. (If the committee wanted to reduce the money supply, it would have these Treasury issues sold in the open market.) Who or what is this open market? It is somewhat of a mystery. The dealers of government bonds in the open market do not reveal the names of the buyers or sellers, but a good guess would be insurance companies, commercial banks, and big business firms.

How does the buying of government bonds in the open market create money? The process operates in the same way that banks create money when they lend money to their customers. It starts with the requirement that banks belonging to the Federal Reserve System—all national banks and most large state-chartered banks—must keep deposits at the twelve Reserve banks equal to a specified percentage of the deposits they hold for their customers. The diagram shows how $100 million, deposited in a commercial bank by a securities dealer who sells Treasury (government) bonds to the New York federal bank, leads to an increase of about $600 million in checking-account money.

After the FOMC sends instructions to the New York bank to buy government bonds (step 1), bank officials buy $100 million in Treasury bills (bonds) from the securities dealer with a check (step 2). The dealer then deposits the check in bank A, and a new $100 million has been injected into the money supply from the Federal Treasury (step 3). As a result, bank A has $85 million in excess reserves to lend to XYZ auto company, or any other company that qualifies for a loan (step 4). (This assumes that the reserve requirement rate is 15 percent.) After this, more new money is created as the lending potential of other banks increases and they make the reserves available as loans to still more customers (steps 5-7).

If in the beginning the FOMC had decided to sell Treasury bonds, a contraction of the money supply would have been set off in the banking system.

2. Changing the discount rate

Another monetary mechanism to change the money supply is the *discount rate*—the interest rate Federal Reserve banks charge on loans to its member banks. The discount rate encourages or discourages banks from borrowing. Lowering the discount rate makes it more attractive for banks to borrow so they can lend more money to their customers. This starts the creation of money.

The Federal Reserve's discount rate eventually affects the interest rates you and I—the public—pay to borrow money from our banks. During inflation, the Federal Reserve is inclined to increase the discount rate in order to discourage member-bank borrowing. When this happens, the member commercial banks raise the interest rates they charge to their customers. This is done both to conserve the scarce funds they have for lending and to maintain their profit margin on loans. The rate that is charged to large corporate borrowers is called the *prime rate*. It is the best interest rate available, and is given to the most preferred customers. This interest rate is kept a little higher than the Federal Reserve's discount rate, and a little lower than the rate charged other customers, including smaller businesses and individuals. When the prime rate is raised, the interest rate is increased for all other buyers and money is tighter (more difficult to borrow).

3. Changing the reserve requirements

The Fed can change the proportion of deposits that a member bank must keep in reserve. If the Federal Reserve wants to tighten credit in the system, thereby reducing the money supply, it can ask Congress for permission to raise the reserve requirement. When this happens, member banks have to increase their reserves. To do this, they must contract their loans and investments. Lowering the reserve requirement creates the opposite effect: credit is easier, banks can lend or invest more funds, and the money supply expands.

The impact of government policies

Monetary and fiscal policy are powerful and controversial tools of the federal government. A decision by the government to spend more money or to increase taxes affects living standards of millions of families. Similarly, the power of the Federal Reserve System is felt in every corner of the economy. When the FED raises or lowers its discount rate, millions of people and billions of dollars are affected—from the bank with huge amounts of money to lend, to the individual with a small savings account. Just one-fourth of 1 percent increase in the discount rate will lead to a decrease of millions of dollars in the economy. There will be less money available for business investments, home building, and the purchases of new cars and televisions. This is why a change in the discount rate makes headlines in newspapers across the country.

Trickle down, trickle up

The economy can be stimulated in one of two ways: by making more money available to producers—the *supply side* of the economy, or by making it available to consumers—the *demand side*. The theory of supply side is that if producers have money available, they will invest it in production and in creating jobs, thus boosting the economy. The expansion of production will *trickle-down* through the economy. The theory of demand side is that if consumers have money to spend, it will create demand for more products which will trickle up, stimulating business growth and expansion of the economy. In either case the multiplier will take effect.

In 1981, President Reagan and his advisors promoted "supply-side" economics. Reagan's economic planners believed that productivity was low because the size of federal taxes discouraged savings, work, investment, and production by individuals and businesses. His policies became known as "Reagonomics." The objective was to stimulate the production—or supply-side of the economic equation—rather than boost the consumption of goods and services, the demand side.

Since the influence of Keynesianism in the 1930s, American economic policy (fiscal and monetary) tended to focus on managing the amount of spending money available to consumers. The supply-side method of filtering money into the economy is reducing income taxes, particularly for people who can afford to spend money for investments, and business taxes. The average worker confronted with high taxes, it is reasoned, is reluctant to put in overtime or take a second job to increase output. And the wealthy seek ways to reduce their taxes, instead of investing to benefit the economy. Lower taxes may encourage people to buy more, but most of all, say supply-siders, they will save and *"invest"* their larger income. This will give business the capital it needs to modernize and expand. The result, according to theory, will be a boost in production, employment, incomes and, incidentally, tax revenues.

Two Theories for Getting
The Economy Moving

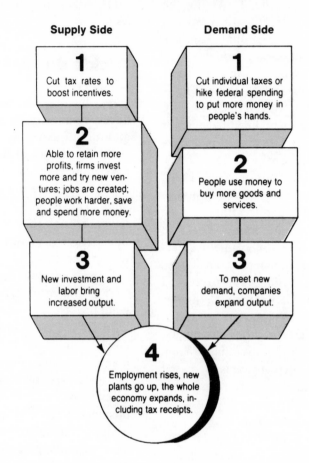

Supply Side

1
Cut tax rates to boost incentives.

2
Able to retain more profits, firms invest more and try new ventures; jobs are created; people work harder, save and spend more money.

3
New investment and labor bring increased output.

Demand Side

1
Cut individual taxes or hike federal spending to put more money in people's hands.

2
People use money to buy more goods and services.

3
To meet new demand, companies expand output.

4
Employment rises, new plants go up, the whole economy expands, including tax receipts.

Chapter 18

Economic classes

> • *Even in a democratic society such as the U.S., there is an economic class system.*
>
> • *Inflation, unemployment and family break-ups have shrunk the middle class, placing more families at a poverty level.*

George and Carol Barker expected to be on their way to acquiring a piece of the American Dream. Both are college graduates; Carol worked as a school teacher for several years after their marriage and before giving birth to their two children; George is an electrical engineer earning $35,000 a year. They used much of Carol's earnings to finance a home they purchased in 1972, and to buy other trappings of the "good life"—a new automobile every few years, a second car, and skiing vacations in Colorado.

Even though the children are still young and Carol would like to stay at home with them, she is going back to work. Several years ago, $35,000 seemed like a great deal of money. Now the Barkers have what appears to be a good income, but they are struggling. The second car may not be replaced, or may be replaced only with a small, cheaper, second-hand model when it wears out. Their vacations also will be much less extravagant. Ten years ago, Carol's working full-time was voluntary. Today, it has become a necessity.

The middle class

The Barkers' experience is common among middle-class families today. They are struggling merely to maintain a constant "standard of living": a minimum of necessities, comforts, or luxuries held essential to a person or a group. Still, the Barkers are doing well compared to many American families. They are part of the vast middle class with a better-than-average income.

The middle class of the early 1980s includes families with incomes ranging from approximately $20,000 to $40,000. The average income is approximately $25,000. George Barker's income has increased steadily, but like other middle-income families, the Barkers are not advancing economically. Gains in family income the past ten years have been eaten away by inflation.

Distribution of income

As a salaried, professional technician, George Barker is earning what might be expected. Many wage earners would envy the Barkers' standard of living. To make ends meet, both husband and wife in many American families have become full-time wage earners.

Despite a progressive taxation system, the distribution of income in our economic system has remained remarkably steady over the years. We are not gradually drifting toward an equality of income. There is a wide disparity between the highest and lowest paid workers in our economic system, and between those in the top one-third income group and those in the bottom one-third.

Determination of income

We often take for granted that people in some occupations earn higher incomes than those in others. Lawyers, for example, earn more than journalists, bankers more than teachers, and doctors more than auto mechanics. There are a number of reasons for the differences in income, but rarely do they totally explain—or justify—high, low, or average income.

One standard economic explanation for different payments to different occupation groups, or individuals, is their relative *productivity*. Some workers have greater job skills or ability because of more training, better training, or experience on the job. This explanation is true to a limited extent, but, in many cases, productivity is difficult to measure.

Another explanation is the *supply* and *demand* conditions in the *labor market*. Sometimes this is closely related to productivity: Workers who have spent more time in training, or have learned more difficult skills, are fewer in number. The supply of these workers, compared with their demand, is likely to be low. Therefore, they can command a high price in the labor market.

Where certain types of workers are scarce (demand exceeds supply), the earnings of those people will be high. Are their larger earnings due to more productivity? Are they deserved? Perhaps, but supply and demand considerations are not much help in determining productivity.

There are other reasons for differences in earnings. Both *race* and *sex discrimination* are factors. It may be true that some of the differences that exist between the incomes of whites and blacks, and men and women are explained by productivity levels, training, and experience. Yet, even when these factors are held constant, and people with equal abilities hold the same positions, there are often differences in the wages paid to workers of different races and sexes.

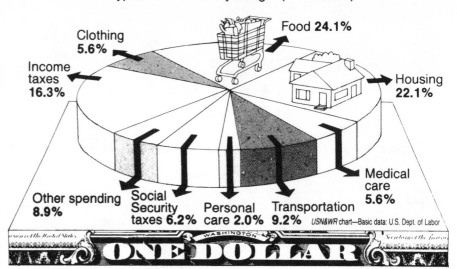

Where the Money Goes
Typical Urban-Family Budget (4 members)

Clothing 5.6%
Income taxes 16.3%
Food 24.1%
Housing 22.1%
Medical care 5.6%
Other spending 8.9%
Social Security taxes 6.2%
Personal care 2.0%
Transportation 9.2%

USN&WR chart—Basic data: U.S. Dept. of Labor

The affluent

Some people have higher earnings because they have invested their savings in the stock market, real estate, or a business. But a person must have sufficient savings to be in a position to earn more this way. Other people inherit money from wealthy relatives. This not only enhances their material life immediately, but the money can be put to use earning even more money. In short, the more money one has, the more one can earn. The rich tend to get richer.

The poor

In our economic system, where there are wide variations in income, some people benefit and others suffer. There are many poor people in the U.S.

The poverty figure shifts with time to keep up with increases in the cost of living. In 1981, the official *poverty income level* was an annual $9,300

Who Is the Middle Class?

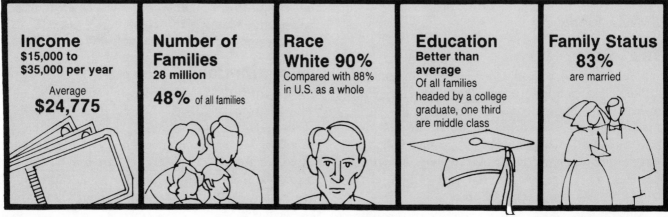

Income
$15,000 to $35,000 per year
Average **$24,775**

Number of Families
28 million
48% of all families

Race
White **90%**
Compared with 88% in U.S. as a whole

Education
Better than average
Of all families headed by a college graduate, one third are middle class

Family Status
83%
are married

USN&WR charts—Basic data: U.S. Dept. of Commerce

Work vs. Prices— Changes Over 10 Years

Estimated on-job time of production workers in manufacturing required to buy these goods and services—

	1971	1981
New home (median price)	41 months	53 months
New car (average price)	26 weeks	28 weeks
Washing machine	71 hr., 10 min.	55 hr., 17 min.
Hospital room, semiprivate, per day	16 hr., 40 min.	22 hr., 14 min.
Week's groceries (family of four)	13 hr., 27 min.	13 hr., 49 min.
Motor tuneup	8 hr., 20 min.	8 hr., 19 min.
Month's electric bill (750 kwh)	4 hr., 23 min.	7 hr., 0 min.
Month's gas bill (100 therms)	3 hr., 23 min.	6 hr., 0 min.
Permanent wave	3 hr., 57 min.	3 hr., 35 min.
Physician's office visit	2 hr., 42 min.	2 hr., 52 min.
Carton of cigarettes	1 hr., 2 min.	47 min.
Coffee, 2 pounds	31 min.	37 min.
Man's haircut	41 min.	36 min.
Dry cleaning, man's two-piece suit	29 min.	30 min.
Movie admission, adult	33 min.	26 min.
Round steak, pound	23 min.	22 min.
Six-pack of beer	23 min.	19 min.
Pork chops, pound	18 min.	17 min.
Butter, pound	15 min.	15 min.
Toothpaste, 8 oz.	17 min.	15 min.
Bacon, pound	13 min.	13 min.
Sugar, 5 pounds	11 min.	13 min.
Gallon of regular gasoline.........	6 min.	10 min.
Potatoes, 5 pounds	8 min.	10 min.
Tuna, 6.5-oz. can	7 min.	8 min.
Eggs, dozen	9 min.	6 min.
White bread, pound	4 min.	4 min.

Note: Average hourly earnings in manufacturing were $3.57 in 1971 and $8.03 in August, 1981; figures based on 40-hour workweek.
USN&WR table—Basic data: U.S. Depts. of Labor, Commerce, Energy; American Medical Association

for a nonfarm family of four, and slightly lower for a farm family.

Recent studies on poverty in America came to the following findings:

● Education, not jobs, is the single most important factor determining who will be poor. The lack of education handicaps not only adults, but also their children. Children raised in a home where the parents, particularly the father, had less than a sixth-grade education, are at a much higher than normal risk of living in poverty.

● Disintegration of families is a major contributor to poverty. When the head of a household dies, or if the parents divorce, the likelihood of poverty increases substantially.

● Rural residents are more likely to be poor than city dwellers.

● Relatively few people stay in the poverty class year after year. Poverty for most people is temporary: More than one-half of poor families are poor only for a limited period. Many people move into poverty—through divorce or by leaving a parental home. Others climb out of the poor class by getting married, changing occupation, or getting more schooling.

While about one of every 11 American families may be classified as poor in any single year, only one-fourth of them are likely to stay poor over a five-year period. These are hard-core poor; they number between six and seven million Americans.

In theory, incomes in a capitalist society are distributed "to each according to his or her ability." In practice, it doesn't work out so neatly. The poor are not necessarily lacking in ability, and the rich are not necessarily talented, gifted or even hard-working. The government manages *redistribution of income* through such measures as welfare, job training programs, and the progressive income tax. The efforts toward and success of redistribution have been modest.

Family Income

Median family income doubled during the 1970s and reached a total in 1980 of $21,023, Census Bureau figures show. But purchasing power of a family with that income in 1980 was only $40 more than in 1970.

In 1980, nearly 30 million people lived under the government's poverty level—real median income plunged 5.5 percent. That meant 13 percent of the population was officially poor, compared with 12.6 percent in 1970.

Family incomes in 1980 varied widely by race, age and education.

How Living Costs Compare Around U.S.

To live in moderate comfort in 1982, an American family of four needed an annual income of $25,661.

According to an annual survey by the U.S. Labor Department, a family of four needed a minimum of $15,323 just to get by, and $38,060 to live very comfortably in the 1982 economy.

All three budgets included food, housing, transportation, clothing, personal care, medical care, Social Security and personal income taxes.

At the moderate-budget level, the biggest single bite was for income and Social Security taxes, which accounted for 24 percent of the total. Food took 23 percent, housing 21.8 percent. Biggest increases from the prior year were 19.3 percent for Social Security and 17.5 percent for income taxes. Food costs went up only 4.9 percent and clothing 3.2 percent.

Moderate Budgets For Family of 4

(by metropolitan area)

Anchorage	$31,890
Atlanta	$23,273
Baltimore	$25,114
Boston	$29,213
Buffalo	$26,473
Chicago	$25,358
Cincinnati	$25,475
Cleveland	$25,598
Dallas	$22,678
Denver	$24,820
Detroit	$25,208
Honolulu	$31,893
Houston	$23,601
Kansas City	$24,528
Los Angeles	$25,025
Milwaukee	$26,875
Minneapolis–St. Paul	$25,799
New York City	$29,540
Philadelphia	$26,567
Pittsburgh	$24,717
St. Louis	$24,498
San Diego	$24,776
San Francisco	$27,082
Seattle	$25,881
Washington, D.C.	$27,352

How Inflation Has Shrunk Family Income

Median Family Income

In Today's Dollars $21,023

$15,000

What It's Worth in 1970 Dollars

$9,867

$10,000

$9,907

0

1970 '72 '74 '76 '78 '80

Thus, despite more than a doubling in income, families now have only slightly more buying power than they had in 1970.

USN&WR chart—Basic data: U.S. Dept. of Commerce

How Education Boosts Income

Family Heads Age 25 or Older	Median Family Income, 1980
Finished college	$32,469
1 to 3 years of college	$24,866
Finished high school	$21,845
1 to 3 years of high school	$16,203
Finished grade school	$14,115
Did not finish grade school	$10,836

Where Families Stand in Income

Based on Median Income in 1980

If Your Family Income Is	You Fall in This Bracket
More than $75,000	Top 2%
$50,000 or more	Top 7%
$35,000 or more	Top 20%
$25,000 or more	Top 39%
$20,000 or more	Top 53%
Less than $15,000	Bottom 33%
Less than $10,000	Bottom 19%
Less than $5,000	Bottom 6%

Pinpointing the Poor

Based on official poverty levels, 29.3 million individual Americans were considered poor in 1980.

Of This Group,	This Share Is Poor
All Americans	13.0%
Whites	10.2%
Blacks	32.5%
People of Hispanic origin	25.7%
People 65 and older	15.7%
People in central cities	17.2%
People on farms	17.5%

When Earnings Reach a Peak

Age of Family Head	Median Family Income, 1980
Younger than 25	$13,792
25 to 34	$20,411
35 to 44	$24,670
45 to 54	$27,256
55 to 64	$23,531
65 and older	$12,881

Black-White Income: Gap Grows Wider

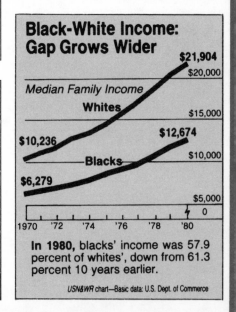

Median Family Income

Whites $21,904

$20,000

$15,000

$12,674

Blacks

$10,236

$10,000

$6,279

$5,000

0

1970 '72 '74 '76 '78 '80

In 1980, blacks' income was 57.9 percent of whites', down from 61.3 percent 10 years earlier.

USN&WR chart—Basic data: U.S. Dept. of Commerce

Chapter 19

Unemployment

- *Automation is taking jobs, especially in the smoke-stack industries.*

- *The U.S. is changing from an industrial society to an information society which means a change from a goods-producing to a service-producing economy.*

During the early 1980s, about 11 million Americans were classified as unemployed. To be unemployed means to be out of work and actively seeking a job. These 11 million would-be workers represented 10 percent of the labor force. (In total, there were nearly 110 million people at work. No one knows how many unemployed people are discouraged and have given up looking for work.)

The unemployment rate of more than 10 percent was the highest since the Great Depression of the 1930s. Unemployment is not just a statistic, but a tremendous hardship in the lives of individuals and families.

How much unemployment is acceptable

Most economists say that 5 percent unemployment is the best that can be expected. (It used to be 4 percent.) There are others who say the policy makers should not be "let off the hook" so easily. With effort, unemployment can be reduced to lower levels. Unemployment figures should not be taken lightly; a change of 1 percent affects jobs for nearly a million people.

Nevertheless, reducing unemployment to 5 percent or below is difficult. Unemployment has fallen below the 4 percent mark only during war years. The major cause of unemployment is a slowdown in production, when businesses operate at less than full capacity. It is rare for business production throughout the economy to be at a maximum level. Even at full capacity there will be some unemployment due to "shifts" in the economy.

Businesses relocate, reducing employment in one location while increasing it in another. It then takes time for new employment to fill the gap where workers have been laid off. In addition, individuals and families are constantly moving. This factor results in some unemployment.

Public service jobs

In the mid-1970s, due to high unemployment rates, Congress passed a bill to create *public service employment* (PSE) jobs. It was the largest federal government attempt to create jobs since the Great Depression. Entry-level jobs were created in the public sector, such as nurses' aides and teacher aides, city and school bus drivers, park and playground workers. Jobs were allocated to communities with the highest unemployment rates. At its peak in 1978, the program employed 750,000 people at a cost of $5.7 billion .

The PSE program was ended in 1981. It was replaced by a *job training program* in 1982 to provide unemployed and displaced workers with skills which are in demand. A budget of $3.7 billion was approved by Congress to train or retrain a million workers for such jobs as auto mechanics, machinists, aerospace equipment assemblers and computer repairers.

The unemployed

In recent years, new forces have been operating to change the employment situation. The economy has steadily grown and employment has increased, but not fast enough to accommodate the burgeoning work force. During the ten-year period from 1966 to 1976, the number of women entering the work force rose by 11.3 million, or more than 40 percent. This pace has been more rapid in recent years. The number of teenagers available for the civilian labor force was greater during the 1970s because of the baby boom. In part, it was also due to the end of the armed forces' draft.

The unemployment rate for both women and teenagers is higher than the overall rate. The teenage unemployment rate is particularly high for several reasons. Increases in the federal *minimum wage* ($3.35 per hour as of 1983) and the spread of unions have priced low-skilled workers out of many jobs. Employers are reluctant to hire unskilled teenagers at the minimum wage. Many chores once performed by teenagers are now done by machines or by illegal aliens who risk deportation should they complain to the government about below-minimum pay.

One major cause of unemployment in the 1980s is the decline of old-line manufacturing jobs in the *smokestack industries*. Steel, auto and railroad companies have lost several million jobs. The U.S. is moving into the *information society* and away from the *industrial society*. It is unlikely that the smokestack industries will employ as many people as they did in the past. Computers and robots are likely to do much of the work in these industries.

There is a heavy human toll for the individuals who are unemployed. But being temporarily out of

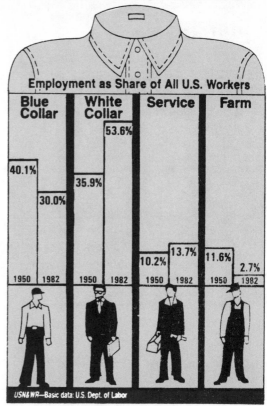

America's Fading Blue Collar

Employment as Share of All U.S. Workers

Blue Collar	White Collar	Service	Farm
40.1% (1950) / 30.0% (1982)	35.9% (1950) / 53.6% (1982)	10.2% (1950) / 13.7% (1982)	11.6% (1950) / 2.7% (1982)

USN&WR—Basic data: U.S. Dept. of Labor

work today is not as agonizing for most people as it once was.

Unemployment compensation, food stamps and other forms of welfare help the idle worker maintain a standard of living above that of the jobless of past decades. In addition, more people are now eligible for unemployment compensation. The federal government has extended this assistance to cover laid-off farm workers, maids, and employees of local government. Medical benefits are not provided.

Some experts contend that unemployment benefits reduce incentives to take available jobs. People are more careful about the employment offers they accept. But job seekers are required to accept positions that match their work skills, or the unemployment compensation is terminated.

Solutions to unemployment

Public service jobs and *public works projects* (on sewage systems, hospitals, schools) are two suggested solutions to unemployment. Crumbling highways, rusting bridges, backed-up sewers, leaking water mains, bursting dams, broken-down buses and subway

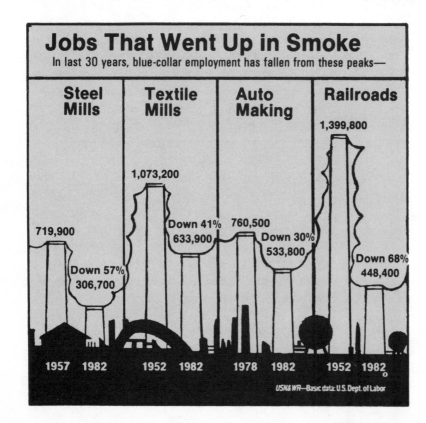

Jobs That Went Up in Smoke

In last 30 years, blue-collar employment has fallen from these peaks—

Steel Mills	Textile Mills	Auto Making	Railroads
719,900 (1957)	1,073,200 (1952)	760,500 (1978)	1,399,800 (1952)
Down 57% 306,700 (1982)	Down 41% 633,900 (1982)	Down 30% 533,800 (1982)	Down 68% 448,400 (1982)

USN&WR—Basic data: U.S. Dept. of Labor

cars are all in need of repair. Public works, known as the *infrastructure* have been neglected. It is estimated that it will cost $2.5 trillion to rebuild America. In addition to providing necessary improvements, which would stimulate the entire economy, millions of jobs would be created.

Other proposals would establish training programs for young people who don't qualify for work that now exists. It has also been proposed that the federal government finance a youth service program. Local needs would determine where to place young people in *community service jobs* (with public or private industry) as apprentices.

Other proposals are aimed at creating more jobs in private industry. One provides *tax incentives* for capital investments by businesses in areas of high unemployment. Another provides a *wage subsidy* to businesses who hire the jobless. Others entail tax reductions: Reducing personal income taxes would stimulate consumer demand for goods and services; reducing corporate income taxes encourages businesses to create new jobs with the added profits.

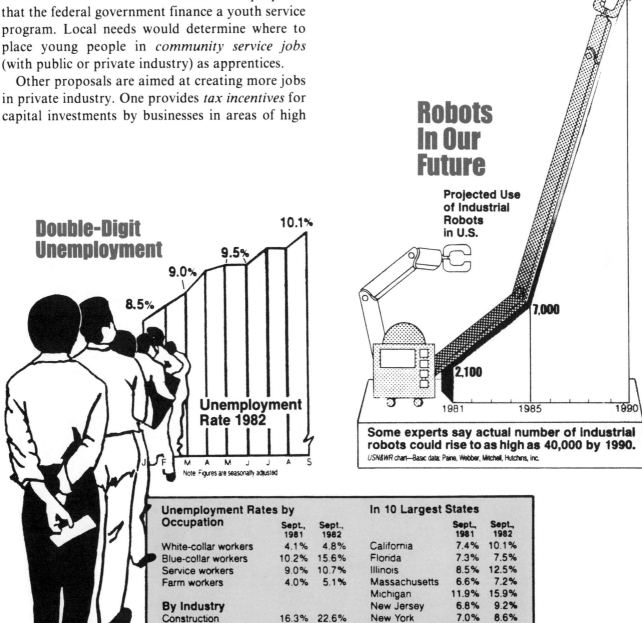

Robots In Our Future

Projected Use of Industrial Robots in U.S.

30,000

7,000

2,100

1981   1985   1990

Some experts say actual number of industrial robots could rise to as high as 40,000 by 1990.

USN&WR chart—Basic data: Paine, Webber, Mitchell, Hutchins, Inc.

Double-Digit Unemployment

10.1%

9.5%

9.0%

8.5%

Unemployment Rate 1982

J F M A M J J A S

Note: Figures are seasonally adjusted

Unemployment Rates by Occupation	Sept., 1981	Sept., 1982
White-collar workers	4.1%	4.8%
Blue-collar workers	10.2%	15.6%
Service workers	9.0%	10.7%
Farm workers	4.0%	5.1%
By Industry		
Construction	16.3%	22.6%
Manufacturing	7.9%	13.8%
Transport, public utilities	4.2%	6.9%
Trade	8.5%	9.8%
Finance, services	6.0%	6.8%
Government	4.7%	4.9%

In 10 Largest States	Sept., 1981	Sept., 1982
California	7.4%	10.1%
Florida	7.3%	7.5%
Illinois	8.5%	12.5%
Massachusetts	6.6%	7.2%
Michigan	11.9%	15.9%
New Jersey	6.8%	9.2%
New York	7.0%	8.6%
Ohio	10.3%	12.5%
Pennsylvania	8.5%	11.3%
Texas	5.5%	8.4%

USN&WR—Basic data: U.S. Dept of Labor

The Leap Toward a Service Society

Since the close of World War II, dramatic shifts have occurred in the ways that Americans earn their livings. From a time when more than 40 percent of nonfarm workers were engaged in production, the U.S. economy has now moved into a period when it is heavily weighted toward services—trade, finance and government, for example. Today's work force of 92 million persons includes only 20.5 million workers in manufacturing—compared with 20.8 million engaged just in wholesale and retail trade. By 1990, even more people will be employed in miscellaneous service-type jobs such as data processing, hotels and restaurants than in all of manufacturing. The charts on this page sharply define the enormous changes and what to expect in years to come.

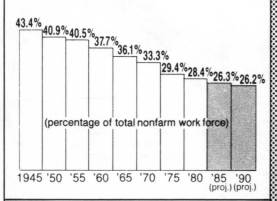

Goods-Producing Jobs Shrink...

43.4% 40.9% 40.5% 37.7% 36.1% 33.3% 29.4% 28.4% 26.3% 26.2%

(percentage of total nonfarm work force)

1945 '50 '55 '60 '65 '70 '75 '80 '85 '90
(proj.) (proj.)

	Mining	Construction	Manufacturing
1945	**2.1%**	**2.8%**	**38.5%**
1950	**2.0%**	**5.2%**	**33.7%**
1955	**1.6%**	**5.6%**	**33.3%**
1960	**1.3%**	**5.4%**	**31.0%**
1965	**1.0%**	**5.3%**	**29.7%**
1970	**0.9%**	**5.1%**	**27.3%**
1975	**0.9%**	**4.6%**	**23.8%**
1980	**1.1%**	**4.9%**	**22.4%**
1985 (proj.)	**1.2%**	**5.3%**	**22.4%**
1990 (proj.)	**1.2%**	**5.0%**	**21.6%**

...As Service-Producing Jobs Swell

56.6% 59.1% 59.5% 62.3% 63.9% 66.7% 70.6% 71.6% 73.7% 73.8%

(percentage of total nonfarm work force)

1945 '50 '55 '60 '65 '70 '75 '80 '85 '90
(proj.) (proj.)

	Transportation, Utilities	Wholesale and Retail Trade	Finance, Insurance, Real Estate	Other Services	Government
1945	**9.7%**	**18.1%**	**3.7%**	**10.5%**	**14.7%**
1950	**8.9%**	**20.8%**	**4.2%**	**11.9%**	**13.3%**
1955	**8.2%**	**20.8%**	**4.5%**	**12.3%**	**13.7%**
1960	**7.4%**	**21.0%**	**4.9%**	**13.6%**	**15.4%**
1965	**6.6%**	**20.9%**	**4.9%**	**14.9%**	**16.6%**
1970	**6.4%**	**21.2%**	**5.3%**	**16.3%**	**17.7%**
1975	**5.9%**	**22.2%**	**5.4%**	**18.1%**	**19.1%**
1980	**5.7%**	**22.5%**	**5.7%**	**19.8%**	**17.9%**
1985 (proj.)	**5.5%**	**22.9%**	**5.6%**	**20.2%**	**16.3%**
1990 (proj.)	**5.4%**	**23.0%**	**6.0%**	**21.5%**	**16.3%**

Note: Figures may not add because of rounding.

USN&WR charts—Basic data: U.S. Dept. of Labor

Chapter 20

Federal subsidies

- *Major political decisions are involved in determining who gets federal subsidies.*

- *Who is entitled to government subsidies? Should it be businesses, consumers, the aged, veterans, students?*

A *subsidy* is a payment or a tax deduction made by a government to a business or individual to encourage or protect a particular economic activity. A subsidy also may be a maintenance payment.

The aim of subsidies is to have a central agent—the local, state, or federal government—collect money from the general body of citizenry and distribute it to those who need economic assistance, including the poor, the aged, disabled veterans, college students, specific businesses, and even entire industries, such as housing.

The home mortgage interest income tax deduction illustrates the subsidy mechanism. By allowing a tax break to home owners, more people can buy houses. This benefits individual families, but it also helps the housing industry. As more houses are built, carpenters, plumbers, electricians and many others are provided with jobs. All of the people who work in this industry in turn spend their money on many things, from food to entertainment—the *multiplier effect* in operation. The result is that the entire economy benefits.

Farm subsidies are offered for a different reason. At times, weather ruins crops, adversely affecting the farmers' sales and income. At other times, under favorable conditions, farmers produce a surplus. The surplus drives farm prices down, forcing some farmers out of business. In times of surplus crops, the government may arrange for farmers to keep a certain proportion of land out of production; and may even pay (subsidize) them to do this. By subsidizing farmers, the government can help them stay in business.

There are two types of federal subsidies: entitlements and tax subsidies or expenditures.

Entitlements

Entitlements are payments or services to individuals because they are eligible for them by law. Entitlement programs include: social security, unemployment assistance, aid to families with dependent children, food stamps, medicaid, medicare, veterans' benefits and federal retirement benefits. Once such programs become law, agencies make payments to eligible recipients without any appropriation from Congress.

Most of the entitlement programs are *indexed*—that is, payments automatically increase periodically when the consumer price index rises. As the population grows older, more people are becoming eligible for certain kinds of payments. Between 1967 and 1982, the annual cost of entitlement programs grew from about $42 billion to about $340 billion.

Tax subsidies

Tax subsidies are tax benefits given to people and businesses to reduce their annual tax. They include exemptions, deductions, credits, deferrals and special rates to reward socially or economically beneficial activities. Between 1973 and 1983, the amount of federal income lost because of tax subsidies grew from about $65 billion to over $270 billion per year. One reason the tax breaks are hard to hold down is that just about everyone benefits: homeowners, investors, the elderly, parents,

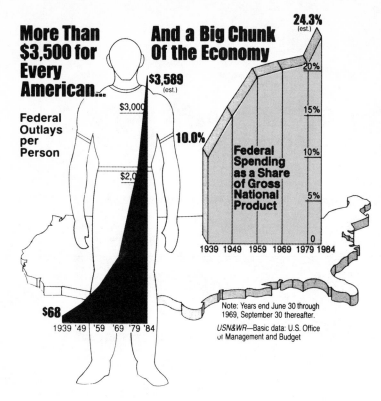

More Than $3,500 for Every American...

Federal Outlays per Person

$3,589 (est.)

$3,000

$2,0

$68

1939 '49 '59 '69 '79 '84

And a Big Chunk Of the Economy

24.3% (est.)

20%

15%

10.0%

10%

5%

Federal Spending as a Share of Gross National Product

0

1939 1949 1959 1969 1979 1984

Note: Years end June 30 through 1969, September 30 thereafter.

USN&WR—Basic data: U.S. Office of Management and Budget

Social subsidies: welfare

A significant percentage of federal subsidies go directly to aid the socially deprived—the poor, aged, blind, and disabled. Federal government aid to these people began in the mid-1930s.

Throughout most of American history, there was no apparent need for assistance from the federal government. Most people lived on family farms and provided much of their own food. Families stayed in one area for generations. The old and infirm were cared for by other family members. The poverty that did exist was equated with criminality. The poor were dispatched to workhouses or county homes where they were required to work long hours at disagreeable tasks that paid little or nothing.

In the late nineteenth and early twentieth centuries, the social fabric of American life began to change. Large cities became giant industrial complexes, fueled by the labor of millions of workers. As young people left rural areas to take jobs in the cities, family ties were broken. Many of the elderly were left to fend for themselves. The growing numbers of industrial workers were totally dependent on the policies of big businesses. If the steel mills, coal mines or railroads shut down in a recession, thousands of people were out of work. On the farm, there had been, at least, food and shelter during bad times. In the cities, there was no

and businesses. Some economists believe that uncollected taxes should not be considered expenditures. Others argue that tax subsidies clutter the tax code, may work at cross-purposes to each other and, sometimes, are irrational and inequitable.

Some of the people entitled to government funds in 1984

People collecting Social Security	36,400,000
People under medicare	29,700,000
Children in school-lunch programs	23,000,000
Medicaid beneficiaries	22,600,000
People receiving food stamps	21,500,000
Members of families receiving Aid to Families With Dependent Children	10,905,000
Workers on unemployment compensation	4,600,000
Veterans or survivors collecting pensions or compensation	4,400,000
Persons in subsidized housing	3,900,000
Aged, blind, disabled receiving aid	3,400,000
Government workers	2,800,000
Military personnel	2,200,000
Civil-service retirees	1,500,000
Military retirees	1,500,000
Railroad-retirement beneficiaries	976,000
Disabled coal miners	413,000

What's more: Millions of Americans are helped by other programs, such as farm-price supports, college-student loans, small-business loans and veterans medical care.

Note: Figures cannot add to a total because many people receive government help under more than one program.

USN&WR—Basic data: U.S. Office of Management and Budget

refuge. The general economic collapse that began in 1929 and led to the Great Depression of the 1930s left more people out of work and in desperate need of assistance than at any other time in American history. A federal *welfare system* became imperative.

Welfare's beginning

The federal government became involved in welfare with the *Federal Emergency Relief Administration* in 1933, which was created to care for the destitute. But the program that eventually grew into today's large program of family aid actually began as an afterthought.

When Congress passed the *Social Security Act* of 1935, it tacked on aid to dependent children. The intent was to place an income floor beneath widows' pensions until the Social Security program became established, then slowly to phase out aid to dependents. Instead, both the number of aid recipients and the amount of money spent climbed, through war and peace, boom and recession.

Expansion of social welfare

Experts blame the increase in welfare on economic and social changes. Automobiles and the construction of good roads made Americans mobile as never before. Family ties loosened. At the same time, millions found themselves qualified for only the lowest-paying jobs in an increasingly complex society.

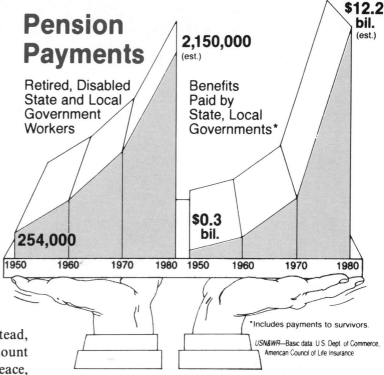

Pension Payments

Retired, Disabled State and Local Government Workers

254,000

2,150,000 (est.)

Benefits Paid by State, Local Governments*

$0.3 bil.

$12.2 bil. (est.)

1950   1960   1970   1980   1950   1960   1970   1980

*Includes payments to survivors.

USN&WR—Basic data: U.S. Dept. of Commerce, American Council of Life Insurance

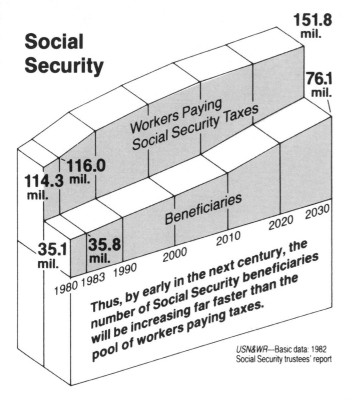

Social Security

151.8 mil.

76.1 mil.

Workers Paying Social Security Taxes

116.0 mil.

114.3 mil.

Beneficiaries

35.1 mil.

35.8 mil.

1980 1983 1990 2000 2010 2020 2030

Thus, by early in the next century, the number of Social Security beneficiaries will be increasing far faster than the pool of workers paying taxes.

USN&WR—Basic data: 1982 Social Security trustees' report

New government programs are credited with improving the standard of living of millions of Americans. Over the years, constantly rising prices have caused a raise in the minimum income level, *the poverty line.* Many people, whose past income classified them as middle-class, today are eligible for public assistance.

During the 1960s, the idea that all people are entitled to a decent standard of living was expressed by a government official. In 1966, Ellen Winston, U.S. Commissioner of Welfare, said: "An affluent society needs and can afford collective social welfare programs which benefit large segments or even its total population by improving the opportunities for happiness and self-development and full participation in the mainstream of activity."

The position that a *minimum standard of living* is a right and not a privilege has been adopted by the government and the courts. As a result, welfare benefits expanded from simple cash payments to other types of aid, including medical care and food stamps.

There are five categories in the present welfare system:

1) *Aid to Families with Dependent Children* (AFDC),
2) aid to the aged, blind, and disabled,
3) health care for the needy, *Medicaid*,
4) food stamps,
5) general assistance.

The programs are administered by state and local governments, but most of the money comes from the federal government.

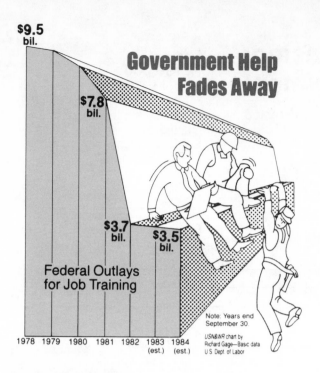

Government Help Fades Away

$9.5 bil.

$7.8 bil.

$3.7 bil.

$3.5 bil.

Federal Outlays for Job Training

Note: Years end September 30

1978 1979 1980 1981 1982 1983 (est.) 1984 (est.)

USN&WR chart by Richard Gage—Basic data U.S Dept. of Labor

Social Security

The *Social Security* system is designed to supplement the decreased income and savings of the elderly. Instituted by the Social Security Act of 1935, the system was designed to be a nationwide retirement insurance program. Workers pay into the fund through a tax deducted from paychecks, under the *Federal Insurance Contributions Act* (F.I.C.A.). The amount of retirement benefits payable to workers depends on their average income during employment years, age at retirement, and family status. A person who averaged $5,000 a year as a worker will receive less than a person who averaged $10,000, but there is an upper limit to the amount of benefits received. Retiring at the age of sixty-two also brings a lower monthly return than retiring at sixty-five. An unmarried individual receives less than one with a dependent spouse. Social Security also provides benefits for survivors of workers who are covered. In 1965, an amendment to the Social Security Act created *Medicare*, a system providing hospital and medical insurance to Americans over sixty-five years old.

Federal pensions

The federal pension fund is another government subsidy. The federal government provides pensions for its employees, both civilians and members of the military. Federal elected officials, such as the President, judges and members of Congress, also receive pensions after serving in office.

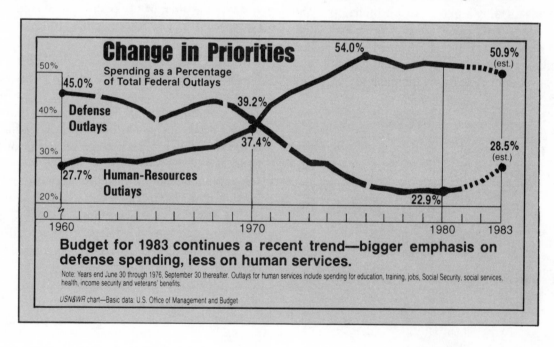

Change in Priorities

Spending as a Percentage of Total Federal Outlays

54.0%

50.9% (est.)

45.0%

Defense Outlays

39.2%

37.4%

27.7% Human-Resources Outlays

28.5% (est.)

22.9%

1960   1970   1980   1983

Budget for 1983 continues a recent trend—bigger emphasis on defense spending, less on human services.

Note: Years end June 30 through 1976, September 30 thereafter. Outlays for human services include spending for education, training, jobs, Social Security, social services, health, income security and veterans' benefits.

USN&WR chart—Basic data: U.S. Office of Management and Budget

Chapter 21

American farm

- *The paradox in American farming is that the more successful the farmer is in growing crops, the lower the price and income.*

- *The small independent farm is being replaced by corporate farms.*

In the colonial period of American history, and in the early days following the Revolution, farming was a way of life. Nine out of ten workers farmed, mostly for the survival of their families. Any crop surplus was sold or exchanged for cloth, tools, and other necessities.

Farming has changed radically. Today, 4 percent of the nation's workers are farmers. This 4 percent produces enough food for themselves, the other 96 percent of Americans, and millions of people in foreign countries.

Throughout American history, the population has continued to rise. At the same time, the number of farms and farmers has fallen sharply. A dramatic rise in farm productivity has enabled today's average farmer to grow enough food and fiber for about sixty people. In 1940, the typical farmer could provide for twelve.

This rise in productivity has been made possible by advances in farm science and technology. Highly specialized machinery has been developed to perform tasks that were formerly done by hand. Crop yields have been increased by improved pesticides, fertilizers, and seeds. Since 1940, food grain output has increased by over 100 percent; vegetable crops, by 33 percent. Farm animals have also been affected by the growth of technology. Cows give 85 percent more milk than in 1940; egg production has increased 300 percent. Animals provide 83 percent more meat.

Modern farm equipment is expensive. To offset these expenses, farmers have increased the acreage under cultivation. A $60,000 tractor, used to culti-vate a 500-acre farm, is more economically viable than one used on a 100-acre farm. As the number of units produced increases (bushels of corn, for example), the cost of production per unit decreases. The farmers with vast acreage and a huge output can afford the expensive, modern equipment that small farmers cannot. As a result, the modern farm is far larger than farms of the past, and far more expensive. Farm assets, which averaged $8,500 per farm in 1947, zoomed to over $125,000 by 1982. Large farms are often referred to as *agribusinesses,* and they are considered to be "factories in the field." Agriculture is the nation's biggest industry with annual sales of over $150 billion.

Supply and demand on the farm

To maintain massive farm enterprise requires a great deal of money. This money is raised by selling farm products. While the costs of running a farm have increased, the prices for farm goods have not increased at the same rate. The demand for farm products is "inelastic." Families consume about the same amount of food, regardless of price. Some foods are more *inelastic* than others. If the price of bread increases, consumers may grumble, but the amount of bread consumed will remain almost constant. Other products are relatively *elastic*. If the price of steaks rises too high, consumers switch to poultry or fish.

There is little that farmers can do to increase the demand for their products. Advertising campaigns encouraging people to "eat more" are unfeasible in a land where many are concerned about the size of

2.4 Million Farmers: Their Impact...

On Jobs

Every farm worker creates jobs for **5.2 other workers** who make things farmers use or who handle farm output. That's about **21 million jobs**, or one fifth of all civilian employment.

On People's Spending

Americans last year spent **$350 billion** on food—one fifth of all personal spending. Of each dollar, farmers got about 35 cents, a sharp drop from 44 cents in 1972. The rest went to packagers, transporters, processors, wholesalers and retailers.

On Government Outlays

Federal outlays to subsidize farmers may reach a record **$21 billion** this year—more than five times as much as in 1981. An additional **$20 billion** is spent on government outlays for food, which tend to prop up prices.

On Foreign Trade

Without farm exports, America's balance-of-trade deficits would be enormously greater. Farm goods account for about **20 percent** of all exports. A farm trade surplus of **$166 billion** since 1972 offset much of the trade deficit in oil and autos.

On Finance

Farm assets, mainly real estate, amount to a bit more than **$1 trillion**—up 61 percent since 1977. In that same period, farmers' debts more than doubled and now total **$218 billion**. It costs farmers $23 billion a year to pay interest on that debt.

On Productivity

Farmers are models of efficiency. Their output per hour of work grew **4.4 percent** a year in 1972-82—more than **six times** the rate of growth among nonfarm businesses. In 1972, one farmer produced food for 53 persons. Today, one farmer feeds 78.

Though they number but 1 percent of the U.S. population, farmers affect the lives and pocketbooks of Americans far out of proportion to their numbers.

USN&WR artwork by Richard Gage

their waistlines. When one segment of the food industry convinces consumers to eat or drink more of its products, it is accomplished at the expense of other products.

Farmers are at the mercy of nature. Too much rain, not enough rain, a sudden hailstorm, a freeze at the wrong time of the year, an infestation of grasshoppers—any of these incidents can ruin a year's crops. On the other hand, if all the conditions are satisfactory, many farmers will have good crops, and the market will be flooded. Prices will go down, which may be good for the consumer, but is a disaster for the farmer.

Who Gets the Food Dollar

Farmer
35¢

Retailer
19¢

Transporter
6¢

Wholesaler
9¢

Processor
31¢

USN&WR—Basic data: U.S. Dept. of Agriculture

The farm problem

The unpredictability of supply and demand and the high cost of modern farming have put many farms on the brink of bankruptcy.

On December 14, 1977, hundreds of tractors rolled down Pennsylvania Avenue in Washington D.C., signaling the start of a national farmer's strike. The farmers were protesting their poor economic position. Farmers are often caught in a vicious economic squeeze, but in the 1980s it reached its worst level in many years.

Farmers have turned to the government for help with their problems. The government has always aided the farmer. In early history, it provided land, built railroads for transporting farm products to market, and subsidized agricultural colleges. Direct aid to stabilize prices came about in 1933, with the creation of the *Agricultural Adjustment Administration.* Its purpose was to halt the decline in farm prices during the Depression. The AAA was empowered to enter into agreements with

farmers to reduce the amount of their cultivated acreage. In this way, the total output of wheat, cotton, corn and tobacco was decreased. Farmers were paid *subsidies* to compensate for the land they didn't farm. Reducing the acreage planted had the desired effect. Farm prices began to rise.

In 1938, a new AAA bill was passed. This law provided for additional benefits to farmers who held acreage out of production. It guaranteed farmers that if they could not sell their crops, the government would store their goods and "lend" them the money their stored crops were worth. If prices rose, the farmers could buy back their products and resell them on the open markets. If prices remained below the level guaranteed by the government, the farmers kept the "loan."

The price level guaranteed by the government is the *parity price.* Parity insures that the buying power of a farmer's goods remains the same in a changing economy. In fixing parity, government economists return to the price levels of 1910-1914, a time called the "golden era of agriculture."

How parity works

The *Department of Agriculture* compares current prices for crops and livestock with those of the 1910-1914 era. It then compares farm expenses with those of that same period. If costs of running a farm have doubled, prices should also double. If it cost $2.00 to grow a bushel of wheat in 1910-1914 and wheat sold for $2.50 a bushel, and it costs $4.00 to raise a bushel of wheat today, wheat should sell for $5.00.

In recent years, parity level has been less than

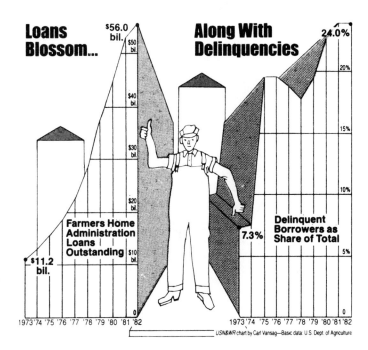

Loans Blossom... Along With Delinquencies

$56.0 bil.

$11.2 bil.

Farmers Home Administration Loans Outstanding

Delinquent Borrowers as Share of Total

7.3%

24.0%

1973 '74 '75 '76 '77 '78 '79 '80 '81 '82

1973 '74 '75 '76 '77 '78 '79 '80 '81 '82

USN&WR chart by Carl Vansag—Basic data: U.S. Dept. of Agriculture

100 percent. Farmers have asked that parity levels be returned to 100 percent, but government economists claim that if parity were returned to 100 percent, food prices to consumers would rise 20-25 percent.

In early America, farmers marketed their goods directly, avoiding *middlemen*. Then, as many farmers moved west, it became necessary for others to assume the role of processing and delivering farm goods to the populous markets in the East. Middlemen handled more and more farm commodities. The advent of supermarkets further widened the gap between farmer and consumer.

Price supports

There are several methods to achieve a desired parity level. Primarily, the government will guarantee a price for a commodity, or several commodities. As a result of this higher price, consumer demand will decrease. At the set price, the market supply is greater than demand. The government responds by filling this demand gap: It buys up the surplus product. In effect, the government provides enough demand for the farm products to maintain the desired price level. What happens to the surplus? The government can store grains in bins, provide food for school lunch programs, distribute it as aid to underfed nations, or sell it to other countries.

American farmers help feed many people

Many countries of the world depend on U.S. agricultural products to help feed their people. In turn, American farmers depend on commodity exports to stay in business. American farmers export over $40 billion of their products annually, far more than any other nation. Every year the United States accounts for about 70 percent of the corn, 45 percent of the wheat, and 80 percent of the soybeans traded on world markets. Thanks to the impressive productivity of the agricultural industry, America is the world's "breadbasket."

It is mainly agriculture that keeps the U.S. *balance of trade* from sinking deeper into a deficit. America's powerful agricultural position is sometimes used as a tool of foreign affairs. The Soviet Union is a large purchaser of American grain. Upon occasion, there has been political opposition to selling grain to Russia. An *embargo* in grain sales to Russia hurts American farmers.

Although the prices farmers receive for corn, soybeans, and wheat have risen in recent years, their costs have gone up even more. The price of fuel and fertilizer soared during the early 1980s. To pay the bills and maintain their equipment, farmers increased their borrowing. The high interest rates on these loans added greatly to the farmer's problems.

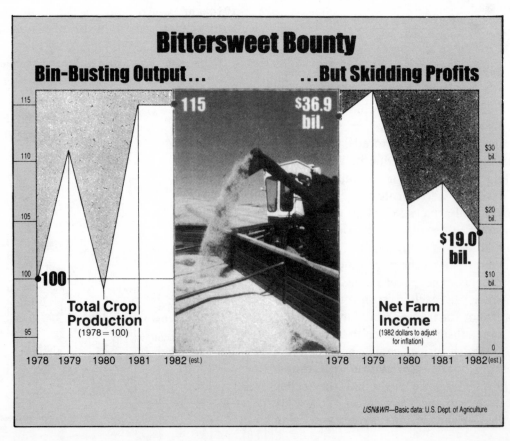

Bittersweet Bounty

Bin-Busting Output... ...But Skidding Profits

Total Crop Production (1978 = 100)

1978 1979 1980 1981 1982 (est.)

Net Farm Income (1982 dollars to adjust for inflation)

1978 1979 1980 1981 1982 (est.)

USN&WR—Basic data: U.S. Dept. of Agriculture

Chapter 22

Foreign trade

- *The U.S. is a large world trader and our economy is directly dependent on imports and exports.*

- *The U.S. is losing "comparative advantage" in some areas, but gaining in others.*

As big, rich and varied as it is, the U.S. economy cannot efficiently produce all the goods and services desired by its citizens. Dependence on products from abroad grows yearly. The United States is primarily an *exporter* (seller to another country) of manufactured goods and an *importer* (buyer from other countries) of raw materials. Still, this country exports large amounts of raw materials and foodstuffs while importing a variety of manufactured items.

As American industries have grown, so has the volume of exported manufactured goods increased. Today, they make up 75-80 percent of U.S. shipments abroad; farm products account for the remainder.

Exports are credited with supporting one of every eight jobs in American factories. One-sixth of everything that is grown or made in America is sold abroad. In 1970, just four percent of the nation's total output involved exports. Now they account for about twice that.

While more U.S. production is devoted to export trade, the American share of total world exports has decreased in recent years. At the same time, the amount of goods imported to the United States has risen sharply.

In 1981, the United States imported about $273 billion worth of goods. It exported about $120 billion, including computers and aircraft, together with grain and other agricultural products. The shortfall in exports, known as a *trade deficit*, was nearly $39 billion. The comparison between the value of goods a nation sells (exports) to others

and the value of those it buys (imports) is called the *balance of trade*. If exports are greater than imports, then there is a *trade surplus*. In recent years, the United States has been having a *trade deficit*.

Importance of trade

Foreign trade is a method whereby the demand for more and better goods can be satisfied at lower costs. Small countries, with only a few economic resources, cannot hope to maintain adequate standards of living without engaging in international trade. Large countries, such as the United States and the Soviet Union, are less dependent upon international trade because of their diversified resources. Still, even the economic giants need and depend upon foreign trade.

The U.S.S.R. must import sizable quantities of grain to help feed its growing population. The U.S. must buy petroleum and a variety of minerals and raw materials from abroad. Many U.S. industries would be destroyed or seriously handicapped without imports.

The tremendous development of the U.S. economy has been due in large part to the abundance of natural resources. The expansive growth of American manufacturing rapidly placed new demands on natural resources. The massive array of consumer goods and capital equipment that flood the marketplace today, along with the imcomparable ease with which we heat or cool homes and buildings, stimulates an increasing demand for natural resources—coal, oil, gas, and many nonfuel minerals.

Dependency on other nations

With about 6 percent of the world's population, the United States consumes one-third of the world's mineral output each year—including nearly 60 percent of all natural gas, about 35 percent of the non-communist world's silver and aluminum, and more than 30 percent of all lead.

This country relies increasingly upon other nations to supply metals, minerals, and other substances. The U.S. imports all natural rubber, manganese, cobalt, chromium, platinum, aluminum, tin and nickel.

The United States is involved in a competition with other nations for these scarce resources. The demand of other industrial nations is expected to be even greater than America's. As developing nations industrialize their economies, they will hold on to more of their own raw materials. This competition among consuming nations tends to drive prices up.

The oil crisis. An especially notable decline in American self-sufficiency is in the area of energy resources—coal, oil, and gas. The United States has about 30 percent of the world's coal reserves, but mining it presents environmental problems. Oil, other petroleum products, and natural gas are widely used to fuel homes, automobiles, and industry.

The United States has become increasingly dependent upon foreign producers for petroleum. In the early 1970s, the oil-exporting nations placed an embargo on their products, then raised prices considerably. Less fuel was available for industry, transportation companies, home heating, and auto-

mobiles. The prices of goods requiring large amounts of fuel in their production increased sharply.

America's crude-oil imports increased to more than one-third of the nation's total consumption by the mid-seventies. This dependence on imported oil made the United States increasingly subject to the international crude-oil *cartel*, OPEC, (the Organization of Petroleum Exporting Countries). The function of a cartel is to regulate the purchasing, production, or marketing of a product to the mutual advantage of its members.

Law of comparative advantage

Countries import some items and export others because it is more efficient. The *law of comparative advantage* states that some countries can produce certain goods more cheaply than others. They may have better access to raw materials or markets, special skills, or workers who can produce the same output at lower wages (or more output for the same wages).

In practice, the United States and most other countries import some things that they also produce. Sales of foreign autos, clothing, shoes, and steel are just a few examples of how the market tests the relative ability of nations to produce efficiently.

Changing technology affects the ebb and flow of trade. At one time, Swiss watches held a large share of the U.S. market. American watchmaking declined drastically. Then the invention of the digital watch shifted the industry to Japan and the Far East.

The role of trade in the economy is growing. In 1960, imports and exports together were equal to 10 percent of total U.S. goods and services. By 1977, that figure was up to 19 percent.

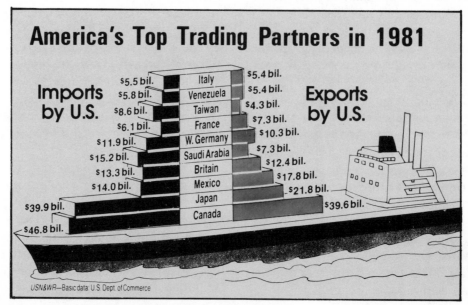

America's Top Trading Partners in 1981

Imports by U.S. / Exports by U.S.

	Imports by U.S.	Exports by U.S.
Italy	$5.5 bil.	$5.4 bil.
Venezuela	$5.8 bil.	$5.4 bil.
Taiwan	$8.6 bil.	$4.3 bil.
France	$6.1 bil.	$7.3 bil.
W. Germany	$11.9 bil.	$10.3 bil.
Saudi Arabia	$15.2 bil.	$7.3 bil.
Britain	$13.3 bil.	$12.4 bil.
Mexico	$14.0 bil.	$17.8 bil.
Japan	$39.9 bil.	$21.8 bil.
Canada	$46.8 bil.	$39.6 bil.

USN&WR—Basic data: U.S. Dept. of Commerce

What We Buy and Sell

10 Biggest Imports in 1981 . . .

Petroleum	$78.5 bil.
Motor vehicles, parts	$27.4 bil.
Iron, steel	$12.1 bil.
Electrical machinery, parts	$ 9.4 bil.
TV, radio, sound products	$ 9.2 bil.
Clothing	$ 8.0 bil.
Nonferrous metals	$ 7.1 bil.
Natural gas	$ 5.8 bil.
Chemicals	$ 5.6 bil.
Special-purpose machinery	$ 5.3 bil.

. . . And 10 Biggest Exports

Motor vehicles, parts	$16.2 bil.
Aircraft, parts	$14.7 bil.
Industrial machinery	$11.5 bil.
Electrical machinery	$11.5 bil.
Office machinery, computers	$ 9.8 bil.
Power-generating machinery	$ 9.5 bil.
Chemicals	$ 9.2 bil.
Corn	$ 8.0 bil.
Wheat	$ 7.8 bil.
Soybeans	$ 6.2 bil.

USN&WR—Basic data: U.S. Dept. of Commerce

The multinational corporation

Foreign trade is not the only way the American economy is tied to the global economic system. All around the world, U.S. firms have invested in mines, factories, and stores. Today, these investments are worth more than $225 billion. Much of this investment is by *multinational corporations* who do business around the world without much regard for national boundaries.

American investments abroad are not only advantageous to investors, but they are a payoff to the rest of the economy. Foreign investments stimulate production and higher living standards in other countries. These nations, particularly the developing nations, are able to carry out more trade with the United States, importing American goods that they need, and exporting raw materials for industry in this country.

The multinational corporation, with branches and factories in many countries, symbolizes the way in which the economies of the United States and other nations are being knit more closely together.

U.S. trade policy

How can the large trade deficits of the United States be reduced or prevented? Some people suggest limiting foreign imports. They believe that American producers need *protection* from foreign producers who are able to sell merchandise more cheaply than we can. The principal reason cited is the lower cost of foreign labor. Requests for protection come from American makers of textiles, clothing, sugar, shoes, automobiles, and ball bearings—to name a few—and from labor unions in these industries.

Government officials are not overly concerned about the recent deficit, and economists are rarely influenced by the protectionist argument. The deficit, officials point out, is no indication that American industry is unable to compete effectively in world markets; if it were, then there would be cause for alarm. Many American industries remain competitive. The trade deficits incurred in recent years are due mostly to America's large appetite for imported oil, without which the United States would run a trade surplus.

In those cases where our industries are not competitive, the economy as a whole is actually better off importing products. Consumers benefit from lower-priced goods, and if resources (capital and labor) were allocated to more efficient industries, American businesses and workers would also benefit, from greater sales and higher wages.

The argument that low foreign wages result in unfair competition, and endanger the jobs of American workers, is debatable. An industry's ability to compete depends on several factors: One of these is low wages, but others are the cost of materials, machinery, and borrowing money. Likewise, labor productivity, management efficiency, and technology are important production factors. Wages should increase as productivity increases. In those industries where labor productivity is higher than average—such as machinery, aircraft, and chemicals—the United States competes easily in world markets, despite high wages. When higher wages are not accompanied by greater productivity—as is the case with shoe, television, and automobile production—American industry is in trouble.

Protecting domestic industry

The United States does protect some industries from foreign imports. The most commonly used barrier to foreign trade is the *tariff*—a tax imposed by the government on imported products. Another major measure is the *import quota*, which limits the total volume or total value of particular goods allowed into the country. America's trading policy has selectively used tariffs and quotas to benefit industry and the economy.

During the colonial period of American history, foreign trade followed the classic pattern of developing nations: Manufactured goods were imported from Europe and paid for by exports of farm products and raw materials. The import tariffs were modest (about 5 percent) and regarded chiefly as a source of revenue.

During the early years of the new nation, tariff duties were increased to protect *infant* manufacturing industries—largely New England manufacturers and the textile industry. Southern planters and farmers of cotton, tobacco, and rice feared that high duties would damage their profitable sales in England.

During the 1800s, tariff rates fluctuated, as one interest group or another influenced Congress. Tariff barriers were also influenced by the condition of the federal treasury: Higher duties were used as a source of revenue in times of need. After the Civil War and through the early 1900s, Congress enacted high tariffs to protect American industry. The **McKinley Tariff** of 1890 was, at the time, the highest tariff in the nation's history. With the **Tariff Act** of 1897, protective rates reached a new high, averaging 57 percent.

U.S. Jobs That Depend Upon Trade

	1982 Trade-Related Jobs	Percentage of total Employment
Alabama	70,800	5.0%
Alaska	5,700	3.4%
Arizona	47,400	4.5%
Arkansas	38,000	4.4%
California	518,000	5.1%
Colorado	46,500	3.4%
Connecticut	107,900	7.2%
Delaware	14,200	5.5%
District of Columbia	4,800	1.6%
Florida	141,700	3.9%
Georgia	107,900	4.9%
Hawaii	6,800	1.8%
Idaho	14,300	3.7%
Illinois	285,800	5.8%
Indiana	143,800	6.3%
Iowa	56,600	4.2%
Kansas	44,400	4.0%
Kentucky	57,300	4.0%
Louisiana	52,600	3.4%
Maine	18,500	4.2%
Maryland	59,100	3.1%
Massachusetts	157,300	6.0%
Michigan	237,000	6.6%
Minnesota	85,100	4.2%
Mississippi	36,800	4.0%
Missouri	90,500	4.3%
Montana	5,900	1.7%
Nebraska	19,800	2.7%
Nevada	5,500	1.6%
New Hampshire	23,600	5.8%
New Jersey	176,900	5.5%
New Mexico	7,900	1.6%
New York	377,100	5.2%
North Carolina	154,600	6.1%
North Dakota	6,300	2.2%
Ohio	298,900	6.6%
Oklahoma	44,300	3.5%
Oregon	58,700	5.1%
Pennsylvania	285,500	5.9%
Rhode Island	30,600	7.5%
South Carolina	79,000	6.2%
South Dakota	6,400	2.0%
Tennessee	94,100	5.1%
Texas	267,200	4.4%
Utah	17,900	3.1%
Vermont	10,800	4.8%
Virginia	91,900	4.0%
Washington	114,100	6.7%
West Virginia	28,600	4.3%
Wisconsin	119,800	5.7%
Wyoming	2,800	1.3%
United States	**4,778,900**	**5.0%**

Note: Employment figures are for manufactured exports only.
USN&WR—Basic data: U.S. Dept. of Commerce

Industrial development was explosive near the turn of the century, and treasury surpluses grew. Protectionists attributed much of this growth to the high barriers, but the surplus spurred sentiments

124

for freer trade. In 1913, President Wilson called a special session of Congress to change tariff policy. Rates were lowered from about 40 percent to 29 percent.

After World War I, protectionist sentiments drove tariffs up again, initially to aid a struggling farm industry, although manufacturers succeeded in including many of their products. In 1930, the *Hawley-Smoot Tariff*, one of the highest in U.S. history was enacted. This set off an outburst of tariff-making activity around the world.

The depression of the 1930s also helped trigger a barrage of tariff increases and import quotas throughout trading nations. By 1932, world trade dropped to about one-third of the 1929 level. Instead of stimulating economic development, the trade barriers contributed to the downward spiral—dramatic evidence that world economies were *interdependent*.

Under President Franklin Roosevelt, the *Reciprocal Trade Agreements Act* of 1934 was passed, beginning a reduction of tariffs and other barriers around the world. This act gave the President authority to negotiate *reciprocal trade agreements*, lowering tariff duties by as much as 50 percent. The act was renewed several times, with the addition of even more liberal trade-agreement powers for the President. By 1939, U.S. foreign trade had risen 30 percent. From 1934 to 1961, the value of international trade increased fifteen times, as the average U.S. tariffs dropped from nearly 50 percent to 12 percent.

By the 1940s, many nations began to take a global view of economic trade. Allowing for some selective restrictions, nations saw that free trade was an economic advantage to everyone in the long run. As part of an effort to ease post-World War II economic problems, the U.S. and 22 nations established the *General Agreement on Tariffs and Trade* (GATT) in 1947, at Geneva, Switzerland.

Directions of Merchandise Trade

JAPAN $21.8 bil. U.S. $51.4 bil. EUROPEAN COMMON MARKET $37.6 bil. $41.4 bil.

Note: Figures are for 1981.
USN&WR—Basic data: U.S. Dept. of Commerce

Where U.S. Is Ahead in Trade . . .

Merchandise Trade in 1981

	Exports	Imports	Balance
Nonelectrical machinery, parts	$ 41,043 mil.	$ 15,846 mil.	$25,197 mil.
Food, feed, beverages	$ 37,888 mil.	$ 18,113 mil.	$19,775 mil.
Chemicals	$ 17,962 mil.	$ 5,966 mil.	$11,996 mil.
Aircraft, engines, parts	$ 13,467 mil.	$ 3,749 mil.	$ 9,718 mil.
Industrial supplies, materials	$ 25,677 mil.	$ 17,804 mil.	$ 7,873 mil.
Computers, office equipment	$ 10,562 mil.	$ 5,204 mil.	$ 5,358 mil.
Other electrical machinery	$ 12,920 mil.	$ 9,452 mil.	$ 3,468 mil.
Trucks, buses, auto parts	$ 13,982 mil.	$ 11,968 mil.	$ 2,014 mil.
Other items	$ 16,887 mil.	$ 13,906 mil.	$ 2,981 mil.

. . . And Where It's Behind

Petroleum, related products	$ 10,725 mil.	$ 82,058 mil.	− $71,333 mil.
Automobiles	$ 4,005 mil.	$ 17,768 mil.	− $13,763 mil.
Other consumer durable products . .	$ 6,975 mil.	$ 20,766 mil.	− $13,791 mil.
Consumer nondurable products	$ 8,336 mil.	$ 14,928 mil.	− $ 6,592 mil.
Iron and steel	$ 3,390 mil.	$ 11,262 mil.	− $ 7,872 mil.
Other metals	$ 9,920 mil.	$ 12,514 mil.	− $ 2,594 mil.
Total	$233,739 mil.	$261,305 mil.	−$27,566 mil.

Note: Totals may not add because of rounding.
USN&WR—Basic data: U.S. Dept. of Commerce

This agreement established a forum and procedure for nations to negotiate trade agreements. The United States concluded exchanges with these other countries in less than seven months.

The expansion of international trade agreements continued. The so-called *Kennedy Round* of negotiations that began in May, 1964 and ended in June 1967, was the most extensive negotiation. As a result of this agreement and other efforts under the *GATT treaty*, the United States achieved the lowest general tariff rates in its history.

Most people recognize the benefits of international trade. With it, nations enjoy a wider array of higher quality goods than when there are trade restrictions.

Chapter 23

Balancing our accounts

> • *In balancing accounts, the U.S. has had a deficit for a majority of years in the last decade.*
>
> • *The U.S. is still an industrial giant, but is facing competition from other growing economies in the world.*

In transactions with other nations, accounts are kept to determine how much money nations owe each other. This is known as *balance of payments*. The trade account (*balance of trade*) is the major element in America's balance of payments. The United States has been running a substantial *trade deficit* in recent years, but the balance of payments includes many favorable transactions with other nations.

The balance of payments includes, in addition to imports and exports, many items, such things as money spent for travel by tourists and the cost of transporting goods by ships and airplanes. When the entire balance of payments account is reviewed—including earnings on investments by American firms around the world and capital invested by foreign investors in U.S. companies, the deficit is considerably less than when considering trade alone.

The United States's balance of payments deficit started during the decade of the 1960s. A deficit was incurred in seven of the ten years. There was pressure to reduce spending abroad. Steps were taken to discourage foreign travel, American business investments abroad, and the number of American civilians employed by our industries in other countries. The government also encouraged other nations to buy more from the United States, while encouraging American business firms to sell

more in international markets—policies it has continued to pursue in recent years.

International exchange

To keep all international transactions flowing smoothly, a foreign-exchange market has developed. Widely spaced financial centers, in cities including London, New York, and Hong Kong, are linked electronically to form one huge market. To see why such a market is needed, consider the case of an American firm that imports Scotch whiskey from Britain and has to pay for the purchase in British pounds:

The U.S. firm usually has only dollars on hand. To complete the transaction, the importer has to exchange dollars for pounds in the foreign-exchange market. By doing this, he increases the supply of dollars on the open market and reduces the supply of pounds.

At the same time, British businessmen are exchanging pounds for dollars in order to buy things from the United States, or to make investments here.

Exchange rates. The number of dollars it takes to purchase a single British pound is established by the exchange rate, which varies constantly. When the dollar is rising against the pound, it takes fewer dollars to buy the same number of pounds. When the dollar is falling, the opposite is true.

What causes these shifts? It is the law of supply and demand as it applies to the number of dollars in world markets.

When the United States runs a deficit in its trade and investment accounts with the rest of the world, the supply of dollars in the hands of foreign traders increases. Other things being equal, the exchange rate of the dollar then tends to decline. The opposite happens when the United States runs a payment surplus.

Governments are concerned about exchange rates. Sharp changes have a major impact on economic activity. When the exchange rate declines, it takes fewer pounds, marks, yen, and other currencies to buy one U.S. dollar. This means foreign buyers need less of their own currencies to pay for American goods, so they are likely to buy more. Foreign buyers usually pass such savings on to their own customers; as a result, the prices of American exports fall in other countries even though there has been no change in prices here at home. Thus, the weak dollar can be good news for exporting industries and their workers. The lower prices make U.S. goods more competitive with foreign-made goods, so that American companies can sell more abroad.

A decline in the value of the dollar simultaneously raises the cost of the goods that the United States imports, because it takes more dollars to buy a mark, yen, pound, or franc. The costlier imports add to inflationary pressures at home.

The opposite happens when the dollar gains in value against other currencies. Imports become cheaper and are encouraged; exports become more expensive and run into stiffer competition.

World money standards

In the not-too-distant past, currency exchange rates were set at fixed levels. They were changed only when a nation chose to devalue its currency.

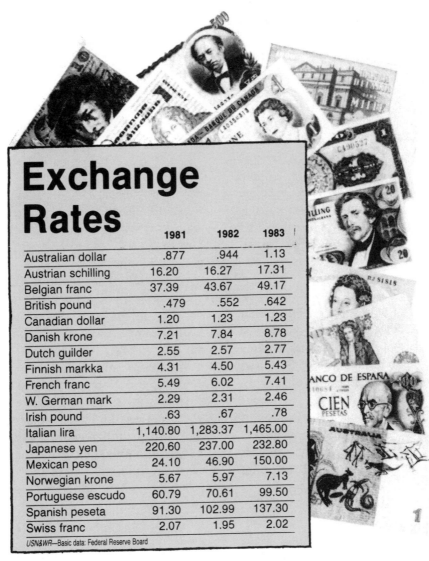

Exchange Rates	1981	1982	1983
Australian dollar	.877	.944	1.13
Austrian schilling	16.20	16.27	17.31
Belgian franc	37.39	43.67	49.17
British pound	.479	.552	.642
Canadian dollar	1.20	1.23	1.23
Danish krone	7.21	7.84	8.78
Dutch guilder	2.55	2.57	2.77
Finnish markka	4.31	4.50	5.43
French franc	5.49	6.02	7.41
W. German mark	2.29	2.31	2.46
Irish pound	.63	.67	.78
Italian lira	1,140.80	1,283.37	1,465.00
Japanese yen	220.60	237.00	232.80
Mexican peso	24.10	46.90	150.00
Norwegian krone	5.67	5.97	7.13
Portuguese escudo	60.79	70.61	99.50
Spanish peseta	91.30	102.99	137.30
Swiss franc	2.07	1.95	2.02

USN&WR—Basic data: Federal Reserve Board

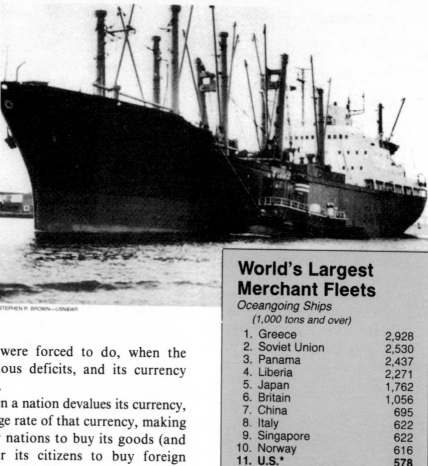

World's Largest Merchant Fleets
Oceangoing Ships
(1,000 tons and over)

1.	Greece	2,928
2.	Soviet Union	2,530
3.	Panama	2,437
4.	Liberia	2,271
5.	Japan	1,762
6.	Britain	1,056
7.	China	695
8.	Italy	622
9.	Singapore	622
10.	Norway	616
11.	**U.S.***	**578**
12.	Spain	509
13.	W. Germany	473
14.	Netherlands	444
15.	Cyprus	395

*Includes government-owned ships.
USN&WR—Basic data: National Maritime Council

This they did, or were forced to do, when the nation ran continuous deficits, and its currency was priced too high.

Devaluation. When a nation devalues its currency, it lowers the exchange rate of that currency, making it cheaper for other nations to buy its goods (and more expensive for its citizens to buy foreign products). Because of its balance-of-payments problems, Great Britain, for a number of years, had to monitor the value of the pound. On several occasions it was forced to devalue the pound, encouraging other nations to buy British products.

For years, the situation in the United States was just the opposite of Great Britain's: America had a solid trade and payments surplus. In the 1960s, the tide changed for the U.S. At first, the trade surplus turned to a deficit, but receipts from services and other international accounts still left the United States with a favorable balance of payments. Gradually this eroded. Today, America runs a payments deficit.

Breaking from the gold standard. The dollar and the pound, along with gold, were considered the primary international currencies by trading countries. Nations were content to hold U.S. dollars because they knew they could be used in trade; in any case, the United States would exchange dollars for gold at the rate of $35 an ounce. But as nations held more dollars and the U.S. payments deficit increased, many decided to exchange their dollars for gold. Our gold supply dwindled and the dollar became overvalued at the fixed exchange rates.

This situation aggravated our trading position. At the fixed exchange rates, our goods were overpriced. In 1971, the United States devalued the dollar by raising the price of gold from $35 an ounce to $38 an ounce. In other words, the dollar was worth less in gold. At the same time, the United States announced that foreign-held dollars could no longer be freely exchanged for gold.

As a result of devaluation, dollars bought less in foreign countries, but American exports were cheaper for foreign buyers. Still, the payments position worsened, and official gold prices were raised to $42.22 an ounce in 1973—a second devaluation of the dollar.

When a nation attempts to improve its world currency position, it does so at the expense of other nations and their currency. After the U.S. devalued its dollar, most major nations responded by abandoning their attempts to keep exchange rates set at the old fixed rates. At this point, the relative values of the various currencies—the pound, yen, franc, mark, and others—were established daily by market forces. Today, there are *floating rates.*

THE INTERNATIONAL MONETARY FUND AT A GLANCE

WHO BELONGS TO THE IMF—

Over 140 countries: most of the non-Communist world, plus Rumania, Yugoslavia, Cambodia, Laos and Vietnam.

WHAT THE FUND DOES—

1. **Oversees foreign-exchange market** to make sure countries do not manipulate currency-exchange rates.
2. **Makes short-term loans** to member countries that are running deficits in their payments with the rest of the world.
3. **Advises borrowers** on how to improve their balance of payments.
4. **Creates its own money,** known as Special Drawing Rights.
5. **Sells gold** from its reserves and uses part of the proceeds for interest-free loans to needy members.

WHO RUNS IT—

Appointed managing director

Board of governors, one from each member country, usually its finance minister, meets once a year.

Interim committee of 20 finance ministers sets policy between sessions of the board of governors.

Executive board of 20 civil servants elected by the members functions full time in Washington, passing on loans and other operations.

The International Monetary Fund

With floating exchange rates, the fate of a nation's world trade is left to forces in the market. This fuels the temptation for a nation to improve its trading position in times of economic stress by charging tariffs, imposing quotas or tampering with the value of its currency.

The International Monetary Fund (IMF) was established to facilitate world trade. It is charged with several functions, among them, monitoring foreign exchange markets. It also makes loans to countries in financial difficulty so that they will be less likely to set up trade barriers or manipulate exchange rates.

The IMF also sponsors a new type of international currency called *special drawing rights* (SDRs). This so-called paper gold is transferred among nations by bookkeeping entries.

SDRs reduce the reliance of trade on gold, dollars and other heavily used currencies. In effect, they could become the true global currency shared by all nations in world trade. The use of SDRs also would discourage speculation and wild exchange rate fluctuations of individual national currencies.

The result of this is that the health of the U.S. economy is affected to a greater extent than ever before by events overseas. And other countries are even more affected by business trends in the United States.

International trade and finance is a major influence in bringing nations closer together. Nations are now interdependent. International economics is bringing us closer to being "one world."

Growth of the Industrial Giants

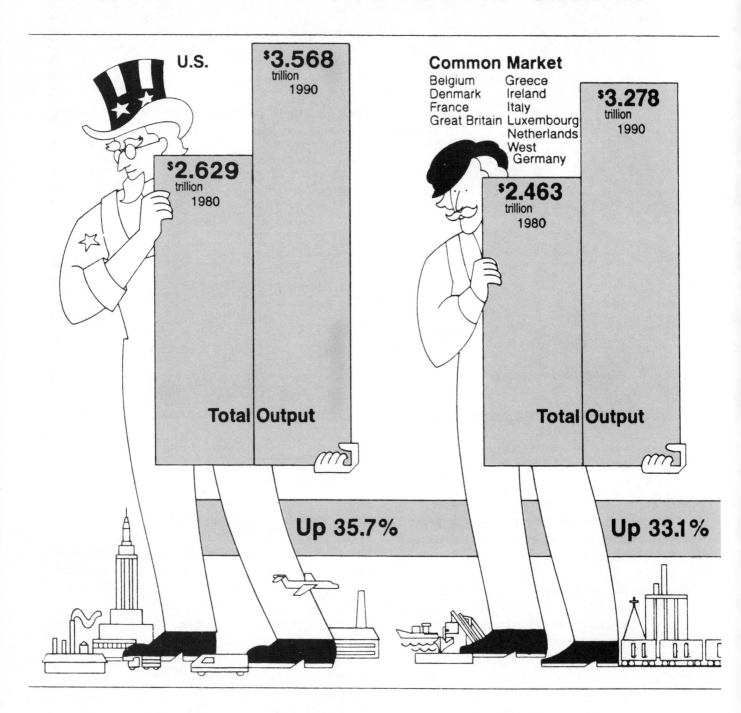

U.S.

$3.568 trillion 1990

$2.629 trillion 1980

Total Output

Up 35.7%

Common Market

Belgium
Denmark
France
Great Britain

Greece
Ireland
Italy
Luxembourg
Netherlands
West
Germany

$3.278 trillion 1990

$2.463 trillion 1980

Total Output

Up 33.1%

Total output of goods and services, adjusted for inflation, if trends of past decade continue until 1990—

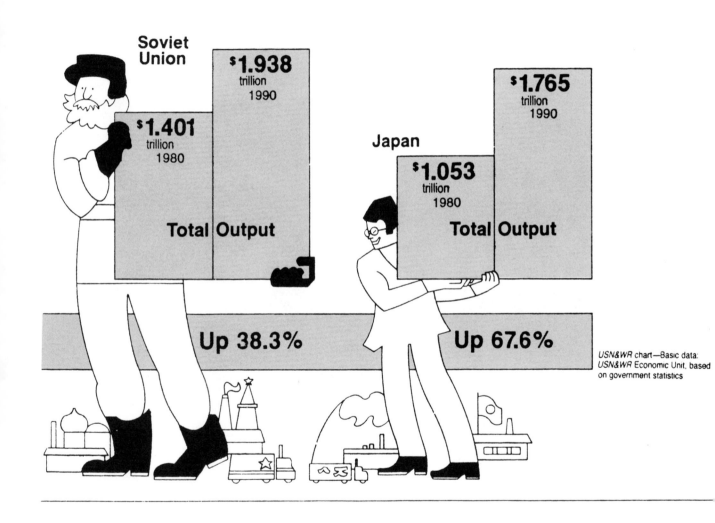

Soviet Union

$1.938 trillion 1990

$1.401 trillion 1980

Total Output

Japan

$1.765 trillion 1990

$1.053 trillion 1980

Total Output

Up 38.3%

Up 67.6%

USN&WR chart—Basic data: *USN&WR* Economic Unit, based on government statistics

INDEX

A

AFL. *See* American Federation of Labor
Ability to pay, 68
Abundance, 1, 2
Accelerator effect, 86-8, 101
Ad valorem tax, 74
Advertising, 17
Affluence, 82, 106
Agency shop, 53
Aggregate demand, 84, 99, 101
Agricultural Adjustment Administration, 119
Agriculture, U.S., 39-44, 45, 117-20
Aid to dependent children, 115
American Federation of Labor, 53
Antimonopoly legislation, 46
Arbitration, labor, 54
Assets, 38
Automation, 50, 111
Automobiles: industry, 86, 122, 124; ownership, 2

B

Balance of payments, 38, 126
Balance of trade, 120, 121, 126
Banking, 56-60, 84, 102-3
Bankruptcy, 26, 27
Base year, defined, 20
Benefits received, 68
Black Americans, income, 108
Blacklisting, 53
Bonds: corporate, 33-4, 38; government, 61, 100, 102
Boycott, 54
Budget, federal, 63-7, 116
Business, 30-8: cycle, 91; enterprises, defined, 1, 5, 30; family, 36-7; terms, defined, 38; types, 31

C

CIO. *See* Congress of Industrial Organizations
Capital, defined, 7, 38. *See also* Investment
Capitalism, 10-13. *See also* Free enterprise; Private enterprise
Cartel, 122
Cash reserve, 58
Caveat emptor, 17
Checkbook money, 56, 58
Child labor, 49
Circular flow of money, 77
Clayton Antitrust Act, 46, 52
Closed shop, 53
Collective bargaining, 52, 54
Commercial banks, 58-9
Commodities market, 34, 38
Common Market, European, 130
Communism, 12
Community service jobs, 111
Company unions, 53
Competition, 11-12, 45, 122
Complementary goods, 41
Congress of Industrial Organizations, 54
Consumer price index (CPI), 4, 19-21
Consumer Product Safety Commission, 17
Consumer protection agencies, 17-18
Consumerism, 15-18

Consumers, defined, 5, 15
Consumption, 77-8
Cooperative, business, 31
Corporate: debt, 28, 33-4; subsidy, 48; taxes, 70, 74
Corporations, 30-1, 45
Corporations, multinational, 123
Cost of living, 19-24, 108. *See also* Consumer price index
Cost of production, 7, 40, 42
Craft union, 53
Credit, 25-9, 38
Credit cards, 26
Currency, U.S., 56-9, 126-7; World, 126-8. *See also* Dollar

D

Das Kapital, 10
Debt: consumer, 25, 29; corporate, 28, 33-4; government, 27-8, 83, 100-1
Decreasing returns, 35
Defense spending, 116
Deficit financing, 38, 101
Demand, 15, 16: deposits, 58, 59; elasticity, 42-4, 117; shifts, 41-2, 45; side, 103-4. *See also* Supply and demand
Democratic socialism, 13-14
Dept. of Agriculture, 119
Depletion allowance, 74
Depreciation, 38, 74
Depression, 38, 92
Depression, the Great, 93-7, 99-100, 109
Devaluation, currency, 38, 128
Discount rate, 38, 58, 103
Discrimination, race and sex, 106
Disequilibrium, economic, 84
Disinvestment, 88
Disposable income (DI), 38, 76
Distribution of goods, 5
Distribution of income, 105-8
Dividends, 31, 38
Dollar: buying power, 2, 19, 21; exchange rate, 126-7. *See also* Currency, U.S.

E

EFT. *See* Electronic funds transfer
Earnings, 22-4, 106, 108. *See also* Wages
Economic classes, 105-8
Economic cycles, 91-3, 99
Economic goods. *See* Goods; Manufactured goods
Economic growth, 82-90. *See also* U.S. economy, growth
Economic indicators, 3, 4
Economic questions, 5-7
Economic recovery, 91, 92
Economic services. *See* Services
Economic stability, 99-104
Economic systems, 10-14
Economics, science of, 1-3
Economies, mixed, 14
Education, 2, 68, 106, 108. *See also* Jobs, training
Elasticity of demand, 42-4
Electronic funds transfer, 56
Embargoes, 120
Employer-worker relationship, 49-55

Employment, 84. *See also* Jobs; Unemployment
Employment Act (1946), 100
Employment index, 4
Energy resources, 122
Engels, Friedrich, 10
Entitlements, 113
Entrepreneur, defined, 7, 30
Environmental problems, 84, 86
Equilibrium, economic, 84
Equilibrium price, 41
Equity capital, 32
Eurodollars, 38
Europe, economies, 12-13, 130-1
Exchange rates, 38, 126-7
Excise tax, 74
Expenditures, 77
Exports, U.S., 78, 120, 121-5

F

FOMC. *See* Federal Open Market Committee
FTC. *See* Federal Trade Commission
Fair Labor Standards Act, 49
Family income, 15, 25-6, 105-8
Farm subsidies, 118, 119
Farmers' strike (1977), 119
Farming. *See* Agriculture
Federal Assistance. *See* Public service employment; Subsidies; Welfare
Federal Emergency Relief Administration, 115
Federal expenditures, 61-7, 75, 116
Federal Insurance Contributions Act, 116
Federal Open Market Committee, 101-3
Federal Reserve banks, 57, 60, 101
Federal Reserve Board, 58, 100
Federal Reserve notes, 58
Federal Reserve System, 58, 59-60, 92-3, 101-2
Federal Trade Commission, 18, 46
Fiscal policy, U.S., 38, 100-1, 103
Flat tax, 74
Flextime, 51
Floating currency rates, 128
Flows, economic, 77, 79
Food and Drug Administration, 18
Food prices, 21, 98, 119. *See also* Supply and demand, agricultural
Foreign exchange market, 38, 126-7
Foreign trade. *See* Trade
Free enterprise, 3, 11. *See also* Capitalism; Private enterprise
Fringe benefits, 52, 55
Futures contracts, 34

G

GATT. *See* General Agreement on Tariffs and Trade
GNP. *See* Gross national product
Galbraith, John Kenneth, 16-17, 30
Gas: prices, 20; taxes, 68
General Agreement on Tariffs and Trade, 125
Gold, 56-7
Gold standard, 128
Goods, economic, 1, 39. *See also* Manufactured goods

Credits

Cover photos: James Stanfield, Black Star
                  Joseph Sterling
                  Grant Heilman
                  Yale Joel, Life Magazine, © 1970, Time Inc.
                  Ted Spiegel, Black Star

Cartoons: George Peltz